Wirtschaftssoziologie und Politische Ökonomie
Economic Sociology and Political Economy

edited by

Prof. Dr. Alexander Ebner,
Goethe-Universität Frankfurt am Main

Prof. Dr. Stefanie Hiß,
Friedrich-Schiller-Universität Jena

Prof. Dr. Konstanze Senge
Martin-Luther-Universität Halle-Wittenberg

Volume 8

Thomas Jackwerth-Rice

The Praxis of Collaborative Innovation

A Comparison of Six Innovation Projects in the Wind Energy Industry

Nomos

Lower Saxony Ministry of Science and Culture (MWK) with advance funds from the Volkswagen Foundation

The Deutsche Nationalbibliothek lists this publication in the Deutsche Nationalbibliografie; detailed bibliographic data are available on the Internet at http://dnb.d-nb.de

a.t.: Oldenburg, Univ., Diss., 2019

Universität Oldenburg **DE-715**

1st Edition 2025

Published by
Nomos Verlagsgesellschaft mbH & Co. KG
Waldseestraße 3–5 | 76530 Baden-Baden
www.nomos.de

Production of the printed version:
Nomos Verlagsgesellschaft mbH & Co. KG
Waldseestraße 3–5 | 76530 Baden-Baden

ISBN 978-3-7560-0112-5 (Print)
ISBN 978-3-7489-4722-6 (ePDF)

DOI https://doi.org/10.5771/9783748947226

Online Version
Nomos eLibrary

To Max and Tom

Table of contents

List of tables

1. Introduction

Collaborative innovations are realized by networks of different organizations. Because of the technological interdependencies between the components of a technological system, such as a car or a wind turbine, the development of such technologies involves different component specialists. In addition, technologies must be adapted to individual customer needs and regulatory requirements, drawing on complementary knowledge from different disciplines, such as information technology, sensor technology, or new materials. As a result, innovation processes in technology-based industries such as wind energy tend to involve specialists both inside and outside the innovating organization.

However, as postulated by the management paradigm of open innovation (Chesbrough, 2003, 2006a), collaborative innovation is not simply achieved by increasing knowledge flows across the organizational boundaries of the innovating firm. If technical standards are not compatible or if development partners do not have a common set of rules to facilitate collaboration, the opening up of firm innovation processes may be hindered. The argument of this book is thus: The management of collaborative innovation is largely based on a social praxis. In fact, the authors of this book argue that the process of establishing shared norms is a key competence required of innovating firms.

The establishment of a collaborative innovation praxis is particularly important when pursuing radical innovations. That is, any project that aims to introduce a complex technology based on knowledge from new fields of expertise must successfully define common social norms that are shared by organizations from other fields. Such an innovation praxis is then expected to provide, first, the skills necessary to adapt existing technical standards to solve new technical problems that may arise during the innovation process (cf. Berger & Luckmann, 2009, pp. 44–45) and, second, the power to normatively integrate representatives of different organizations with different interests, bodies of knowledge, and worldviews.

The author of this book assumes that firms only risk to create innovations, to deviate from established paths of technological development and even to implement radically new technologies if there is an innovation praxis based on inter-organizational shared norms, as Esser (2000, p. 17) might put it. This argument is tested by comparing cases of incremental, radical and emerging technologies in the wind energy industry in the empirical part of the book. It will be shown that the outcome of collaborative innovation is less the result of managerial decisions than of field structures, which influence the extent to which innovation partners are able to establish a shared innovation praxis. This chapter introduces the reader to the topic of the book.

While scholars of innovation management are primarily interested in increasing the efficiency of innovation processes, the author of this book analyses the 'rules of the game' or 'ways of doing things' that are shared between different organizations. In essence, the author argues that the process of institutionalizing shared working standards of collaborative problem-solving influences the outcome of innovation projects. In the specific context of innovation projects, shared working standards can be seen as institutional elements that are powerful enough to bind the involved professionals together despite different cognitions and interests, as Esser (2000, p. 3) indicates:

> *Institutions are rules for solving everyday problems, they 'define' what is possible and meaningful, and soon gain an objective power over people's actions that they can hardly escape, even though they have created the rules and the institutions based on them and constantly reproduce them through their actions (Esser, 2000, p. 3).*

This study seeks to advance our understanding of managing collaborative innovation from a social science perspective. As will be shown in *chapter 2*, the debate on open innovation in particular overestimates the commercial benefits of collaboration. It neglects the institutionalized conditions for which specific strategies must be found. Management scholars like to postulate: Open Innovation, if actualized, will increase the competitiveness of firms. However, from a sociological point of view, collaborative innovation is based on a social praxis that is based on working standards that are shared by the professionals representing the different organizations. Engaging in time-consuming technical discussions or micro-politics due to conflicting interests can lead to unintended outcomes that are not predicted by the normatively connoted image of open innovation, whose perspective is limited to capturing business value from knowledge sharing (cf. Langhof et al., 2014). Therefore, in order to better understand the outcome of innovation projects, one needs to look at the social process of establishing a collaborative innovation praxis.

Looking at institutional barriers is a particularly appropriate research strategy to identify more clearly the 'rules of the game' or 'ways of doing things' that shape innovation strategies (cf. Edquist, 2005; Elster, 2007; North, 1990, p. 427). From a management perspective, such barriers can be identified against the 'iron triangle' of initially defined time, cost and quality targets. However, taking a sociological perspective, Sage et al. (2013) suggest that within organizations, even criteria for project failure are "*negotiated, even pre-configured, to favor or disfavor particular actors, their interests, agendas and identities*" (p. 284). This perspective underlines that rules or standards of collaborative innovation might also be a social construction (cf. Bijker et al., 1987; Rammert, 2007). They can include or exclude actors from collaborative innovation.

The author of this book expects institutional barriers – understood as rules or norms that hinder innovation process to achieve their objectives – to be strongly related to regulatory, normative and cognitive-cultural elements. They are more or less shared between experts representing different organizations (Habersang et al., 2018; Scott, 2008). For a sociologist, the study of institutional barriers to collaborative innovation is particularly revealing. As Ortmann (2014, p. 32) puts it, such a perspective on barriers – Ortmann even speaks of failures – provides insights into the more or less shared 'ways of doing things' or 'rules of the game' that are expected to make the outcome of an innovation project understandable.

> *I am concerned here with that particular type of failure which is not – not primarily, not ultimately – attributable to individuals, but to (initially imperceptible) shifts and ultimately to a failure of the basic social safeguards for success, namely institutions as 'rules of the game' and organizational sets of rules, norms and routines.*

From this perspective, the author of this book identifies the institutional barriers to collaborative innovation. Due to their complexity and related uncertainties innovation projects need to find strategies to overcome these barriers. The author evaluates this assumption by analyzing six empirical cases of innovation projects in the wind energy industry. It is expected that excessive time delays or serious quality defects can be related to institutional barriers. By looking at this more or less established innovation praxis, the observed outcomes are analysed. Thus, the following research question guides the empirical analysis:

> *What are the institutional barriers to collaborative innovation?*

1.2 The social process of collaborative innovation

From a sociological perspective, the introduction of a new technology cannot be reduced to a single point in time, such as the signing of a purchase contract for a new product or production facility. It is necessary to look at the social processes that preceded this moment. New technologies are introduced through an evolutionary process involving sequential events (Dosi & Nelson, 2010; Williams & Edge, 1996). In the early stages, an innovation process is highly contingent. It is undetermined and open to new inputs. In later stages, the process becomes streamlined around a shared and more or less congruent technological frame[2] that guides how agents think, practice and decide (Bijker,

2 Frames contain the underlying assumptions, expectations and knowledge of actors regarding a new technology (Orlikowski & Gash, 1994).

2010; Davidson & Pai, 2004; Hughes, 1987). In an ongoing sequence of events, professionals collectively decide what a new technology will look like. The results are then manifested in technical drawings, specification sheets, 3D animated designs or prototypes. Collaborative innovation are thus based on a social process in which powerful interest groups make decisions. In the process, alternative technical solutions are gradually excluded, which leads to social closure.

If unintended outcomes occur, this can be explained by decisions made under specific institutionalized conditions. Sociology has argued that new technologies cannot be understood as material objects that are developed and universally applied regardless of the context in which they are used (cf. Edgerton, 2008). Instead, technologies are defined as "*material artefacts that are socially defined and socially produced, and thus relevant only in relation to the people who engage with them*" (Orlikowski, 2010, p. 131). From this perspective, outcomes are produced during the social process of collaborative design, construction and testing of a new technology. Due to the high degree of uncertainty involved in innovation processes and the interdependence of innovation partners, collaborative innovation are hardly controllable by central authorities. Nor are their outcomes predictable. Rather, the praxis of collaborative innovation is characterized by interactions in which meanings, interests and authority systems are socially constructed (cf. Dougherty & Dunne, 2011; Maitlis & Christianson, 2014; Weick et al., 2005). Therefore, we need to look at the praxis of collaborative innovation to identify the institutional barriers.

The innovation praxis is typically characterized by horizontal relationships or based on the image of concerted action,[3] which is why networks of organizations have been established as the primary site of innovation (Powell et al, 1996).[4] As knowledge becomes more specialized and dispersed, complex technologies such as renewable energy are often introduced through such

3 Such an image might question established models of hierarchical control, centralized authority and top-management leadership that are typically associated with mechanistic or bureaucratic forms of organizing (cf. Dougherty, 2001). Instead, the image of collaborative innovation can include experts from different organizations who concentrate on technical problems and define standards of how to solve them.

4 Within such networks, specialists from different organizations and professional communities such as marketing managers, product and production engineers or project controllers work together. Across organizational boundaries (which are defined by the formal structures of organizations), these specialists are integrated through similar working issues. For example, specialists might deal with problems such as those arising during product development and manufacturing, basic and applied research or quality control and commercialization (Dokko et al., 2012, p. 697). Such networks are particularly suited for introducing radically new ideas. As Hage & Hollingsworth

networks (cf. Dougherty & Dunne, 2011).[5] Besides markets or hierarchies of individual organizations, the network literature considers networks as typical institutional arrangements that coordinate the economic behavior of formally independent organizations on the basis of a long-term orientation and shared norms of reciprocity. In this book, collaborative innovation are assumed to be based on such networks, in which professionals belonging to formally independent organizations work together to introduce a new technology.

Despite the often horizontal character of networks, power asymmetries are common in collaborative innovation. This is due to the fact that professionals belonging to different organizations pursue egoistic motives, self-interests and often conflicting goals. These are linked to the position of their organization in the network or the field. For example, strong power asymmetries prevail when a dominant technology firm defines technical specifications for suppliers of components or materials (Hollingsworth, 2000; Powell, 1990; Windeler, 2001).[6]

Besides power asymmetries, collaborative innovation are shaped by social norms and authority systems. Network knowledge is not freely available. Instead, formal or informal norms of knowledge protection, such as intellectual property rights, copyrights, licenses or confidentiality, define who has access to the knowledge created within a network (Baldwin & von Hippel, 2011). As a result, collaborative innovation are expected to be characterized both by horizontal relationships between professionals sharing their expertise and by power asymmetries, with incumbent actors controlling the technical standards and the 'rules of the game' (cf. Edquist, 2005).

(2000) point out, the successful introduction of radically new products depends on frequent and intense communication across different areas of expertise.

5 The increasing specialization of knowledge drives the emergence of networks. Firms reorganize their internal structures as well as the interfirm division of labor with other partners. They downsize internal R&D capacities, spin off specialized organizational units and collaborate with research institutes that master little pieces of the knowledge that is used in an innovation process. As a result, the number of potential collaboration partners grows and firms must use the knowledge of an increasing number of sub-specialists for developing and introducing new technologies (Hage & Hollingsworth, 2000).

6 A single organization engages in networks for two reasons. First, the network partners assume that the knowledge of the partners complements their own competences, thereby creating synergy effects. Second, through network ties, organizations expect to strengthen their power position by gaining access to, or control over, additional resources (Kappelhoff, 2014; Meyer, 2016; Powell et al., 1996; Sydow et al., 2016; Windeler, 2014). Networks are thus not static interorganizational structures, but highly dynamic; organizations actively decide to establish new ties or withdraw from partnerships to pursue strategic interests.

All in all, from a sociological point of view, collaborative innovations are realized by professionals working together in spite of different interests and cognitions that are linked to the position of their organizations in a network. The author of this book argues that the normative power necessary to bind such professionals together is exerted by working standards for the design, construction and testing of a new technology. In turn, uncoordinated 'rules of the game' or 'ways of doing things' that arise when professionals from different organizations are not sufficiently integrated into the project can lead to unintended outcomes.

By taking a sociological perspective, the author of this book advances our understanding of innovation management. This debate has so far been dominated by management scholars, who often perceive institutionalized rules, routines or standards as merely instrumental means to increase the efficiency of learning and innovation. The sociological perspective adopted here rejects this view and analyses the (management of) collaborative innovation as a largely social process of establishing common working standards across organizations.

1.3 A sociological approach to innovation management

After the introduction to the sociological perspective on collaborative innovation, this section is a brief overview of the management perspective on this issue.

In the management literature, collaborative (or open) forms of innovation are intensively discussed. The main question is how firms can use external knowledge to transform their own ideas into new technologies. In particular, scholars explore the organizational ability to use external knowledge efficiently to improve products or processes under the heading of "absorptive capacity." Management scholars seek routines that enable firms to identify, acquire and assimilate knowledge from the firm's external environment (Cohen & Levinthal, 1990; Ebers & Maurer, 2014; Egbekokun & Svin, 2015; Lewin et al., 2011; Volberda et al., 2010).

The classical concept of absorptive capacity focuses on individual organizations. Contributions to the open innovation debate emphasize that new technologies are developed by collectives of organizations. These scholars ask how firms can manage knowledge flows in more open forms of innovation (Bengtsson et al., 2017; Chesbrough, 2003). For example, Chesbrough (2003) postulates his belief that in the 21st century, innovating firms depend on increasing collaboration and knowledge flows across organizational boundaries to ensure their survival: "*[c]ompanies that don't innovate, die*" (p. xxvi). From this perspective, open innovation is the new paradigm of innovation management.

In a similar vein, other scholars of innovation management believe that the ability to develop new technologies is embedded in inter-organizational relationships with external partners who have different interests and are specialized in different ways. This implies that an innovating firm is embedded in inter-firm relationships and operates in networks of organizations. As a result, it is no longer at the center of the innovation process. Instead, innovation management is expected to shift 'towards distributed or community-based models of innovation' (Salter & Alexy, 2014, p. 27). This has led to an intensification of the discussion about how companies should manage such open forms of innovation.

Unfortunately, because innovation management is rooted in economic theory, the view of the firm underlying the literature on innovation management is often rather simplistic.[7] This makes it difficult to understand how the innovation praxis actually influences the outcomes. Companies operate in perfect markets and make rational decisions based on cost-benefit calculations, while social norms seem to have no effect on economic behavior, according to the neoclassical economic view. However, some economists criticize their own discipline for lacking analytical tools to understand how the management of inter-firm relations affects the outcome of collaborative innovation. Productivity gains, for example, can result not only from investment in tangible goods but also from investment in intangible assets such as knowledge creation or diffusion processes (Freeman & Soete, 1999, pp. 1–25). At the same time, the monopolization of learning and innovation in large, professionalized R&D departments, as suggested by Freeman & Soete (1999), is seen as an innovation strategy of the past, practiced by technology firms such as General Electric, Kodak or AT&T that dominated the 20th century (Chesbrough, 2003; Powell & Giannella, 2010; Takeichi, 2002).

Obviously, the institutionalized 'rules of the game' or 'ways of doing things' in innovation projects seem to have become more sensitive in the management literature (as well as in the absorptive capacity literature). Particularly in the mid-1990s, the economist Robert M. Grant was the founder of the knowledge integration management approach. He emphasized (cf. Kogut

7 Economists recognize that institutions are a means of controlling economic behavior in organizations in an instrumental way. For example, North & Thomas (1976, p. 1) state: "*Efficient organization involves the establishment of institutional arrangements and property rights that create incentives to channel individual economic effort into activities that bring the private rate of return close to the social rate of return.*" Sociologists such as Swedberg & Granovetter (2018) criticize that this economic conception of organizations and institutions remains fixated on efficiency gains.

& Zander, 1992) that knowledge is the primary strategic resource of firms. Instead of maximizing shareholder value, firms should focus on building internal capabilities for the coordination of knowledge integration (Grant, 1996b, a). According to Grant (1996a, p. 377), "*organizational capability is defined as the ability of a firm to repeatedly perform a productive task related either directly or indirectly to the firm's ability to create value by transforming inputs into outputs.*" As the term 'repeatedly' suggests, management scholars appear to acknowledge that a more or less institutionalized praxis somehow reproduces the results achieved, such as solving technical problems by using external knowledge.

For management scholars, one way to increase the efficiency of learning and innovation within firms is through institutionalized routines, rules or standards. Management theorists argue that coordinating mechanisms such as rules and guidelines, the sequencing of decisions, or problem-solving routines "*explain and predict*" why some firms are more competitive than others (Grant, 1996a, p. 100). Grant has established the concept of knowledge integration, which emphasizes that firms can 'manage' the efficient learning of the professionals who work together in the firm. However, the classical conception of knowledge integration has been criticized for its methodological individualism (cf. Tell, 2017, p. 38). It also remains fixated on learning within firms and on management priorities such as efficiency, competitiveness and business success.

In contrast, this book's author takes a broader perspective. He argues that managing innovation projects can be better understood as an ongoing social process of establishing working standards shared by professionals from different organizations. To evaluate this assumption, the author analyzes the 'rules of the game' or 'ways of doing things' that are expected to make the outcome of innovation project understandable

More recent contributions to the debate on the management of knowledge integration emphasize the need for such a social analysis, as well as the need to look beyond the organizational boundaries of firms to networks of organizations (cf. Berggren et al., 2017). In addition, these management scholars also look at complex technologies as an example of the integration of knowledge. Empirical studies show that firms in technology-based industries (defined as industries that rely on complex technologies) must know how to integrate expertise from different organizations (Berggren et al., 2011a). More specifically, it is argued that new technologies emerge through "*a process of collaborating and purposefully combining complementary knowledge*" (ibid., p. 7). In the globalized economy, knowledge is increasingly distributed along value chains as well as between scientific and engineering communities. Therefore, management scholars assume that knowledge integration practices need to be in place to 'bridge' or 'cross' knowledge boundaries.

In the context of collaborative innovation, management scholars have identified knowledge combinations as a mechanism for 'bridging' knowledge boundaries. In fact, according to Tell (2017): Combining knowledge means configuring technical knowledge in two ways. The first way is through the incremental improvement of technologies – within its technology life cycle (Foucart & Li, 2021). For example, an innovating firm uses the knowledge of partners, decomposing and creatively (re)combining it to define the technical specifications of a module that is intended to improve the technological architecture. A second possibility is to create an entirely new technological architecture by decomposing it and re-configuring the way in which the modules or components interact with each other (Foucart & Li, 2021). The result is the creation of new design rules. These must be coordinated with the partners responsible for the other subsystems of the architecture (Hofman et al., 2016).[8]

In short, management scholars suggest that the strategy of knowledge integration differs across contexts. Innovation projects decompose knowledge, either through its transformation into new modules or through the reconfiguration of a technological architecture. However, these combinations remain at the micro level of professionals working together, as described in the management literature. It tells us little about how knowledge combinations are influenced by the 'rules of the game' or 'ways of doing things' that are more or less institutionalized in the organizational field in which an innovation project takes place. The author of this book will fill this research gap by analysing the institutional barriers to collaborative innovation and knowledge integration.

The literature on knowledge integration, which has its roots in economic theory, would emphasize that the combination of knowledge is essential for innovation. The idea that new technologies are the result of new combinations of knowledge has its origins in the work of the economist and sociologist Joseph A. Schumpeter. He understood economic change as the result of individual entrepreneurs with unique characteristics such as visionary thinking and assertiveness, which enable them to introduce innovative ideas against social resistance (Blättel-Mink, 2015; Schumpeter, 1934). However, the majority

---

8 When an engineering project is set up to solve technical problems, such knowledge combinations are often supported by digital tools such as Computer Aided Design (CAD), CFD or Finite Element Analysis (FEA), which can be used to model, simulate and visualize technical designs (Arthur, 2007; Dodgson & Gann, 2014). To solve technical problems, knowledge is then combined in a virtualized environment. The first prototype is produced and ready for testing. However, it is outside the virtual environment that a social practice is established that facilitates technical problem solving.

of innovations are not radically new, but introduce novelty through creative combinations of elements that have been produced in the past (Edgerton, 2008; Schumpeter, 2006). A basic definition of innovation is: "*New creations of economic significance, either tangible or intangible. They may be entirely new, but are often created by combining existing elements in a new way*" (Edquist, 2002, p. 219). For example, Henry Ford's assembly line for the production of the Ford Model T was a novelty in the automotive industry. It combined existing technologies of the electric motor, continuous flow production, the assembly line and interchangeable parts. As Salter & Alexy (2014) point out, the iPhone, which was mainly a product of the visionary power of Steve Jobs, was a breakthrough in the telecommunications sector not because of its innovative design, but because of the creation of a market for knowledge combinations that constantly innovate software applications (apps), leading to what Teece (2018) calls an innovation platform. These software innovations are based on combinations of existing technologies. They complement the look and feel of the iPhone, thereby enhancing its overall commercial success.

From this perspective, knowledge combinations represent first and foremost a type of economic behavior whose goal it is to create new technologies that can be sold on markets or introduced into production processes. This economic perspective which is limited to capturing business value from innovation, however, tells us little about the social dynamics that are inherent in the social 'production' of new technologies. In addition, person-centered 'stories' about the development of the Model T Ford or the iPhone barely tell us anything about the institutionalized conditions of innovation.

In order to improve our understanding of the management of collaborative innovation, the author of this book adopts a sociological perspective. Empirical cases are used to show how social norms influence the outcome of such projects. The study rejects any 'best practices' or technocratic thinking of innovation management, but rather acknowledges the social dynamics inherent in such processes (cf. Luhmann, 2006; Mattes, 2014; Ortmann, 1999).

Thus, based on sociological theory (Berger & Luckmann, 2009), the author of this book will argue that the management of collaborative innovation must be understood as a social process of norming a shared praxis of technical problem-solving. As Elster (2011, p. 196) argues, this process can be expected to exert the normative power needed to bind professionals together, despite likely differing cognitive frameworks and vested interests:

> *Social norms are social both because they are maintained by the sanctions the others impose on norm violators and because they are shared – and known to be shared with others (Elster, 2011, p. 196).*

In particular, the social process of establishing shared working standards is expected to normatively bind professionals representing different organizations together, creating a shared consciousness of being sanctioned in the case of standard-violating behavior. In particular, the social process of establishing common working standards is expected to bind together professionals representing different organizations in a normative way and to create a common awareness that norm-violating will be sanctioned.

1.4 The praxis of collaborative innovation

A closer look at the praxis of innovation is needed to identify the barriers to collaborative innovation and knowledge integration. Practice-based conceptions of organizations show how professionals working together on the development and introduction of a new technology institutionalize 'rules of the game' or new 'ways of doing things' (cf. Orlikowski, 2010). In fact, research has shown that innovation projects institutionalize working relations and power structures through the daily practice of collaborative work (cf. Ortmann et al., 2000).[9] In this book, the author expects that this praxis largely makes the outcomes of collaborative innovation understandable.

Indeed, practice-based conceptions of organizations assume that innovation projects socially construct both new technologies and organizational rules based on shared practices (cf. Jackwerth, 2009; Orlikowski, 2001, 2007). From this perspective, the knowledge that is created in innovation projects does not stick, leak or flow, nor can it be captured, stored or transferred (Ortmann et al., 2000; Sydow, 2014b).[10] Instead, innovation projects integrate knowledge by establishing shared praxis of designing, building and testing a new technology (cf. Brown & Duguid, 2001; Giddens, 1984; Orlikowski, 2010). Therefore, to

---

9 In his seminal work, Barley (1986) introduced new technologies as an "*occasion for structurating*" work relations. The author took a similar perspective on organizing collaborative innovation. However, he focused on the introduction of technologies within organizations, analyzing the introduction of new computer tomography in two American hospitals. Barley (1986) showed that such innovation projects are an occasion for reorganizing work relations. He stated that the application of technologies can disrupt existing professional knowledge, introduce new power relations among technical experts and doctors, and lead to new processes of taking decisions during medical examinations. The author of this book takes a similar perspective, but assumes that to be successful, the introduction of a new technology depends on establishing a division of innovative labor that facilitates the coordination of knowledge integration across organizations.

10 In contexts of innovation-related problem-solving, information sticks to a locus if it is costly to transfer, acquire or use (von Hippel, 1994).

identify the rules or norms that may hinder (or promote) innovation projects, we look at the practices involved in the introduction of new technologies.

There are several different conceptions of practices in the literature. Some management researchers adopt Reckwitz's (2002) definition of practice, which states that 'practices' refer to shared routines of behavior, including traditions, norms and procedures for thinking, acting and using 'things' (Whittington, 2006, p. 619). The author of this book adopts a different perspective and understands practices as typical, ongoing, shaped and regulated activities of social actors dealing with technical problems, such as the development of a new technology (Giddens, 1984; Orlikowski, 2002; Windeler, 2014).

This perspective implies that in order to understand the outcomes of collaborative innovation, it is crucial to look at organizational practices. Specifically, practice-oriented research argues that socially skilled individuals can manipulate meanings and identities through their cognitive, empathic and communicative skills to create, maintain or disrupt institutionalized ways of doing things (cf. Fligstein & McAdam, 2011, 2012; Lawrence, 2010; Lawrence & Suddaby, 2006). Such knowledgeable agents or socially skilled individuals practically exclude, improvise, modify and reject established 'rules of the game' or 'ways of doing things' in solving problems, making decisions, setting deadlines or assuming roles. In the context of collaborative innovation where members of different organizations work together, professionals are expected to actively and strategically establish not only working relationships but also an innovation praxis (cf. Sydow, 2014b; Windeler, 2001; Ortmann et al., 2000; Giddens, 1984).

The establishment of an innovation praxis has been the subject of empirical studies. For example, Mariotti & Delbridge's (2012) longitudinal empirical study of the European motorsport industry found that firms take strategic actions to form new or reactivate existing ties. Interestingly, the authors found that motorsport firms view reactivating latent ties as a quicker and smoother approach to problem-solving than working with unfamiliar partners. Problem solving goes more smoothly when the network partners share the same standards of work, such as "*unique expertise, high reliability and quality of work*" (p. 525). While in this example the agents are reacting to the network ties, other examples show how the agents are creating common practices. Powell & Giannella (2010) argue that when a future technological path is unknown, individuals form communities of practice in which even experts pursuing "*competing intellectual property interests*" (p. 578) are integrated and engaged in collective invention.[11] In other words, when the future technological path is unknown, individuals form communities of practice in which even experts pursuing "*competing intellectual property interests*" (p. 578) are integrated and engaged in collective invention.

Thus, based on practice-based conceptions of organizations managing collaborative or open innovation projects means establishing an inter-organizational shared praxis of collaborative innovation. The process of establishing such a praxis then follows a logic of negotiation and compromise with regard to "*formal and informal rules of co-operation*" (Sydow, 2010, p. 397). Scholars of network management consider negotiations as a "*functional requirement*" or "*constitutive element*" of networks: "[T]*hey bring together diverse individual and collective actors with a variety of interests, cultures, histories or belief systems that form the basis for ongoing processes of bargaining and negotiation*" (Sydow et al., 2016, p. 21). Thus, as Mayntz (1993, p. 13) points out, negotiation is not directed towards maximizing egoistic self-interest, but towards achieving collective outcomes and generally accepted compromises:

> *The network logic of negotiation is a logic of compromise. It has the advantage of permitting cooperation in spite of conflicting interests, but also the possible disadvantages of painful slowness, suboptimal results, and even stalemate.*

Establishing a praxis of collaborative innovation in a reflexive and active way is then the 'management' of innovation projects. An established innovation praxis implies that standards are in place for negotiating solutions and structurally excluding actors who deviate from the shared standards of design, construction and testing of a new technology (cf. Ortmann et al., 1990; Stones, 2009). Such standards then narrow down the design rules, the choice of project partners, the technical ideas, the quality standards and so on. In daily meetings, workshops or discourses, development partners may negotiate such design rules, define intellectual property rights (IPR) or agree on sanctions in case of norm violation, thus controlling risks or zones of uncertainty (Bijker, 1995; Crozier & Friedberg, 1979; Davis & Eisenhardt, 2011). It can be predicted that an innovation project is likely to suffer from unintended outcomes if such 'rules of the game' (North, 1990) or 'ways of doing things' (Elster, 2007) are not shared by development partners.

The author of this book empirically analyses how a less widely shared innovation praxis influences the outcome of collaborative innovation. Such a praxis includes the power to cognitively and socially complete an innovation process, despite the high level of uncertainty involved. Power should not be

---

11 "*Collective invention is technological advance driven by knowledge sharing among a community of inventors who are often employed by organizations with competing intellectual property interests*" (Powell & Giannella, 2010, p. 578)

understood as something owned or possessed by individuals who might use it to satisfy egoistic motives such as status, freedom, wealth or happiness. In the context of inter-firm collaboration, Huxham & Beech (2010) see power as a relational concept that involves agents from different organizations (cf. Windeler & Sydow, 2001). Power is rooted in social norms. It does not result from top-down rational planning, centralization of authority and hierarchical control to maximize individual profit gains. Rather, innovation projects derive their power from a system of norms that mobilize knowledge and resources, thereby creating opportunities but also structurally excluding those who are not members of the social system of collaborative innovation (Knights, 2009). The social process of establishing a shared innovation praxis thus draws organizational boundaries around the relevant development partners through the definition of shared working norms. This excludes outsiders.

In summary, the author of this book seeks to identify the institutional barriers to collaborative innovation. The social process of establishing a collaborative innovation praxis involving professionals from different organizations is analyzed to answer this question. In essence, it is argued that establishing shared working standards strongly shapes the outcome of innovation projects, because it facilitates the definition of technical specifications, excludes alternative development options, and thus socially and cognitively closes the innovation process, creating organizational boundaries around the relevant innovation partners and excluding outsiders. The author analyses six empirical cases of innovation projects in the wind energy industry to evaluate this argument.

1.5 Structure of this book

There are eight chapters in the book, which are briefly reviewed below. *Chapter 2* introduces two management approaches of 'open innovation' and 'knowledge integration', both of which discuss how firms should manage knowledge flows across organizational boundaries. The chapter critically assesses what management research tells us about the institutional conditions of (open) innovation processes. The chapter concludes by presenting the research gap that informs the present study, which relates to the institutional barriers of collaborative innovation.

Chapter 3 introduces the book's own approach. Drawing on field theory, it argues that unintended outcomes such as excessive time delays or quality defects are understandable by uncovering the institutional conditions of innovation projects. In particular, it is theorized that common working standards, like social norms, bind innovation partners together despite differences in expertise (cognitions) or self-interest (positions in the relevant field of technology development). For three types of innovation, namely incremental innovation, radical innovation and innovation in an emerging field of technology development, different strategies of establishing an innovation praxis.

Chapter 4 is a presentation of the methodology and empirical data on which this research is based. A multiple case study design was used as this book seeks to understand the institutional barriers to collaborative innovation and knowledge integration. The empirical part of this thesis is based on a case study of an innovation project in the wind energy industry. The data collection was part of the COLLIN research project at the University of Oldenburg. For the present work, six cases have been selected and grouped into three pairs that represent three different types of innovation: incremental innovation, radical innovation, and emerging technologies. The explanatory objective of the present empirical evaluation is met by an embedded multiple case study design.

The *Chapters 5 to 7* analyse three pairs: increment, radical and emerging technologies. In chapter 5, the examples of two different component suppliers working with a large European windmill producer (WTM) show how distributed knowledge is integrated in incremental innovation projects. However, neither case shows strong signs of collaborative innovation. On the contrary, the cases show how coercive rules reduce the innovation potential of collaborations between component manufacturers and system integrators. A WTM that imposes its technical expectations on supplier firms tends to control both innovation projects centrally. The examples illustrate how WTMs use standards as an instrument to control technology development. They reduce innovation projects to a rather simple form of development, instead of collaboratively creating innovative technologies. In these cases, coercion can be identified as the dominant strategy of technology development.

In *Chapter 6*, two examples of radical innovation will be presented. In the first case, a rotor blade factory of a large European WTM introduces a robot-based rotor blade coating system. In the second case, a small German start-up company develops a 'wooden wind turbine'. In both cases, the focal firms collaborate with various specialists from different fields of expertise (e.g. component and material suppliers, testing and certification institutes), thus creating a new innovation network. However, both cases suffer from serious quality defects (rotor blade coating system) or project delays (wooden wind turbine). It was found that in both projects not all relevant partners, including the customer or the approval authorities, were involved in the development praxis. The cases thus provide empirical evidence that an innovation praxis which does not involve all relevant partners can lead to unintended outcomes. In both cases, the focal firm relied on personal trust to gain some control over technology development, rather than establishing a shared innovation praxis. The findings point to personal trust as an alternative strategy to the development of radically new technologies.

Finally, *Chapter 7* presents two examples of engineering service providers trying to establish a position as system suppliers in an emerging technological field. Firstly, the cases show how public regulations for the protection of marine fauna by the German authorities gave rise to a new field of technology development in the offshore wind energy industry. Most importantly, the two cases show how innovating firms struggle to introduce their product ideas because they are unable to establish a power position in the new field of offshore wind energy technologies through collaboration with incumbent energy firms. In terms of their innovation strategy, the two engineering service providers studied are completely different. In the first case, an entrepreneur relies on his individual skills to quickly invent new technical solutions. In the second case, an offshore specialist uses professional engineering skills to realize a technology transfer from the offshore oil and gas industry to the wind energy industry. In both cases, however, a coherent approach to co-innovating together with strong local partners could hardly be identified. At least at the time of the research, both companies remained excluded from innovation networks that were powerful enough to set a new technical standard in the emerging field of offshore wind energy technologies.

Chapter 8 summarizes the empirical findings of this book. The answer to this question is given in the form of testable hypotheses. In addition, the chapter discusses three degrees of openness of the innovation praxis as a critical factor for understanding the outcome of innovation projects, which can be realized depending on the regulatory, normative and cognitive-cultural conditions of technology development in a given field. Finally, there will be a critical assessment of the theoretical and practical relevance as well as the limitations of this study.

2. The management of collaborative innovation

This book examines the barriers to collaborative innovation. Firms establish social relationships with other formally independent organizations rather than developing and introducing complex technologies in isolation. As shown in the introductory chapter, from a management perspective, the introduction of a complex technology is primarily a matter of its commercialization in markets or its application in production lines (Dodgson et al., 2014; Edquist, 2005; Fagerberg, 2005). However, this chapter critically assesses what management research tells us about the barriers to collaborative innovation, as management scholars are intensively discussing how firms should manage knowledge flows across organizational boundaries.

Innovation management research tends to focus on how collaboration enhances firms' ability to innovate or solve problems. Since the seminal work of Chesbrough (2003), the concept of open innovation has postulated that inter-firm collaboration is a straight path to commercial success, so the first part of this chapter reviews the debate on open innovation. This means that although the open innovation literature does not explicitly address institutions, management scholars analyse how firms manage interfirm relationships. They also analyse how firms can use external knowledge to increase their own innovativeness, and how formal and informal rules of knowledge protection can affect a firm's propensity to collaborate with external stakeholders.

Another management debate, that of knowledge integration, is introduced in the second part of this chapter. This approach has less normative connotations than open innovation. Its proponents take a more nuanced view of the benefits of collaboration. They acknowledge that innovation projects can lead to unintended outcomes. More importantly, while open innovation remains a management ideology, the knowledge integration approach is more theory-driven. It is mainly based on the knowledge-based view of the firm (KBV). Rather than simply looking for success stories, the theory allows us to derive hypotheses about the outcomes of innovation projects that can be systematically tested using empirical data.

At the end of the chapter, the research gap of this study is presented. This book contributes to the debate on innovation management by identifying the institutional barriers to collaborative innovation. The author of this book will argue that managing innovation projects can be better understood as a social process: in order to 'bind' specialists together, despite their potentially conflicting cognitive orientations and self-interests, innovation partners need to establish a shared praxis of collaboratively designing, building and testing a new technology (cf. Lawrence, 2010; Lawrence & Suddaby, 2006). Institutional barriers may then explain unintended outcomes.

2.1 Open innovation – A straight road to success?

In the introductory chapter, the introduction of complex technologies was described as being dependent on the collaboration of formally independent organizations. In the field of innovation management research, the concept of open innovation is prominently discussed as how focal firms (that initiate innovation processes and commercialize a new technology) collaborate with heterogeneous partners. This debate on open innovation is hard to ignore. Since its introduction, the number of contributions has increased significantly. A review by Chesbrough & Bogers (2014) found thousands of new contributions each year, citing Chesbrough's (2003) seminal work.[12] Therefore, the author of this book only reviews studies that provide insights into the praxis of collaborative innovation.

The open innovation literature identifies various potential collaborators, such as material or component suppliers, technology users or customers, universities or research institutes, competitors and intermediaries.[13] The latter provide knowledge-intensive services.[14] Open innovation scholars consider

12 For a literature review, see West et al. (2014); a review of quantitative studies of open innovation is provided by Schroll & Mild (2012).

13 The literature considers intermediaries as particularly helpful for SMEs because they provide support in establishing collaboration networks and rendering cooperation among partners effective (Lee et al., 2010; Katzy et al., 2013). Intermediaries can actively contribute unique knowledge-intensive services to new product development (NPD), such as scouting new technologies and markets, generating concepts and designs, and supporting engineering and testing (Czarnitzki & Spielkamp, 2000). Technology transfer offices, business incubators or entrepreneurship centers provide complementary knowledge that smaller firms do not possess (Katzy et al., 2013).

14 Different forms of more or less collaborative innovation are referred to in the management literature. For example, open innovation is distinguished from other forms of distributed (or horizontally integrated) innovation processes by Alexy & Dahlander (2014). For example, in contrast to user innovation, the open innovation approach is concerned with producer firms that create new technological designs and deliver them to consumers in the form of goods and services (cf. Baldwin & von Hippel, 2011). In some cases, the producing firm may use existing technological solutions developed by external parties to improve its own technologies. In other cases, a producing firm might use product concepts from research institutes as inputs and transform them into a marketable good (Bogers & West, 2012). Alternatively, a producer firm may be in search of new needs that fit with internally

collaboration imperative. They argue that in today's business environment, the job mobility of highly skilled workers is increasing, private venture capital for the commercialization of new products is more readily available, the time-to-market span of innovations is becoming shorter, the technological expertise of firms' customers and suppliers is increasing, and internet-based communication and social media facilitate collaborative work across organizations (cf. Dodgson & Gann, 2014; West & Bogers, 2014). As a result, management scholars are anticipating the advent of the open innovation era.

For sociologists, the open innovation approach is insufficient for the analysis of innovation processes in firms. Blättel-Mink & Menez (2015, p. 191), for example, criticize the management approach for relying on success stories that 'prove' the coming paradigm shift towards open innovation, rather than deriving theory-based assumptions about interfirm collaboration. Indeed, there are management scholars who euphorically see openness as "*a new dimension of competition*" (Henkel et al., 2014, p. 879) or express the superiority of this innovation model compared to closed ones. Collaboration is seen as a management strategy to increase innovativeness, as Cheng & Huizingh (2014, p. 1248) argue: "*Involving external parties in innovation projects, acquiring or exploiting intellectual property, and actively managing a firm's various collaborative relationships seems to be an effective means to increase innovation performance.*" Despite these highly normative associations between collaboration and innovativeness, empirical examples of open innovation provide some insights into the praxis of managing learning and innovation across organizational boundaries.

The basic idea of open innovation is quite simple: its proponents assume that knowledge flows across organizational boundaries increase innovativeness if they are purposefully managed. Through collaboration, innovative firms can take advantage of external knowledge and transform it internally into new products or services that can be sold in markets (Bogers & West, 2012; Chesbrough, 2006a). From this perspective, a collaborative innovation is successfully introduced once a focal firm has commercialized a new technology that contains external inputs (such as ideas, concepts, solutions, needs). As summarized in the following definition, a firm's innovation process is considered to be 'open' if intellectual property (IP)[15] flows deliberately into and/or out of the firm:

---

available ideas. In any case, open innovation assumes that interfirm collaboration is the locus of innovation.

15 Intellectual property is defined as "*registered or unregistered IP ownership and usage rights, which control the commercial use of the shared knowledge*" (Granstrand & Holgersson, 2014, p. 20).

> *Open innovation refers to managing "the use of purposive inflows and outflows of knowledge to accelerate internal innovation, and expand the markets for external use of innovation, respectively. Open innovation assumes that firms can and should use external ideas as well as internal ideas, and internal and external paths to market, as they look to advance their technology."* (Chesbrough, 2006a, *p. 1)*

As Table 1 shows, the literature distinguishes four types of openness. First, firms can acquire a new technology through purchase or license from markets. Second, they can source ideas by collaborating with private or public actors such as start-up firms or external professional or scientific communities. Third, firms may simply sell their products or services on markets or, last but not least, they may reveal their ideas to outsiders (Alexy & Dahlander, 2014). Coupled innovation describes innovation processes where an innovating firm combines different openness. Instead of the dominance of one firm in the innovation process, coupled innovation is typically associated with knowledge interdependencies and complementarities between innovation partners (Chesbrough & Bogers, 2014).[16]

Table 1: Types of open innovation processes

	Inbound innovation	**Outbound innovation**
Pecuniary	Acquiring	Selling
Non-pecuniary	Sourcing	Revealing

(Alexy & Dahlander, 2014; Dahlander & Gann, 2010)

However, the open innovation approach hardly addresses the question of how to explain the outcome of innovation processes, as this book aims to do. Instead, it provides studies that support the highly normatively connotated image of an imagined future in which all firms must open up their innovation processes to external knowledge.

16 In coupled innovation, knowledge is ostensibly controlled by different partners who together form dyadic partnerships or networks (Alexy & Dahlander, 2014; Chesbrough, 2006a; Tucci et al., 2016; West & Bogers, 2014). For example, two or more organizations may collaborate in strategic alliances, joint ventures or R&D consortia. They may also collaborate in more informal networks. However, Cassiman & Valentini (2015) critically discuss the complementarity of inbound and outbound innovation activities (e.g. buying and selling) in an empirical study on Belgian manufacturing firms. The authors do not find any confirmation of a relationship of complementarity. In fact, "*how the different types of openness are related to each other*" (Alexy & Dahlander, 2014, p. 447) is considered to be a research gap in the field of open innovation.

Already in his seminal work, Chesbrough (2003) notes that in the twentieth century, the establishment of sophisticated internal R&D laboratories has been the dominant innovation strategy of large firms such as General Electric (cf. Idelchik & Kogan, 2012). This also entailed creating barriers to entry and defining clearly delineated organizational boundaries between insiders and outsiders of corporate innovation processes (Dahlander & Gann, 2010; West & Bogers, 2014; West et al., 2014). This supposedly old-fashioned model of 'closed innovation' suggests that innovating firms keep their R&D labs closed and their best people in-house. They protect their intellectual property and improve their organizational capabilities, thereby increasing the efficiency of their innovation processes and maintaining their position as technology leaders. The working relations in such firms are typically characterized by a hierarchical organization of decision making as well as a close temporal sequence of managerial control (Bogers & West, 2012).

However, open innovation proponents argue that this closed model is outdated. In the 21st century, large and established technology firms in all industries are increasingly required to open up their internal knowledge silos to external stakeholders and to manage the flow of knowledge in and out of the firm. The reward for doing so is likely to be shorter innovation cycles and reduced internal R&D efforts. By leveraging external knowledge through collaboration, firms accelerate internal innovation processes, improve efficiency by minimizing investment in internal R&D facilities, reduce time-to-market, discover technological alternatives faster, and specify design features or technical interfaces more easily. Empirical evidence seems to prove that the age of open innovation has arrived (Alexy & Dahlander, 2014). Even technology companies such as Intel, Microsoft, Sun, Oracle or Cisco are increasingly using the "*research discoveries of others*" (Chesbrough, 2003, p. xix). For example, technology companies such as IBM, Novell or NOKIA use software knowledge created by open source communities (Alexy & Reitzig, 2013). Pharmaceutical companies such as Bayer actively use the "*creative potential of external partners*" (Dekkers, 2014, p. 69) by collaborating with members of scientific communities or integrating innovative start-ups into their product development processes (cf. Nakagaki et al., 2012). In all industries, as management science claims, open innovation is a straight path to commercial success, but "*little is known about the failures of open innovation*", as West & Bogers (2014, p. 828) point out in their literature review on open innovation.

Studies provide empirical evidence that collaboration is positively related to higher innovation performance.[17] However, some management scholars

17 Open innovation scholars often link collaboration to innovation performance. For example, Cheng & Huizingh (2014, p. 1235), based on empirical data from a large

show that this relationship cannot be simply assumed. For example, using survey data from 221 Belgian manufacturing firms, Faems et al. (2005) found that collaboration increases sales of new or improved products. However, the innovation outcome differs depending on the type of collaboration. While collaborating with customers or suppliers increases the innovating firm's ability to exploit existing technologies, collaborating with universities and research centers makes it easier to benefit from exploring new technical knowledge.

Based on panel data from Irish manufacturing firms, Love et al. (2013) found that the positive effect of collaborating does not need to be present from the start. Rather, firms must learn to improve their innovation performance through collaboration on the basis of prior experience. Thus, the link between collaboration and innovation performance postulated by the open innovation approach cannot simply be assumed. Rather, innovating firms may – over time – learn to exploit external knowledge through collaboration with heterogeneous partners. They will then have a better understanding of how to select appropriate partners or how to manage multiple relationships.

Another study by Walsh et al. (2016) points in a similar direction. They also find that the link between collaborating and innovating cannot be simply assumed, because the praxis of collaborating differs. For example, using survey data on inventions by US firms, the study shows that vertical collaboration between firms and their suppliers or customers during the invention phase increases the likelihood of successful commercialization of an innovative technology. Horizontal collaboration, especially with universities, does not. This may be because vertical collaboration provides the innovating firm with more specific knowledge of customer needs or supplier capabilities, whereas collaboration with universities provides knowledge that is much broader (cf. Nieto & Santamaría, 2007; Un et al., 2010).

More analytical approaches to the management of open innovation ask the question of why top managers should voluntarily give up control over their intellectual property (Alexy et al., 2017). If technology firms are defined as bundles of valuable, rare, inimitable and non-substitutable resources such as knowledge and information-as predicted by the knowledge-based view of the firm (KBV)-firms must control these resources to remain competitive (cf. Henkel et al., 2014). Empirical evidence shows that firms like IBM, Novell or NOKIA share proprietary knowledge with outsiders like OSS communities (Alexy & Reitzig, 2013).

---

service firm in Taiwan, found that open innovation activities positively affected four measures of innovation performance: "new product/service innovativeness, new product/service success, customer performance, and financial performance".

An explanation for these findings can be found in the management literature. It views firms as bundles of complementary resources and concludes that the creation of a common resource pool that can also be shared with rivals (e.g. source codes in software communities) and the separation of this common resource pool from exclusive, internal knowledge could influence a firm's propensity for collaborative innovation. In this way, there is no contradiction in established management theory with strategic openness. On the contrary, a firm might gain superior information or complementarities from competitors if it succeeds in creating a common resource pool that can be shared even with rivals. Thus, management scholars conclude: 'strategic openness' can be seen as an economically rational management decision to selectively appropriate external knowledge. In practice, collaboration with research consortia or cooperative standardization may be established as a new industry norm to appropriate knowledge and outperform those competitors who are excluded from the shared knowledge pool.

In conclusion, empirical findings suggest that an increase in collaborative innovation cannot simply be assumed, as is often done by open innovation scholars, in contrast to the highly normative image of open innovation. Moreover, collaborating does not automatically lead to (commercially) successful technological innovations. Instead, the outcome of collaborative innovation may be influenced by the structural characteristics of collaborations, such as the specificity of the knowledge exchanged or the type of collaboration. These findings support the author's main argument: Institutionalized 'rules of the game' or 'ways of doing things' strongly influence the outcome of innovation projects.

2.1.1 Rules and practices of IP management

The previous section introduced the management approach of open innovation. It was shown that the positive relationship between collaboration and innovativeness, which has a strong normative connotation, *cannot* be simply assumed. Empirical studies suggest that structural conditions such as the type of collaboration (vertical, horizontal) or knowledge specificity (broad, specific) have an impact on the outcome of open innovation projects. The author of this book argues that in order to identify the institutional barriers to collaborative innovation, it is necessary to understand the 'rules of the game' or 'ways of doing things' of innovation projects.

To the best of the author's knowledge, the open innovation literature rarely discusses the praxis of collaborative innovation. Management scholars only suggest that the extent to which innovating firms open up their innovation processes to outsiders may be affected by formal and informal knowledge protection practices. The implication is that firms have to establish effective appropriability rules in order to minimize the risk of knowledge leakage that might occur in collaboration with outsiders (Alexy & Dahlander, 2014; Henttonen et al., 2016) Such rules of knowledge protection then increase firms' propensity for collaboration.

Collaboration as a business strategy paradox is discussed by other open innovation scholars. If it is true that collaborating is the best way to succeed, collaborating is the best choice. However, opening up the firm's boundaries to outsiders increases the risk of unintended knowledge spillovers. This can weaken an innovating firm's ability to capture value from proprietary knowledge. This risk has been referred to as the paradox of openness by Laursen & Salter (2014). For example, knowledge leakage can occur when a partner who has been part of a joint innovation project collaborates with a competitor after the project has been completed (Ortmann, 1999; Takeichi, 2002). There is discussion in the literature about practices and strategies for dealing with this 'paradox of openness'.

Firms are faced with two choices. On the one hand, a firm can prevent knowledge spillovers by protecting its intellectual property, defining the ownership of exclusion rights (patenting, licensing) and securing rents from innovations (cf. Bogers et al., 2012; Veer et al., 2016). In the day-to-day praxis of open innovation, such formal or informal rules of knowledge protection might reduce a firm's risk perception of collaboration with outsiders and thus increase its propensity to share proprietary knowledge. On the other hand, a firm might have the perception that too much knowledge protection would make it less attractive as an innovation partner. In this case, it might give up control over parts of its intellectual property (Alexy et al., 2017). Management scholars call this strategic openness. They consider it a rational decision.

There is empirical evidence in the literature to support both strategies. Arora et al. (2016) conclude that a firm's decision to adopt one of the two strategic options depends on its technological leadership in a sector, based on survey data from UK firms that use patents at different intensities. The authors find that technology leaders, who face a higher risk of knowledge spillovers, are more likely to patent than technology followers, who have less proprietary knowledge. These findings suggest that a firm's position in the industry, e.g. as a technology leader, may influence its decision to use formal precautions to protect knowledge.

Other scholars discuss the extent to which formal rules for protecting knowledge increase firms' propensity to engage in collaborative innovation. These scholars have found that in R&D projects the risk of imitating knowledge is not evenly distributed, but depends on the stage of the innovation process as well as the partners involved (Veer et al., 2016). Moreover, even when appropriability regimes exist, "*[n]oncontractual social relations are important complements to contractual relations*" (Granstrand & Holgersson, 2014, p. 25). Apparently, the existence of formal appropriability regimes alone does not sufficiently explain the conditions under which firms decide to collaborate with outsiders and share proprietary knowledge.[18] The management literature acknowledges that informal relationships, non-contractual agreements, trust and secrecy may also influence the degree of openness.

Veer et al. (2016) criticize that the link between appropriability regimes and openness is often discussed in the context of dyadic relationships. However, open innovation research analyses portfolios of heterogeneous organizations engaged in joint R&D projects. Here, informal knowledge protection mechanisms such as trust or secrecy may be even more important than formal knowledge protection measures (Henttonen et al., 2016). Even patents do not necessarily have to facilitate collaborative innovation. They can work both ways, as both enablers and inhibitors of open innovation (Laursen & Salter, 2006). Only for industry newcomers, patenting of proprietary knowledge may act as an incentive to engage in collaborative innovation in order to gain access to complementary knowledge and resources (Zobel et al., 2016).

A coherent understanding of how appropriability regimes influence firms' propensity to collaborate is not provided by the empirical findings summarized above. Nor do they have any bearing on what influences the outcome of innovation projects. This is why some management scholars call for more theory-led studies on how appropriability regimes relate to managing open innovation. Alexy & Dahlander (2014), for example, stress that legal definitions of ownership and use rights are not effective in all contexts. Intellectual property rights (IPR) may facilitate the contractualization of collaboration between innovation partners in contexts of "*clearly delineated boundaries*" (ibid., p. 451). On the other hand, if the boundaries between innovation partners are unclear and partners have difficulties in defining what knowledge they have used in other projects, the legal conditions for collaboration may prove problematic.

Granstrand & Holgersson (2014) take a similar view. They emphasize that in coupled innovation contexts, characterized by high knowledge interdependence and reciprocity between partners, knowledge use rights and ownership can be easily distributed between different organizations. The authors acknowledge that in empirical reality, different forms of IP management are conceivable. Thus, managers need to negotiate appropriate practices that fit

18 Appropriability regimes are defined as conditions such as the ownership of exclusion rights (patents) which determine how firms can create value from innovation (Pisano & Teece, 2007).

Another concept of managing complex innovation projects is introduced in the next section. Knowledge integration management explicitly considers theoretical considerations such as knowledge boundaries as institutionalized barriers to collaborative innovation, in contrast to open innovation. Such scholars look for "*more or less formal mechanisms for the coordination of behavior and the achievement of goals when operating in the context of changing and uncertain contingencies*" (Tell, 2017, p. 8). How innovation projects are managed, and why they produce unintended outcomes may be better understood through this more social theory-led approach.

Table 2: Factors influencing the outcome of open innovations

Factors	**Authors**
Type of collaboration (e.g. vertical, horizontal)	Faems et al., 2005; Walsh et al., 2016
Specificity of the knowledge exchanged among partners	Annique et al., 2010; Nieto and Santamaría, 2007
Appropriability regimes and knowledge ownership rights (e.g. licensing, patenting)	e.g. Alexy and Dahlander, 2014; Henttonen, 2016; Laursen and Salter, 2014
Rationality of openness as a management decision to outperform competitors	Alexy et al., 2017, Alexy et al., 2016;
Organizational practices that mediate the use of external knowledge	Alexy and Reitzig, 2013; Foss et al., 2011

2.2 Key objectives of collaborative innovation management

Management research underscores the importance of integrating external knowledge and technologic sub-systems in achieving a competitive advantage for the company and enhancing the innovative capacity of business partners along the value chain (Gurca et al., 2020; Grant, 1996 a, b). This viewpoint lends support to the author's rationale behind the adoption of a social science perspective, which aims to examine the institutional barriers to collaborative innovation and knowledge integration.

As mentioned in the preceding section, the open innovation approach provides empirical insights into how firms manage knowledge flows across organizational boundaries. However, it must be noted that the approach is 'blind' to the institutionalized conditions of collaboration, as it is preoccupied with the highly normatively connoted positive association between collaboration and innovation.

In contrast to open innovation, the knowledge integration management debate recognizes that institutionalized conditions, in particular epistemic communities, can act as barriers to collaborative innovation. How firms can rely on routines, rules or standards to increase the efficiency of learning and innovation. Therefore, the integration of knowledge is considered to be a primary objective of collaborative innovation (Caccamo et al., 2023; Tell, 2011).

2.2.1 Knowledge boundaries – The cognitive barriers of collaborative innovation

The management approach of knowledge integration is rooted in management theories. In particular, the knowledge-based view of the firm (KBV). From this perspective, firms are bundles of "*valuable, rare, inimitable and non-substitutable (VRIN) resources*", including intangibles such as knowledge or information (Alexy et al., 2017, p. 4). Firms are not seen as static, black-box entities that are part of abstract economic production functions, but as internally building 'competencies'[19] or 'capabilities' that enable them to manage tacit knowledge sharing better than buyer-seller relationships in markets or loose informal collaborations (Cohen & Levinthal, 1990; Grant, 1996 b, a; Håkanson, 2010). From this perspective, firms instrumentally use decision-making rules, problem-solving routines or standards for testing or production to coordinate knowledge sharing within and across firms.

The management literature emphasizes specialization as a problem of innovation management. In modern economies, knowledge is becoming more and more specialized and dispersed. As a result, management scholars argue: The strategic challenge for firms is to build capabilities to integrate specialized knowledge. The management of learning and innovation within firms is directly affected by increasing specialization. On the one hand, the efficiency of intra-firm problem solving increases as a result of knowledge specialization and more complex division of labor. According to management theory, efficiency is the primary goal of economic organizations.[20] On the other hand, the specialization of knowledge within and across firms creates social groups that

19 Competence is defined as follows: "Competence is a generative ability of actors or systems to master concrete tasks and solve problems, but in doing so to make use of general knowledge that transcends the situation (own translation)" (Sydow, 2014a, p. 311).

20 For example, strategic management scholars such as (Grant, 1996b, p. 115) point out: "*[E]fficiency in organizations tends to be associated with maximizing the use of rules, routines and other integration mechanisms that economize on communication and knowledge transfer, and reserve problem solving and decision making by teams to unusual, complex, and important tasks.*"

are cognitively separate. Sociologists have referred to these groups as epistemic communities. This is because their members share rather exclusive cognitive frames of reference, as the definition below makes clear. Management scholars now believe that such institutionalized differences between experts such as engineers, scientists, lawyers or top managers need to be 'bridged' in order to achieve knowledge integration.

> *Epistemic communities consist of individuals with identical or similar "frames of reference" and cognitive "orientation systems." These are associated with specific social roles, such as those of different occupational groups, and are acquired in a process of cognitive socialization, usually through a combination of formal training and on-the-job experience.* (Håkanson, 2010, *p. 1807)*

In the classical concept of knowledge integration management, tacit knowledge in the heads of experts is seen as a management problem. More recent contributions to knowledge integration management point to institutionalized structures such as the epistemic communities mentioned above. Typically, such communities consist of those belonging to a professional or scientific discipline and interacting on a regular basis. Within such communities, interactions run rather smoothly because the members of the community are similar in terms of their epistemic backgrounds in terms of individual training, tacit knowledge, personal experiences, theories, language, identities and value systems. Overall, they share a common frame of reference. This makes it easier for them to reach agreements or compromises. Thus, within such communities, the theory predicts, it is easier to justify and legitimize technical solutions than it is across these communities, as summarized by Tell (2017, p. 22):

> *Specialization into epistemic communities creates knowledge boundaries, which, in turn, creates the need for knowledge integration. These knowledge boundaries arise from the knowledge frames shared by epistemic community members. These frames, which are applied by individuals, imply the existence of shared cognitions and social processes involved in justification and legitimacy.*

Conversely, management literature suggests that the daily activities of knowledge sharing can become problematic when complex problems arise, such as the introduction of a new technology, and experts from different professions and organizations with different epistemic backgrounds have to work together. Due to the expected cognitive differences, which scholars such as Tell (2017) metaphorically describe as knowledge boundaries, communication, interactions and collaborations may be disrupted or even turn into political conflicts.[21] The management literature argues that the establishment of shared cognitions is a crucial task in the context of complex technologies.

---

21 The literature makes several suggestions of how to conceptualize boundaries among (potential) innovation partners. In the case of product development teams within

From this perspective, the whole process of collaborative innovation is influenced by cognitive structures (frames). Reconciling potentially conflicting assumptions, expectations and knowledge about how the future technology will work and be used in a particular context may then be a critical management task. Orlikowski & Gash (1994, p. 178) describe this task as achieving technological frame congruence:

> *A technological frame contains "the assumptions, expectations, and knowledge [people] use to understand technology in organizations. This includes not only the nature and role of the technology itself, but the specific conditions, applications, and consequences of that technology in particular contexts."*

For example, in the context of technology development projects in companies, Carlile (2004) distinguishes three types of knowledge boundaries that can hinder collaboration between experts: The incompatibility of codes, routines or protocols (syntactic knowledge boundaries), difficulties in translating meanings to others (semantic knowledge boundaries), and a lack of common interest in transforming each other's knowledge (pragmatic knowledge boundaries) (cf. Rau et al., 2015). Shared frames are then understood as a prerequisite for knowledge integration between experts from different professions and organizations. Barriers to collaborating could be attributed to incongruent frames.

Management scholars such as Håkanson (2010) adopt the concept of epistemic communities from the sociologist Holzner (1972). They argue that once members of the same epistemic community have mastered the shared theories, codes, tools and practices, they can easily collaborate across time and space. These individuals can share their knowledge regardless of the intensity of their interactions. These interactions can be face-to-face or technically mediated through Internet-based communication. Knowledge sharing could also occur

---

firms, for example, Carlile (2004) has established a typology of syntactic, semantic and pragmatic boundaries. The author argues that knowledge boundaries refer to differences in lexicon (syntactic), meanings (semantic) and interests (pragmatic) among project partners. Collaboration is disturbed as soon as domain-specific knowledge (e.g. functional units) becomes increasingly complex (in terms of differences, dependencies, novelty) (cf. Carlile, 2002; Carlile & Rebentisch, 2003). In contexts of open innovation, Bengtsson et al. (2017) suggests three other types of boundaries: organizational, knowledge and geographical. The authors ascribe these boundaries to differences among organizational units (organizational boundaries), dissimilarities of knowledge among organizations (knowledge boundaries) and geographical distances among organizations (geographical boundaries). Finally, to advance future research on knowledge integration, Tell (2017) suggests to differentiate five types of boundaries: individual, task-related and domain-related as well as spatial and temporal boundaries.

regardless of geographical proximity, e.g. by contacting each other from a distance or interacting closely. Based on such theory-guided assumptions about collective behavior. management scholars suggest that knowledge boundaries (cognitive frames) must be 'bridged' to implement collaborative innovation.

Scholars of knowledge integration suggest that incongruent frames have direct consequences for the strategic management of knowledge. Knowledge boundaries emerge around groups of experts working on specific tasks. According to the literature, the incompatibility of cognitive frames or "*incongruence of technological frames*", as Orlikowski & Gash (1994, p. 180)[22] put it, could explain unintended outcomes of innovation projects. However, knowledge boundaries do not necessarily hinder collaborative innovation. In the context of technology development, knowledge boundaries can be 'bridged' when agents specialized in different knowledge domains share a common set of knowledge that enables them to better assess each other's domain-specific knowledge and understand their cognitive differences (Carlile, 2004). This also implies that in order to achieve minimal knowledge overlap and secure business objectives, cognitive structures such as language, meanings, motivations or interests can be manipulated.

In summary, in contrast to open innovation, the management of knowledge integration implies a more social science approach to collaborative innovation. It argues that a key goal of collaborative innovation is the management of knowledge integration. Simultaneously, it argues that a barrier to collaborative innovation is incongruent cognitive frameworks across professions and organizations, as specialization accentuates cognitive differences across professions and organizations. This results in knowledge boundaries that can hinder collaborative innovation. From this perspective, a praxis of collaborative innovation then requires establishing knowledge integration processes to 'bridge' specialized knowledge by achieving minimal cognitive overlap between members of different epistemic communities to overcome these barriers.

This book is an analysis of these knowledge barriers. Therefore, the next chapter is a summary of the state of the art in research.

22 "Incongruence implies important differences in expectations, assumptions, or knowledge about some key aspects of the technology. For example, a frame incongruence is apparent when managers expect a technology to transform the way their company does business, but users believe the technology is intended to merely speed up and control their work."

2.2.2 Types of barriers to collaborative innovation and knowledge integration

Before presenting a sociological analysis of institutional barriers, we summarize the types of barriers to knowledge integration at the interorganizational level of collaborative innovation that are most relevant to this analysis.

A first barrier is referred to as a *semantic barrier*. These barriers arise when different actors interpret the same information differently, regardless of the context in which the communication takes place. Recent research emphasizes that collaborative innovation requires a shared understanding of vocabulary, concepts, signs or symbols so that semantic barriers do not lead to misunderstandings, hinder the sharing of knowledge or cause external solutions to be forgotten prematurely (Lyng & Brun, 2020; Wojciechowska-Dzięcielak, 2020; Zasa & Buganza, 2024). In addition, an insufficient understanding of customer needs and market requirements, a lack of clarity about the benefits of cooperation and the distribution of risk between the partners can promote semantic barriers (Ates, 2022). By establishing a common understanding, companies can mitigate the effect of semantic barriers and thus overcome different organizational cultures and practices more easily (Rossoni et al., 2024). Boundary objects such as shared documents, prototypes or models can then facilitate knowledge integration by providing an interpretive framework for interactions to translate information or facilitate joint negotiations (Vuillemot et al., 2021).

Research also highlights *pragmatic barriers* as obstacles to collaborative innovation and knowledge integration. Pragmatic barriers occur when the collaboration partners interpret the context of the collaboration differently and, for example, doubt the relevance or benefits of the collaboration (Bø Lyng & Brun, 2020). This means that they pursue different interests and goals in relation to the common context, as they fear that their own competitive position will otherwise be weakened and therefore focus on asserting their own interests instead of negotiating common goals (Lyng & Brun, 2020; Zasa & Buganza, 2024). Recent studies such as that by Zhang et al. (2019) show that aligning objectives, for example by developing a common strategy and building alliance capability, can overcome pragmatic barriers. Thus, pragmatic barriers highlight differences in the interpretation of the shared context of collaboration.

Third, *legitimacy barriers* refer to the acceptance and credibility of external knowledge within an organization. If one organization does not view another as a legitimate partner, this can reduce the willingness to share knowledge (Bø Lyng & Brun, 2020). Research shows that legitimacy barriers pose a particular challenge because even when semantic and pragmatic issues are resolved, knowledge integration can stall because the new knowledge is not perceived as credible or is not compatible with prevailing beliefs. These barriers show that organizations may initially be skeptical and doubt the validity of the new knowledge until it has been validated internally due to asymmetrically distributed information, lack of industry standards or the novelty of the technology (Bjornali et al., 2017). In interorganizational collaboration, this barrier, which is characterized by a large institutional distance between partners, is exacerbated, manifesting itself in a lack of trust and recognition of expertise (Lyng & Brun, 2020; Zasa & Buganza, 2024). These barriers make it clear that, especially for established organizations, as Grigoriou & Rothaermel (2016) show, knowledge sharing alone is not enough, but new knowledge must first be made connectable internally. At the same time, the study by Horn et al. (2023) on "relative expertise" points out that tolerance towards the knowledge of others and one's own knowledge boundaries can also be a question of personal attitude. In more recent studies, internal trust specialists are then discussed as translators of external knowledge or the demonstration of quick wins as a way of validating external expertise.

The last barrier to be mentioned here relates to *power-based barriers* to knowledge integration. Such barriers arise where power asymmetries lead to the establishment of interpretive sovereignty, from which the validity of external knowledge can easily be challenged. In this regard, Baumstark (2020) points to specialization as a source of power asymmetries. Engstrand & Enberg (2020) clarify the link to legitimacy barriers and show that power can be used to create legitimacy barriers, as interpretations can be actively constructed (Engstrand & Enberg, 2020). In the context of interorganizational cooperation, larger firms can then dictate the terms of collaboration to smaller firms, so that the knowledge of the smaller partner is lost. Recent studies confirm this: Egalitarian forms of collaboration strengthen knowledge integration, while power asymmetries are problematic. Venkataramani and Tang (2023) show that teams within organizations are more likely to benefit from external knowledge if their internal network is more decentralized and no team member monopolizes problem solving. Opening one's own innovation routines to external knowledge, higher incentives for external knowledge collaboration, and systematic knowledge management are then approaches to overcome power-related knowledge barriers (de Faria et al., 2020). Thus, this research shows the influence of the power of collaboration partners as both facilitator or barrier to knowledge integration. This means that legitimacy barriers can be strengthened or weakened by power, which is flexible and negotiable, as shown by Collien (2021) using the example of boundary spanning.

Table 3 summarizes the knowledge barriers relevant to this study that come into play in inter-organizational collaboration and innovation processes.

Table 3: Barriers to collaborative innovation

Barriers	Institutional aspects
1) Semantic barriers	Differences in interpretation of information, regardless of the context of the collaboration
2) Pragmatic barriers	Differences in the interpretation of the goals and benefits of collaboration
3) Legitimacy barriers	Differences in the credibility given by the organizations to external knowledge
4) Power-based barriers	Differences in interpretive sovereignty which is constantly negotiated

As will be explained in more detail below, knowledge integration is particularly important in the context of collaborative innovation and the introduction of technologies that are new to a sector. In these contexts, new collaborations need to be established, and firms typically face unusual problems that they cannot solve by relying on existing competencies and partners and replicating what they already know. Instead, companies need to establish collaborations with new, unfamiliar partners.

3. Establishing technology fields

This book explores the institutional barriers to collaborative innovation. As a starting point, the previous chapter has introduced management strategies that have an impact on collaborative innovation processes. While open innovation essentially postulates that firms should exploit external sources of expertise and enrich their internal innovation processes by acquiring or sourcing external knowledge, knowledge integration scholars suggest that firms need to be able to establish routines, rules or standards for combining knowledge across boundaries. From this perspective, more or less institutionalized processes of integrating knowledge influence the outcome of innovative projects.

However, this hardly improves our understanding of institutional barriers to innovation. The highly normative approach of open innovation simply postulates that collaboration increases the innovativeness of firms. It does not take a closer look at the 'rules of the game' or 'ways of doing things' that are established in innovation projects. Knowledge integration scholars, without specifying how projects 'produce' a social outcome point to institutionalized processes and 'bridging' mechanisms.

This book takes a sociological perspective to advance our understanding of the management of innovation projects. It argues that, similar to social norms (Elster, 2007, 2011),[23] the social process of establishing common working standards normatively binds innovation partners and creates a common innovation praxis. This means that the establishment of such standards requires an informal process of constantly negotiating and monitoring the 'rules of the game' or 'ways of doing things' that inform project partners about the consequences of violating standards. For example, deviating from technical standards in order to increase innovativeness, fear of loss of reputation by violating established professional norms, or playing by the rules in order to secure future follow-on projects are possible motivations that drive the actions of experts in collaborative innovation projects, despite possible differences in cognitive frameworks and self-interests.

In short, the social process of establishing inter-organizational working standards is expected to have a strong impact on the outcome of innovation projects. In the empirical part of this book, this argument is evaluated on the

---

23 In contrast to legal norms, which have an obvious instrumental character and sanctions for violation are formally defined, social norms convey social meanings, their compliance is monitored by a social collective, and sanctions often remain diffuse (Elster, 2011).

basis of six technology development projects in three different institutional contexts of the wind energy industry.

Before doing so, the main argument of the book will be specified in this chapter. First, the concept of organizational fields is introduced to theoretically link working standards (which can be more or less institutionalized in a larger field of technology development) with practices of knowledge integration (section 3.1). Second, working standards are introduced as a particular type of rule that regulates an innovation praxis (section 3.2). Third, this book argues that depending on the prevailing type of innovation (incremental innovation, radical innovation or emerging technology), innovation projects are realized in three different ways. This argument is specified in terms of three propositions that will guide the empirical analysis (section 3.3).

3.1 The institutional elements of innovation projects

This book explores the institutional barriers to collaborative innovation. Unintended outcomes such as excessive time delays or serious quality defects are understood here as organizational phenomena which can be traced back to the innovation praxis and the application or non-application of standards for coordinating innovation projects. This section introduces the concept of organizational fields, which can be used to describe theoretically how work standards shape the everyday praxis of innovation and collaboration across organizational boundaries. This will serve as a basis for clarifying how the process of establishing shared norms works.

The author of this book assumes that complex technologies are introduced by at least three formally independent organizations. These innovation partners need to integrate knowledge across professional, organizational and/or sectoral boundaries. In the process of technology development, standards work to normatively bind the innovation partners together, despite any differences in the cognitive frames and self-interests attached to these actors' position in the field. The concept of organizational fields takes collectives of heterogeneous organizations as the unit of analysis and theories how the collective behavior of members of different organizations is regulated. Therefore, this concept is used here to show how the process of establishing such an innovation praxis might regulate the collective behavior of actors in innovation projects (cf. DiMaggio & Powell, 1983). According to Scott (2008, p. 86),

> *An organizational field refers to those organizations that collectively constitute a recognized domain of institutional life: key suppliers, consumers of resources and products, regulators, and other organizations that produce similar services or products.*

It should be noted that field theory has been developed to explain the behavior of organizations independent of the interests or decisions of individuals. The concept assumes that organizations cannot be understood as aggregates of human beings pursuing only selfish interests, constantly seeking to optimize their personal utility and acting on the basis of economically calculated rational decisions (DiMaggio, 1988). Instead, the field perspective assumes that institutions, understood as the taken-for-granted structures of society, influence the behavior of organizations. In the case of technological innovation, examples include 'best practices' for organizing innovation processes or 'blueprints' for successful product development. Institutions such as standards shape, mediate and channel collective choices and thus, according to the theory, lead organizations to act on "*a narrowly defined set of legitimate options*" rather than on efficiency criteria (Krücken, 2016; Wooten & Hoffman, 2008, p. 130). The dynamics of a social field unfold through networks, which are understood as "*the skeleton of fields*" (Owen-Smith & Powell, 2008, p. 596). For example, through networks, field members create hierarchies or coalitions through which actors can shape institutions.

The field concept has been applied to the analysis of technology development. Hoffman (1999) emphasizes that fields emerge around a common issue, which may be markets or technologies. Once members of different organizations interact regularly, exchange significant amounts of information and are aware that others are working on the same common issue, a field emerges (DiMaggio & Powell, 1983; Scott, 2008). Over time, a field acquires its own rationality and meaning system, leading scholars to refer to a field as a "community of organizations" (Wooten & Hoffman, 2008, p. 141). Within fields, competitors can also be members, as they are "bound together" by a common issue despite conflicting self-interests (cf. Meyer, 2016, p. 150). According to the seminal work of DiMaggio & Powell (1983), field organizations align their practices and become increasingly similar because coercive rules, mimetic behavior or social norms exert isomorphic pressure to conform to collective expectations or 'rationalized myths' (Boxenbaum & Jonsson, 2008; Krücken, 2016).[24]

From this perspective, it is not the aggregation of individual choices but more or less institutionalized 'rules of the game' (North, 1990, p. 3) or 'ways of doing things' (Elster, 2007, p. 427) that regulate innovation projects. For

---

24 According to Meyer & Rowan (1977, pp. 343–4), myths control the formal structures of organizations. Myths are defined as "impersonal prescriptions that identify various social purposes as technical ones and specify in a rule like way the appropriate means to pursue these technical purposes rationally. (...) [T]hey are highly institutionalized and thus in some measure beyond the discretion of any individual participant or organization."

example, innovation partners cannot freely choose product designs, development partners, manufacturing processes or R&D partnerships. Their options are limited by the regulative, normative and cultural-cognitive elements of institutions, such as technical standards or common design rules, which define a set of legitimate options for innovation projects. From this perspective, rules, social norms or shared beliefs can thus explain why innovation partners can work together despite differences in cognition or self-interest.

According to field theory, the regulative, normative and cultural-cognitive elements of institutions provide classes of mechanisms that explain how collectives of organizations behave (Lawrence, 2008). As Table 4 illustrates, such mechanisms include 'regulative rules' (coercion),[25] 'binding expectations' (social norms) or 'constitutive schemes' (mimesis). They limit social choices to legal, legitimate or believed options.

Table 4: The institutional elements of fields

	Regulative	**Normative**	**Cultural-cognitive**
Basis of compliance	Expedience	Social obligation	Taken-for-grantedness, shared understanding
Basis of order	Regulative rules	Binding expectations	Constitutive schema
Mechanisms	Coercive	Normative	Mimetic
Logic	Instrumentality	Appropriateness	Orthodoxy
Indicators	Rules, laws, sanctions	Certification, accreditation	Common beliefs, shared logics of action, isomorphism
Affect	Fear guilt / innocence	Shame / honor	Certainty/confusion
Basis of legitimacy	Legally sanctioned	Morally governed	Comprehensible, recognizable, culturally supported

(Scott, 2008, p. 51)

In order to analyse social collectives of organizations working together to adopt a new technology, this book looks at collaborative innovation. In such cases, it may be inappropriate to exaggerate the importance of isomorphism, conformity and homogeneity. Rather, innovation projects are characterized by heterogeneity of knowledge and interests, experimentation and contingent ac-

25 Coercive power is achieved by defining, monitoring and sanctioning rule systems or 'rules of the game' (North, 1990, p. 4).

tion, and deviance (cf. Wooten & Hoffman, 2008). In their empirical research on semiconductor manufacturing, Schubert et al. (2013) showed that new technologies do not simply emerge from interacting with each other. Rather, the establishment of a technological path is "*highly managed and reflexively mediated*" (ibid., p. 1402) (cf. Meyer, 2016).[26] In another empirical study of the German engineering industry, Beck & Walgenbach (2005) argue that firms' decisions on the organization of production processes may even be decoupled from their institutional environment.[27] The authors argue that the likelihood of an organization adopting an institutionalized approach decreases if internal routines bring higher efficiency (cf. Sandholtz, 2012). Thus, not only the institutional environment but also social processes play an important role in the management of innovation projects, as shown by Beck & Walgenbach (2005).

Isomorphic pressure implies homogeneous partners and stable fields. Agency underlines the influence of entrepreneurial action and institutional change. Regardless of which of the two social forces is dominant in a specific empirical case, it can be concluded that, from a field theory perspective, the management of innovation projects is also a regulatory process of institutionalization of rules, social norms or shared beliefs that are shared by the members of heterogeneous organizations (e.g. private firms, public agencies or universities), as Scott (2008, p. 52) claims:

> *[R]egulatory processes involve the capacity to establish rules, inspect others' conformity to them, and, as necessary, manipulate sanctions – rewards or punishments – in an attempt to future behavior.*

---

26 "*A technological path is understood here as the patterned development of a technology that is, due to increasing returns and other positive feedbacks, difficult – if not impossible – to reverse*" (Schubert et al., 2013, p. 1391). With his notion of "innovation paths", Meyer (2016) takes a broader perspective. The author combines the historical context with micro-processes of institutionalizing technology development: "*Innovation pathways are industry or field-wide developments that not only affect a specific artefact, but also describe a general development trend.*" (p. 2; own translation)

27 This observation is supported by neo-institutionalist conceptions of organizations stating that organizations such as firms, universities or public agencies tend to pretend that their formal organization meets the expectations expressed by public opinion, thereby signaling conformity with the rules of the game and securing legitimacy, while inside the organization, the daily praxis might be different. Organizational practices can be decoupled from external expectations, as Meyer & Rowan (1991, p. 58) conclude: "*[D]ecoupling enables organizations to maintain standardized, legitimating, formal structures while their activities vary in response to practical considerations. The organizations in an industry tend to be similar in formal structure – reflecting their common institutional origins – but may show much diversity in actual practice.*"

In this book it is assumed that in innovation projects the regulative rules, the binding expectations or the constitutive schemes that bind the actors together according to the field theory, are embodied in common standards of work.

In summary, from a field theory perspective, innovation projects are organized around working standards. These are established and controlled in two ways: First, they can be imposed in the form of coercive rules, social norms or mimetic conduct. Second, they can be established through strategic agency or by socially skilled individuals who fashion shared meanings and identities. In this book, it is argued that in the context of technological development, standards are a special kind of rule. They function as 'rules of the game' or 'ways of doing things' that regulate the network of innovation and can explain the outcome of the development of technology.

3.2 Standards of technology development

On the basis of field theory, the previous section concluded that, despite potential differences in cognitive frameworks and self-interests, innovation projects can be co-organized on the basis of the imposition of coercive rules or social norms, or through mimetic behavior. In addition, new ways of doing things can also be established through the use of strategic agency. This book argues that in innovation projects, the social process of coordinating and monitoring the ongoing (re)creation of shared working standards is the normative power that binds innovation partners together (cf. Lawrence, 2010; Lawrence & Suddaby, 2006). In this section, we specify how such standards structure the interactions within innovation projects and thus create an innovation praxis.

First of all, in the literature, standards are associated with industrial norms. It is important to note that these types of standards are different from regulations. While regulations are legal restrictions enforced by government authorities, standards are introduced by private organizations such as the International Electrotechnical Commission (IEC) that regulate technologies (e.g. in terms of design, development, reliability or safety) (cf. Blind, 2012; Gallini, 2014; Narayanan & Chen, 2012; Tassey, 2000). For example, in the wind energy industry, the industry standard 'IEC 61.400' is a guideline for the construction of wind turbines. It also contains strict specifications for subcomponents such as gearboxes, or for the design of offshore wind turbines.

In addition to industry standards, another type of standard is widely discussed in the literature, namely technical standards, which are established by officially accredited organizations. These standards can be industry standards, but they are more detailed definitions of technologies and development processes. Similar to 'design rules', technical standards define the architecture of technologies, how components interact (interfaces) or test procedures (cf. Hofman et al., 2016). Their main function is to ensure the compatibility and interoperability of technologies. They restrict the variety of technologies, limit the options for product development and force the integration of technologies into a common architecture or platform (Tassey, 2000). As Garud et al. (2002, p. 198) put it,

> *Standards are codified specifications that detail the form and function of individual components and the rules of engagement among them. Together, specifications about the components' form and function and the rules determining their interaction define a system's 'architecture'.*

The main function of technical standards is to impose compatibility between technologies and components, and thus to a large extent to pre-define an innovation project, as the above quote emphasizes. However, this potential to impose the rules of the game for a given innovation project is likely to depend on the type of innovation in question. For example, in mature markets where a technical infrastructure exists and innovation is often incremental, standards increase the conformity of firms to an established technological path, but also ensure the efficiency of innovation processes. In uncertain markets, where different technological paths compete with each other, technical standards can increase firms' ability to innovate because they provide firms with direction for technological development (Blind et al., 2017). Under such uncertainties, new standards may even be the result of co-operation between competitors. The parties involved may have a common interest in pooling patents and use this patent pool as a basis for their own innovation projects (cf. Gallini, 2014).

Thus, in contrast to their inherent function of imposing conformity, not only in mature markets, technical standards need not necessarily determine innovation processes, stifle creativity and reduce innovativeness, as firms may fear that new solutions outside existing standards are incompatible (Allen & Sriram, 2000; Garud et al., 2002; Ortmann, 2014). On the contrary, since technical standards constrain development options, they not only provide direction, as in the case of catalytic converters for automobiles. They also encourage creativity and experimentation by firms to optimize technologies beyond the technically defined limits and to discover profitable market niches.

It is interesting to note that standards have recently been discussed in organizational science as a tool for organizing the collective behavior of organizations (Brunsson et al., 2012; Ortmann, 2014). This book takes up this perspective. It argues that the social process of establishing shared working standards for the development and introduction of a new technology could function as mechanism. The organization literature emphasizes that the social process of norming implies that the management of innovation projects cannot be reduced to a central authority that coercively imposes conformity on development partners, for example by defining technical standards that must be met. A sociological approach broadens this perspective. It implies that such working standards can structure innovation projects as they are negotiated and monitored in the everyday praxis of collaboration.

Brunsson et al. (2012) argue that standards should be understood as voluntarily adopted rules.[28] From this perspective, professionals working together in innovation projects do not apply a standard because of the hierarchical authority of an external standardizer, but because of the relevance, legitimacy or normative pressure of an actor who monitors compliance. Standard-setting organizations are a typical example of the latter, but an incumbent technology firm could also fulfil this role (Ahrne & Brunsson, 2010). For example, ISO quality standards adopted by a technology firm do not contain legally defined sanctions, but compliance could be mandatory for firms wishing to work with an ISO-certified partner. This example shows that the process of establishing common working standards can create a collective consciousness shared by organizations. Standards thus shape the behavior and identity of actors in an organizational field.

Ortmann (2014) takes a similar perspective. He also refers to recent debates on organizational routines as processes (cf. Feldman, 2016; Feldman & Pentland, 2003). In innovation projects, once institutionalized, standards could provide 'examples, models, levels or norms' that make it easier for the innovation partners involved to evaluate and assess development options, the actions of the partners or the outcomes of the project. From this perspective, standards could structure innovation projects because they impose design rules that are codified in technical standards, or because, once negotiated and established, they impose a praxis of innovation that is loaded with social norms.

Based on these theoretical considerations about standards in organizational life, the social processes of establishing an innovation praxis can be further specified. In fact, two variants, which are driven by social processes of establishing standards, can be distinguished. While the first refers to the

---

28 This understanding of voluntarily decided rules neglects other types of standards such as de facto standards. The latter describe a more or less consciously adopted uniform technical or social solution. This is typically illustrated by the example of the QWERTY layout for typewriters, which has been established as a de facto standard. The "*the concept of de facto standards refers to processes that lead to uniformity, in the sense that all or nearly all potential adopters eventually come to adopt the same solution and turn it into a model (or de facto standard) that it is difficult to deviate from" (Brunsson et al., 2012, p. 617). Such a standard "lacks formal approval by a recognized standards organization or organizations*" (Allen & Sriram, 2000, p. 173).

coercive imposition of technical standards on innovation partners, a second variant underlines the negotiation and monitoring of labor standards. Ortmann (2014) refers to the latter process as a process of establishing collective standards of behavior. These standards of behavior are understood as the generalized imposition of procedures or methods of a normatively connotated praxis, as expressed in the following quotation.[29]

Examples of working standards are practices of 'good management' or professional codes of conduct (Brunsson et al., 2012; Scott, 2008, p. 100). Other examples might be work process standards which have been adapted based on those standards that are monitored by the International Organization for Standardization (ISO) in Geneva in order to protect the environment (ISO 14001), guarantee the quality of products and services (ISO 9001) or provide guidelines of risk management (ISO 31000) or social responsibility (ISO 26000) (Beck & Walgenbach, 2005; Brunsson et al., 2012; Heras-Saizarbitoria & Boiral, 2012; Sandholtz, 2012). Apart from such process standards, Ortmann (2014, p. 34) also speaks of "*various organizational rules*" without further specifying them.

Table 5: Types of standards in innovation projects

	Technical standards	**Behavioral standards**
Logic of regulation	Indirect regulation of collective behavior within innovation networks based on explicit, codified, documented specifications (design rules)	Direct regulation of the collective behavior of innovation partners by establishing a normatively connotated praxis of innovation
Form of power	Coercive rules: imposition of design rules that are derived from the dominant design and which are controlled by third parties such as certifying bodies	Normatively binding expectations: Shared, normatively connoted procedures or methods of designing, building and testing that are established and controlled by the innovation partners

29 The idea that knowledge integration might rely on such behavioral standards is partly supported by research. Sankowska & Söderlund (2015) analysed knowledge integration among professionals (engineers). The authors maintain that the success of knowledge integration is not directly related with a trusted work environment, but – and maybe more importantly – also with the "*perceived value of the assignment*" (p. 5) which facilitates technical problem-solving. In the context of a public construction project, Swärd (2016) found that norms of reciprocity existing at the industry level or being developed in the course of the project suffice to coordinate action.

	Technical standards	Behavioral standards
Examples	IEC norm 61.400 that specifies the design of wind turbines (e.g., performance, safety, testing procedures)	Criteria of risk assessment, norms of professional work, ISO-process norms (product quality, environmental protection)

(own illustration based on Ortmann, 2014; Scott, 2008)

Table 5 illustrates how both standards can structure innovation praxis. In both cases, standards are imposed on technology development. Standards normatively bind innovation partners together despite differences in cognitive frameworks (expertise) or self-interests (tied to power positions in the field). Whether coercively imposed or horizontally negotiated, standards thus operate through shared expectations or collective consciousness and are created through social processes of (re)creating working norms that inform innovation partners about the 'rules of the game' for implementing a new technology, but also about the consequences of violating the 'ways of doing things' established within a given field (cf. Elster, 2011).

In sum, the expectation of being sanctioned for violating standards drives collaborative innovation. As an example of the use of technical standards to regulate technology development, a large technology firm could impose such standards on component suppliers and control that the supplier's products comply with these standards. In the case of behavioral standards, heterogeneous organizations might establish their own praxis for designing, building and testing a new technology, including norms of quality, safety or performance. However, the question remains: which norms are found in innovation projects and how do such norms hinder innovation projects?

The author of this book argues that the social process of establishing shared work norms gives structure and meaning to innovation projects by establishing a system of norms either through coercive imposition or through horizontal negotiation. Particularly in the context of radical innovation, the author of this book argues that the social process of creating shared work norms is key to the introduction of complex technologies. This means that the management of innovation projects is largely an informal process of constantly negotiating and monitoring the 'rules of the game' and the 'ways of doing things' that inform the innovation partners involved about how to implement a new technology in a given field and what happens in case of non-conformity (cf. Elster, 2011, 2007, pp. 353–371). As a result, this social process powerfully and normatively binds innovation partners together, despite any existing differences in cognitive frames (expertise) or self-interests (linked to the respective partners' position in the field).

A key assumption made in this study is that, depending on the type of innovation project, different norms of innovation projects can be found. For example, reflexive adaptation may be particularly important in radical innovation projects, which are typically characterized by high levels of uncertainty and the absence of technical standards. Rather than strictly following rules, playing by the book, or simply adopting a collective rationality or shared perception of what is normal (e.g. regarding acceptable risks or norms of professional work), a reflexive stance means critically assessing whether established rules, collective perceptions, expectations and shared beliefs are effective in dealing with a practical problem at hand. From such a perspective, what Ortmann (2014) calls 'practical drift' leaves the collective rationality or established social order of technology development (e.g. in terms of design rules, technical expectations or shared beliefs) open to improvised local rationalities and organizational change. Thus, because radical innovation projects tend to operate in conditions of institutional uncertainty and lack of applicable technical standards, they are likely to generate an innovation praxis that is characterized by negotiating new working standards and monitoring the collective behavior of the professionals involved. The coercive imposition of technical standards, on the other hand, is most likely to occur in incremental innovation projects located in highly established technology fields.

Table 6: Two forms of norming the innovation praxis

Coercive imposition: rule-following without questioning	**Horizontal negotiations:** *reflexive rule adaptation*
Typical in contexts of incremental innovation	Typical in contexts of radical innovation
Praxis is based on coercive power exercised by an incumbent actor	Praxis is based on the normative power of voluntarily decided rules
Professionals play by the book without reflection, reproducing established standards	Professionals reflect and interpret rules with regard to a given practical problem
Accepting a collective wisdom or rationality of technology development laid out in rules or blue-prints established in the field	Critically reflecting established rules of technology development and deviating from them if problem-solving requires this

As Table 6 illustrates, the norming of the innovation praxis differs according to the type of innovation. This means that in cases of incremental innovation, a logic of playing by the book without reflection and unquestioning acceptance of collective wisdom on how to implement a new technology may be followed in an innovation project where experts rely mainly on technical standards. This kind of project work can also be described as the adoption of a collective rationality, or acting according to the rules or blueprints that have been established in the field. This logic of action stabilizes a social order, such as a project network, because it is formalized in the form of rules. In short, the social processes of establishing an innovation praxis cannot always be reduced to the negotiation and monitoring of standards. They often also imply the reproduction of an already established collective wisdom of technological development controlled by powerful actors in the field.

Conversely, in contexts of radical innovation, professionals work together solely on the basis of newly established standards of work. There is a different logic to the innovation praxis. The process requires a critical perspective on established rules of technology development. The professionals involved will reflect and interpret such rules in relation to a given practical problem, rather than simply playing by the book. Establishing new working standards involves deviating from or breaking rules, which is to be expected especially in fields characterized by a high degree of uncertainty or ambiguity. Ortmann (2014) gives the example of teachers or air traffic controllers who are not able to play strictly according to the rules in order to keep the 'system' running. Another example is that of surgeons who, in the event of complications during an operation, have to deviate from the operation plans and the established routines.

In short, two forms of establishing an innovation praxis can be distinguished. Imposing technical standards implies a logic of acting that can be described as following rules without questioning. The social process of horizontally negotiating working standards, on the other hand, describes a logic of reflexive rule adaptation, which in turn implies adapting rules to situational conditions or the practical problem at hand. In this way, an innovation praxis can emerge that is at variance with the work standards established in the field.

The social process of establishing an innovation praxis, i.e. the reproduction of existing work standards on the one hand or the reflexive adaptation of rules to a given technical problem on the other hand, is a key driver of innovation and new technologies. The question then is: Which institutional conditions favor one of these processes? The author of this book provide answers to this question.

One open question that the author of this book wants to address is whether strict rule-following and playing by the book on the one hand, or the erosion of standards through practice drift or reflexive adaptation of rules on the other, can be found in innovation projects.[30] So far, we have only established that in radical innovation projects, which are typically characterized by deviations from technical standards, project work is structured by the creation

30 Ortmann (2014) illustrates this question by two examples: friendly fire and US combat aircrafts shooting down two other American helicopters in Northern Iraq, and the Challenger catastrophe in 1986.

of shared working standards, whereas in incremental innovation projects the innovation partners involved rely mainly on established technical standards and simply reproduce the rules of technology development established in the field.

If we now assume that innovation projects are managed on the basis of a largely informal process of (re)creation of working standards, different types of innovation projects – incremental or radical innovations as well as emerging technology fields – may reveal different institutional barriers.

In summary, this section has argued that the social process of norming an innovation praxis strongly influences the outcome of innovation projects. This social process functions either on the basis of coercive imposition or on the basis of collaborative negotiation between professionals working together to solve new problems. These assumptions will be evaluated in the empirical part of this book through a comparison of three types of innovation projects: two examples of incremental innovation, two examples of radical innovation and two examples of technology development that is emerging in the German offshore wind energy industry (short: emerging technologies). It will be shown that the institutional configuration of the innovation praxis is an explanation for the dominance of a particular social process. The empirical analysis is guided by three propositions, which are presented below.

3.3 Three strategies of establishing an innovation praxis

The previous section concluded that the process of establishing shared working standards normatively binds innovation partners together in a similar way to social norms (Elster, 2007, 2011). A shared awareness of being sanctioned for violating standards is expected to be the main driver of this social process. In an innovation praxis, such a shared consciousness can be enforced by an incumbent who defines design rules and monitors compliance with them. Alternatively, it can be created through processes of negotiation and compromise.

The author of this book empirically analyses whether such an innovation praxis can be found in collaborative innovation, and how they differ, by looking at technology development in the wind energy industry.

The author of this book empirically analyses whether the social process of establishing shared working standards can be found in innovation projects in the wind energy industry. However, since the projects studied differ in the type of innovation involved, this section proposes three different strategies for establishing technology development standards. The author suggests that innovation occurs differently in different types of fields, drawing on field theory. Fligstein & McAdam (2011, p. 11) state that fields "*tend to move into one of three states: unorganized or emerging, organized and stable but changing, and organized and unstable and open to change*". Here the emerging fields of technology development are related to Fligstein and McAdam's unorganized fields. Fligstein and McAdam's fields that are organized and stable but changing are associated with incremental innovation. Finally, radical innovation is possible in fields that are organized, unstable and open to change.

The empirical evaluation is guided by the following propositions.

3.3.1 Proposition 1: Monitoring technical standards and sanctioning their non-conformity

In incremental innovation projects – technology development within a technology life cycle (Foucart & Li, 2021) – it is common for a project team to improve on a dominant design or on an existing technological architecture (March, 1991; Nooteboom, 2014). In such contexts, the expectation is that technical standards will pre-determine technology development. Collaboration partners mainly use existing knowledge for the improvement of components or sub-systems. The processes of jointly designing, building and testing a new technology are realized through established R&D partnerships or component supplying networks. In such contexts, new technologies are typically introduced based on existing technical standards. Innovation projects reproduce existing technical knowledge and collaboration takes place between trusted partners. Incumbent technology firms are able to impose their technical expectations on other suppliers at the top of an innovation network.

In this context, innovation projects can be expected to be organized around technical standards. However, innovation networks are typically made up of formally independent organizations. They are 'bound' together by interdependencies and knowledge complementarities. For this reason, technical standards can rarely be imposed through hierarchies or through the authoritative directives of one partner alone – Cook & Gerbasi (cf. 2011, pp. 225–228). With regard to inter-firm collaboration, Huxham & Beech (2010) propose a relational concept of power, which means that coercion does not exist as a force that emanates from the external environment of organizations. Rather, power becomes manifest only as it is exercised in the daily interactions between members of different organizations. The authors define power as "the ability to influence, control or resist others' activities" (ibid, p.555). In everyday praxis, innovation partners combine the sources of power they perceive to be available to them and try to shape collective behavior according to their interests or to resist the activities of others (cf. Dörrenbächer & Gammelgaard, 2011).

This means that within innovation networks, partners with a lower position of power also organize cooperation.

All in all, since hierarchical coercion is not sufficient to drive innovation projects even in established technology fields with dominant incumbents, it can be expected that innovation projects are organized through practices of monitoring technical standards and sanctioning non-conformity. The first proposition is based on this theoretical assumption:

> *Proposition 1: The praxis of innovation is mainly shaped by the monitoring of technical standards and the sanctioning of nonconformity when innovation projects are initiated in organized and stable fields.*

3.3.2 Proposition 2: Establishing a praxis of collaborative problem-solving

A praxis of radical innovation – technology development happens beyond the present technology life cycle (Foucart & Li, 2021) – typically deviates from technical standards or changes an existing technological architecture. The technical knowledge needed to innovate is rarely institutionalized and needs to be explored or created from scratch (March, 1991; Nooteboom, 2014). Technologies are radically new when they reconfigure a dominant design. Or when they create what is later called a technological breakthrough. Because radically new technical knowledge is involved, specialists from outside the technological field may be approached and asked to collaborate (Cropper & Palmer, 2009; Johnsen et al., 2009). New social relationships are required.

Collaborating with new partners is associated with two relational risks: (1) hold-up and (2) spillover risks (Nooteboom, 2014). The former refers to investments in relationships. For example, building mutual understanding or personal trust. Hold-up risks also arise when sensitive information has to be exchanged or when new relationships have to be established with new partners. The latter risk refers to the loss of a company's proprietary knowledge as a result of collaboration. This can happen when former developing partners become competitors or when developing partners transfer new knowledge created in the joint project to competitors (Yang & Steensma, 2014).

In the literature, trust building is discussed as one option for the management of such relational risks. Personal trust, for example, is a type of trust that results from repeated personal interactions between agents (Bachmann & Inkpen, 2011; Zucker, 1986). Personal trust is understood as a psychological phenomenon, a state of mind, or an actor's belief that: "the other party has an incentive to act in his or her interest or to take his or her interests to heart" (Cook & Gerbasi, 2011, p. 220). However, since personal trust requires intensive and time-consuming face-to-face interactions, it has been criticized as a basis for the regulation of interfirm relations (cf. Bachmann & Inkpen,

2011; Bachmann et al., 2015; Bachmann & Zaheer, 2014). This is why the literature discusses institution-based trust as another possibility for the organization of interfirm relations. This type of trust results from encountering impersonal institutional arrangements such as "legal regulations, professional codes of conduct that may or may not be legally binding, corporate reputation, employment contract standards, and other formal and informal norms of behavior" (Bachmann & Inkpen, 2011, p. 285). From this point of view, the establishment of common standards of work provides innovation partners with institutional trust.

Huxham & Beech (2010) point out that inter-firm relationships based on institutional trust are less likely to emerge when collaboration is characterized by strong power imbalances. On the other hand, they are more likely to emerge when collaborative relationships are more balanced, which is typically the case in radical innovation contexts. Consequently, norms need to be negotiated and monitored in radical innovation projects, which typically do not have high power imbalances.

The debate on trust points to trust building as an important part of establishing an innovation praxis (cf. McEvily et al., 2003; Zucker, 1986). Therefore, the aim of this book is to understand how the social process of establishing shared normative procedures and methods facilitate collaboration in contexts of radical innovation. Once established, such work norms describe ways of designing, building and testing a new technology in collaboration with new partners. This process of establishing an innovation praxis involves informal rules of conduct for negotiating project goals, seeking compromises on technical solutions, or sharing proprietary knowledge, despite the relational risks involved in any new collaboration. The following proposition summarizes this:

> *Proposition 2: When a radically new technology is being developed, the praxis of innovation is likely to be shaped by newly created procedures and methods for solving collaborative problems.*

3.3.3 Proposition 3: Adapting technical standards from adjacent fields

Finally, a third proposition is introduced. It relates to emerging technology fields. The previous two propositions covered only incremental and radical innovation. However, innovation projects can also operate in emerging technology fields that emerge around a new issue. Typically, such fields emerge as a result of new regulations introduced by public authorities. An example of this is the mandatory use of catalytic converters in cars. A more recent example from the renewable energy sector is the introduction of environmental regulations. These have created new issues and new technology fields in the offshore wind industry.

Projects operating in such environments are unlikely to have access to either technical standards or potential innovation partners for the development of new technology. Instead, they are expected to develop technology from scratch. In order to facilitate the introduction of new technologies, innovation projects adapt technical standards from adjacent fields, which – in the context of offshore wind energy, for example – refers to the oil and gas industry (cf. Mäkitie, 2019). As Fligstein & McAdam (2011, p10) state: "*Adjacent fields are a readily available and generally trusted source of new ideas and practices.*" This is expressed in the following proposition:

> *Proposition 3: When an innovation praxis has to establish itself in an emerging sector, it is likely to adapt technical standards from adjacent fields.*

The three propositions presented above are empirically evaluated in the analytical part of this book. Six cases of innovation projects in the wind energy sector are combined into three pairs of similar cases, (1) two projects of incremental innovation, (2) two projects of radical innovation, and (3) two projects operating in emerging technology fields. For each context, it is shown which innovation praxis emerged and how these findings explain the unintended outcomes of innovation projects.

4. A multiple case study design for understanding innovation projects

To identify standards of collaborative innovation, the author of this book re-analyses six innovation projects covered by the COLLIN research project (see below). The cases provide rich empirical descriptions of unintended outcomes, allowing the social process of creating work standards to be linked to theoretical constructs like knowledge integration (Yin, 2009).

A disadvantage of qualitative case study data is the small sample size. This limits the generalizability of the findings. The relationship between the data and theoretical constructs cannot be tested using statistical methods such as regression analysis because a qualitative case study design does not rely on a representative sample and operationalized variables.[31]

An embedded multiple case study design (Yin, 2009, p. 46) was used in this book to address these drawbacks. This section is an explanation of how this design was constructed. The basic idea behind a multiple case study design is to increase the generalizability of the findings by understanding each case as an opportunity to compare the findings with those of previous cases. The aim of the researcher is then to replicate the previous findings in a stepwise manner, to eliminate results that are idiosyncratic to a particular case, to rule out alternative explanations and to develop a theory (Eisenhardt & Graebner, 2007).

The cases studied are grouped into three pairs (cf. Gerring & Cojocaru, 2016). For each pair of cases, two innovation projects were selected that were similar to each other in terms of the type of innovation: incremental innovation, radical innovation and emerging technologies (the most similar design within the pair and the most different design between the pairs). In doing so, an attempt was made to keep the processes of technology development and knowledge integration somewhat constant for each pair of cases, while allowing for differences in the impact of standards on the outcome of technology development between the pairs of cases.

---

31 A theory test based on statistical estimations is not possible due to the small number of cases and, more importantly, the difficulty of measuring the idiosyncratic social processes involved in knowledge integration across organizations (Bitektine, 2007; Emirbayer, 1997). The quantification of knowledge integration processes has been the subject of only a few attempts by scholars. For example, focusing on recent contributions, Herstad et al. (2015) merge data from innovation surveys with employer and employee registers.

It is plausible to assume that innovation projects that resemble each other in terms of the nature of the innovation will also resemble each other in terms of the practices of knowledge integration, as well as in terms of applying standards, which are more or less institutionalized in a given social context. For example, it was argued in Sect. 3.3 argued that the incremental improvement of an existing technology relies more on regulated processes of knowledge integration than a radical innovation process, which by definition deviates from established standards, so that reliable practices of knowledge integration as well as a common innovation praxis have to be established by the project partners themselves. Similarly, innovation projects operating in an emerging field will find it difficult to draw on either established procedures for knowledge integration or established standards within the field, so it is assumed that focal firms will look for suitable solutions in adjacent fields.

Such a *most similar design*, which is as similar as possible for each pair of cases representing the same type of innovation, increases the validity of the findings for each pair of cases. The *most different design* was realized by contrasting three different pairs of technology projects. This allows us to compare the results. This increases the generalizability of the conclusions that are drawn from the analysis in comparison to a single case study design (cf. Lijphart, 1971).

4.1 The process of "casing"

Casing is the process by which the organizational objectives under study is isolated and the data material that is to be analyzed in detail is defined. Casing requires the researcher to reduce the complexity of the empirical data collected in the course of the investigation, since a case study design aims to illustrate the totality of an organizational phenomenon. The researcher has to decide which organizational objective is to be studied in detail within a social context that is delimited in terms of space and time (Fiss, 2009). In other words, the researcher has to draw a boundary around the empirical observations and focus on certain processes while leaving others to one side.

The authors of this book focus on two activities involved in innovation projects: (1) integrating knowledge from different organizations and disciplines, as well as (2) establishing working standards for developing technology. Unintended outcomes are then the observable outcome. Their social 'production' can be traced back to practices of knowledge integration and the establishment of working standards (cf. Eisenhardt, 1989). Table 7 summarizes the processes and outcomes that have been observed and that have been further evaluated.

Six cases were included in the evaluation. An overview of the organizations and interviews is given at the end of this section. Each pair of cases represents one type of innovation: either an incremental innovation, a radical innovation or an emerging technology.

Cases A and B were chosen as examples of incremental innovation contexts. In both cases, the introduction of a new technology is mainly the result of a collaboration between a component supplier and a large European WTM. The first component is part of the drive train of wind turbines (Case A). The second component is much smaller and is installed in the rotor (case B).

Table 7: The processes and outcomes observed and evaluated

	Integrating heterogeneous knowledge	**Creating shared standards of technology development**	**Institutional barriers to collaborative innovation projects**
Definition	*"process of collaborative and purposeful combination of complementary knowledge"* (Berggren et al., 2011b, p. 7)	*"regulatory process [that] involve[s] the capacity to establish rules, inspect others' conformity to them"* Scott (2008, p. 52)	*"Shifting and ultimately failing the basic social safeguards for success (...), namely (...) organizational rules, standards and routines."* (Ortmann, 2014, p. 32)
Empirical examples	*"[W]e now receive vast amounts of load information (...) that we have to process computationally. (...)."*	*"It takes a certain lead time for a supplier to really fulfil our high quality requirements. It takes time for them to achieve a certain level of process capability."*	*"[The customer] may have planned additional costs for one component that he wanted to compensate for in the other. But he won't let us talk to the manufacturer of the other components to find the optimum solution."*
Measures	A technical concept or design of a new technology that includes technical information from at least three different organizations	Examples, models, levels or norms applied in the daily praxis of organizing the designing, building and testing of a new technology	An ascribed, significant deviation from performance criteria (e.g. excessive time-delays, severe quality defects)

Cases C and D were selected as examples of contexts in which radical innovation is taking place. In case C, a German rotor blade manufacturing site of a large European WTM introduced a robotic coating line. This was mainly done in cooperation with a system supplier specializing in the automotive industry. In case D, an innovative start-up company in Germany introduced a "wind turbine made of wood" and worked with a number of partners to get its innovation approved for construction.

Finally, two offshore wind energy technology cases (Cases E & F) cover a field of technology development in the offshore wind energy sector which arose following new environmental regulations designed to protect marine life during construction in the German North Sea. In Case E, an entrepreneur invented a technical solution that aimed to establish his company as a new system supplier to wind farm planning companies. In case F, a professional offshore engineer, specialized in the offshore oil and gas industry, attempted to transfer an existing technical standard for a relatively quiet foundation method to the offshore wind energy industry.

A number of methodological concerns need to be raised when looking back at the data collection. In each case, the researcher's aim was the inclusion of all partners which were most relevant to the introduction of the new technologies. However, this was not always possible. For example, no interviewee from the system developer could be found in case C, despite several attempts. Similarly, no representative of two large WTMs could be interviewed in the cases of component development (cases A & B), mainly for reasons of confidentiality. These gaps in the empirical data weaken the internal validity of the findings, which is a strict criterion for assessing the extent to which the researcher has been careful to extract causal relationships from the empirical data and whether the inferences drawn from the data are correct based on the underlying theoretical assumptions and empirical evidence (Gibbert & Ruigrok, 2010; Yin, 2009, pp. 40–45).

4.2 The structure of the empirical chapters

Chapters 5–7 of this book are an evaluation of the empirical cases and a summary of the findings. Each of the empirical chapters has a similar structure to the others. That is, the first section analyses practices of knowledge integration. To identify the social processes involved, it is first necessary to collect empirical data on the main actors involved and how they interact. For this reason, an overview of the organizational field in which the innovation project under study was embedded is provided at the beginning of each case description.

How an innovation project was coordinated is discussed in the second section of each chapter. In order to understand the impact of the social process of establishing an innovation praxis, it is particularly important to take into account conditions such as incentives, benefits or legal rights that shape interactions at the level of individuals cooperating in the development of a new technology.

The third part of each chapter traces the institutional barriers. Chapter 8 summarizes the empirical findings of the research, presents the social processes of technology development that could be found in the empirical cases, and answers the research question in the form of three testable hypotheses (cf. Eisenhardt, 1989).

4.3 Discussing rigor criteria

This section reflects on the quality of the analysis. Apart from disclosing how the research was planned and conducted (see below), the quality of a case study design in organizational research should also be assessed on the basis of the following rigor criteria (Gibbert & Ruigrok, 2010; Gibbert et al., 2008): (a) construct validity, (b) internal validity, (c) external validity, and (d) reliability (cf. Easterby-Smith et al., 2007; Yin, 2009, p. 24). Below, these rigor criteria are critically reflected upon for the research design chosen for this book.

Construct validity assesses how the researcher identified a set of operational measures and the extent to which he/she was able to refrain from subjective judgements (Gibbert & Ruigrok, 2010; Yin, 2009, pp. 40–45). Based on multiple interviews for each case, data could be triangulated by drawing on multiple sources of evidence, which is a strategy for increasing construct validity. In addition, planning, conducting and discussing the empirical data in a research team and having key informants review the drafts of the case study reports is another strategy used here. Finally, based on the research proposal, theoretical sampling was aimed at increasing construct validity; however, this sampling strategy could not be fully realized because the type of innovation and the organization of technology development in each case could hardly be identified ex ante. In addition, access to innovation projects was highly dependent on the willingness of companies to participate in the research.

Internal validity assesses whether the researcher was careful in extracting causal relationships from the data. It also assesses whether the inferences drawn from the empirical data are correct based on the theoretical framework and the empirical evidence (Gibbert & Ruigrok, 2010; Yin, 2009, pp. 40–45). In this study, both the sampling and data collection strategy were based on the theoretical framework and hypotheses outlined in Wittke et al. (2012). While the initial theoretical assumptions remained broad, a compelling argument was found by drawing on the literature on knowledge integration and the impact of standards in organizational settings. However, it cannot be ruled out that there may be alternative explanations that would need to be explored in future studies.

A multiple case study design increases the external validity of the research, which is the extent to which the findings can be analytically generalized beyond the observed cases (Gibbert & Ruigrok, 2010; Yin, 2009, pp. 40–45). In particular, comparing findings across cases within pairs and across innovation types increases the generalizability of conclusions. Another strategy to increase external validity is to explain the rationale for case selection. In this book, each innovation project should combine knowledge from at least three different organizations and each project should be characterized as either an incremental innovation, a radical innovation or an emerging technology.

A final rigor criterion is data reliability. This criterion expresses the extent to which another researcher would be able to arrive at the same findings and conclusions if he/she followed the same research procedures (Gibbert & Ruigrok, 2010; Yin, 2009, pp. 40–45). The COLLIN project team carefully documented its research procedures, which increases the reliability of the findings. For each case, the project team wrote a report (documenting the organizations and interviewees contacted, etc.). The use of a (semi-structured) interview guide also increased the reliability of the data.

4.4 Identifying empirical cases of innovation projects

The empirical data used to uncover the institutional barriers to collaborative innovation were collected in the course of the research project 'COLLIN – Collaborative Innovations' (Wittke et al., 2012).[32] The project raised the question of how companies use external knowledge for internal product development processes. Between April 2013 and March 2016, COLLIN investigated

32 The research project 'COLLIN – Collaborative Innovations' was funded by the Volkswagen Foundation. The project idea was supported by the Lower Saxony Ministry of Science and Culture based on the funding program 'Niedersächsisches Vorab'. The joint project was coordinated by Prof. Dr. Martin Heidenreich and Prof. Dr. Jannika Mattes at the Jean Monnet Center for Europeanization and Transnational Regulations Oldenburg (CETRO) of the University of Oldenburg, as well as by Prof. Dr. Jürger Kädtler of the Sociological Research Institute at the University of Göttingen (SOFI). While the working group in Göttingen (Dr. Klaus-Peter Buss, Heidemarie Hanekop, Dr. Patrick Feuerstein) investigated the sector of information technology, the research team at Oldenburg (Dr. André Ortiz, Manfred Klöpper and Thomas Jackwerth) analyzed the sector of wind energy. The project's research design and methodology can be found in the final report (cf. Heidenreich et al., 2017, pp. 45–56).

collaborative innovation processes in innovation projects in two leading sectors of the German economy, wind energy and information technology.

The project originally assumed that innovation projects can be differentiated according to four types of governance: markets, hierarchies, communities and networks (Hollingsworth, 2000; Hollingsworth & Boyer, 1997). For each governance type, the project aimed to collect two cases with about ten experts from different functional units (e.g. project management, R&D, marketing & sales, production, etc.). In total, the 'COLLIN' project collected sixteen cases, eight for each of the two sectors. The author of this book re-analyses six cases from the wind energy industry from a different theoretical perspective.

4.4.1 Wind energy technologies

Wind energy technologies are a suitable example for analysing innovation projects. As is discussed below, modern wind turbines are technological architectures based on a dominant design. Under such conditions, innovations typically take the form of incremental improvements of components or subsystems, albeit requiring collaboration between different actors such as WTM, sub-system or component suppliers, applied research institutes or certifying bodies.

Wind power technologies are not new: the very first wind power technologies were in use on the Persian-Afghan border around 200 BC. The first electricity-producing wind turbine was installed in Cleveland, Ohio, in 1888. Today, countries around the world are considering wind energy technologies as a means of securing their energy supply and reducing their dependence on carbon-based energy (Kaldellis & Zafirakis, 2011).

Wind power technologies are not new: the very first wind power technologies were in use on the Persian-Afghan border around 200 BC. The first electricity-producing wind turbine was installed in Cleveland, Ohio, in 1888. Today, countries around the world are considering wind energy technologies as a means of securing their energy supply and reducing their dependence on carbon-based energy (Kaldellis & Zafirakis, 2011).

In the 1970s, pioneering entrepreneurs, scientists, farmers and local communities began to install wind turbines in rural and politically protected niches in Denmark and northern Germany. Emerging regional networks or clusters provided the social context for these agents to learn about these new technologies, user needs, technical standards and regulatory frameworks. Within these niches, pioneers had the space to deviate from the established technological regime of energy production protected by large incumbents (Fornahl et al., 2012; Karnøe & Garud, 2012; Mautz, 2012; Ohlhorst, 2009; Simmie, 2012).

In the late 1980s, the (onshore) wind energy industry reached a stage of maturity. In Germany, wind energy technologies have been booming since the 1990s. They have been progressively improved and have now become a state-of-the-art renewable energy production system. At the turn of the 21st century, a European offshore sector started to emerge, mainly concentrated in the UK, Germany and Denmark (Rodrigues et al., 2015).[33]

Innovation processes in the wind energy industry are now organized in global networks, geographically decoupled from their Danish and German origins (Jackwerth, 2014; Schaffarczyk, 2013; Silva & Klagge, 2013), whereas the early stages of wind energy in the 1970s and 1980s were characterized by 'bricolage' (Hendry & Harborne, 2011). Large WTMs such as GE Energy, Vestas, Goldwind, Gamesa, Enercon, Suzlon Group, Guodian United Power, Siemens Wind Power and Nordex are dominating the technological innovation (Kumar et al., 2016). For example, Vestas and Siemens Wind Power supply almost the entire global demand for offshore wind turbines.

33 Within the global energy production system, the significance of wind energy technologies is limited, accounting only for 2–3 % of the global electricity supply (Timilsina et al., 2013). Its growth rates, however, are impressive. From 1980 to 2012, the global wind power generation capacity grew from 10 MW to 282 GW, with an annual growth rate of circa 27 %. In Europe, wind energy accounted for 7 % of the European electricity consumption (McKenna et al., 2014).

Figure 1: Technological architecture of wind turbines

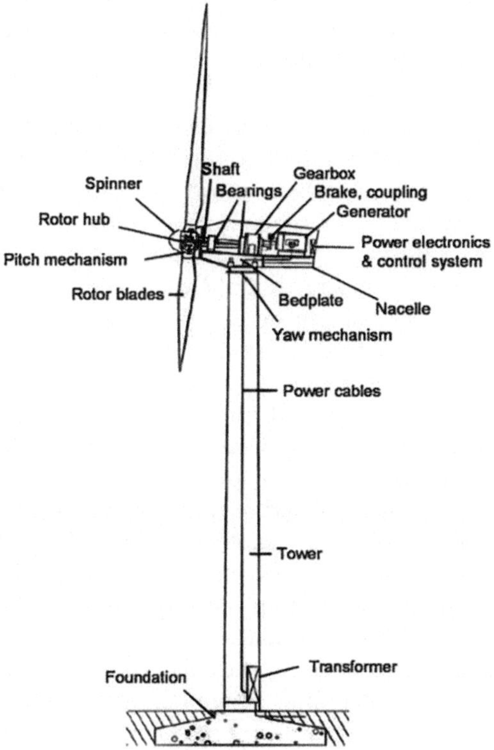

(taken from Huenteler et al., 2016a, p. 1199)

4.4.2 Patterns of technological innovation

Traditionally, innovative energy technologies are rarely developed by energy companies alone, but rather result from combining knowledge established in different sectors: for example, electro-mechanical machinery is used for gas turbines, semiconductors are incorporated in solar panels, and biochemistry provides the basis for biofuel conversion technologies. As wind turbines consist of generators, rotor blades, gearboxes and software systems, the same pattern of technological innovation can be expected for wind energy technologies. In fact, the literature shows that – in contrast to photovoltaic technologies, which are characterized by process innovations aiming at improved large-scale manufacturing capacities – wind energy technologies rely on systemic innovations (cf. Huenteler et al., 2016 a, b). This means that wind turbines are still incrementally improved through collaboration between heterogeneous specialists, such as subsystem or component suppliers.

The architecture of modern wind turbines consists of different subsystems. In general, two different designs can be distinguished. The "Danish design" is characterized by a horizontal rotor axis and three rotor blades (Hendry & Harborne, 2011; Kamp et al., 2004). A second prominent design, the direct drive, was established by Enercon and is often seen in wind farms in Germany (Lema et al., 2014). As shown in Figure 4.3, the architecture of wind turbines includes four sub-systems: the rotor, the drive train, the support structure (consisting of the foundation, tower and nacelle) and the grid connection (cf. Dannenberg, 2013; Schaffarczyk, 2013). Each subsystem in turn comprises various components, so that modern wind turbines contain several thousand of them in total (Huenteler et al., 2016b; Markard, 2011).

Today, as a dominant design has been established, the experimental period has ended and architectural innovation has declined (Huenteler et al., 2016b). Technological innovation has shifted from architecture and core components to subsystems and subcomponents.[34] Technological innovation is mainly driven by increasing size and reliability requirements (for a literature review, see McKenna et al., 2014). Another driver is the adaptation of wind energy technologies to new deployment contexts, such as coastal regions, forests, mountains, near-shore or deep-water locations (Jacobsson & Karltorp, 2013). In particular, the specific conditions of offshore wind turbines – harsh conditions at sea, high maintenance costs, high capital intensity of wind farm projects or production bottlenecks – require new technological and logistical solutions.[35]

34 This means that they are based on "*patents that received more than half of their citations from patents in other subsystems*" (Huenteler et al., 2016b, p. 111). Using empirical data from patent analysis, Huenteler et al. (2016b) found that new technological solutions often rely heavily on knowledge embodied in sub-components or neighboring systems. Indeed, the authors highlight that the share of systemic innovation in wind energy technologies has increased over time, from 49 % in 1980–89 to 58 % in 2000–09. The photovoltaic industry, on the other hand, relies mainly on process innovation.

35 As Jacobsson & Karltorp (2013) explain, the installation, operation and maintenance of offshore wind turbines in particular face harsh environmental and meteorological conditions compared to onshore wind. Due to their increasing weight and size, offshore wind turbines are manufactured close to port facilities. The turbines are built on special foundation structures and their installation requires new grid infrastructure. Suppliers of offshore components are often rooted in the maritime industry. They need to be integrated into supply chains that provide port facilities, specialized vessels and offshore logistics (cf. Fornahl et al., 2012).

In conclusion, wind energy technologies lend themselves to the analysis of collaborative innovation. Wind turbines are technological systems. Innovation in the wind energy sector is often incremental, with improvements realized through collaboration between WTM, component specialists and other partners such as research institutes. However, technological innovation is now mainly driven by increasing size and reliability requirements, as well as a differentiation of application contexts such as offshore, which increases the possibility of radically new solutions.

4.4.3 Data collection and problem-centered interviews

The empirical evaluation in the following chapters is based on expert interviews on six innovation projects collected by the COLLIN research project. One of the major challenges of COLLIN was to identify suitable cases of technology development. This section describes how the data collection was carried out.

In order to gain a better overview of the key players and to discuss current innovation challenges, the research team conducted exploratory interviews with experts from the wind energy industry. As Tab. 4.2 shows, the researchers spoke to 14 experts representing four different actors: associations and political administrations, public and private service providers, electrical plant operators and scientific institutes. In some cases, suitable innovation projects could be identified in this way.

Due to the limited information available on ongoing innovation projects, experts and their contact details were also searched on the Internet. Access to the field was mostly through direct requests for interviews. A mix of approaches was used, including telephone calls, e-mails, formal letters and informal requests at industry trade fairs.

All interviewees were given a one-page overview of the COLLIN research project. Due to the potential sensitivity of the data collected, an official declaration of confidentiality was used in some cases as a 'door opener' for arranging interviews. As the interview locations were often outside of Lower Saxony, extensive travel was required.

In each case, efforts were made to complete the ten interviews originally planned by COLLIN. However, mainly due to difficulties in accessing firms or collaborative innovation projects, the number of interviewees achieved ranged from five to 13 per case. More than five times, access to additional interviewees was denied after the first interview. Consequently, these cases had to be discarded after completion of the first interview.

The empirical data were collected between August 2013 and April 2015. The data collection was based on a semi-structured interview guide according to Flick (2002, pp. 117–145). In designing the interview guide, the two research groups involved from the Universities of Oldenburg and Göttingen defined theoretical categories that were general enough to cover current developments in two different sectors, namely information technology and wind energy technology (Heidenreich et al., 2017, pp. 45–56). The Oldenburg research group was responsible for conducting interviews in the wind energy industry.

One particular case, Case B, served as a pilot case for testing the interview guide. This case helped the researchers to identify underexplored issues (related to collaborative innovation) in the collected data, in particular the influence of coercive power on technology development. It was also Case B that sensitized the author of this book to the role of standards in innovation projects and how they are imposed by powerful actors such as WTM. The case also inspired the author to classify innovation projects according to different types of innovation.

The interview guide consisted of five sections linked to COLLIN's theoretical assumptions and research question (see section 8.7 in the appendix). After a short introduction by the interviewer (aim of the research project, main topics, etc.), the involvement of external specialists in the innovation project was explored in particular.

The interviews were problem-centered, i.e. the questions were oriented towards theoretically relevant problems such as practices of knowledge integration or the coordination of innovation projects based on standards (cf. Flick, 2002, p. 135). Problem-centered interviews are particularly suitable for the analysis of social processes in and across organizations because they address individual actions and increase the researchers' understanding of the underlying meaning or rationality (Witzel, 2000). Questions such as 'why' a project team faced a particular problem and 'how' they worked together to solve it emerged frequently. Both COLLIN's research proposal and the interviewer's personal professional experience provided further impetus for sensitizing concepts (Blumer, 1954), i.e. ideas for questions to be asked in the interviews with the experts.

Each interview lasted approximately 50 to 90 minutes. Due to the often limited time available, and depending on the interviewee's position in the company and his or her insights into a particular innovation project, not all points could be addressed in all cases. In such cases, efforts were made to cover missing items with other members of the same innovation project.

All interviews were transcribed according to a systematic transcription guide. The transcripts were coded using analytical categories derived from three sources: (1) the interview guide, (2) COLLIN's theoretical framework, and (3) unanticipated themes that emerged from the empirical data (cf. Schmidt, 2004). MAXQDA coding software was used for the pilot study and the most relevant interviews for the other cases. Later in the research process, relevant quotes were inserted directly into the case reports.

The interview material was summarized in eight case reports. For this book, six cases with a total of 55 interview transcripts were re-analysed after the completion of COLLIN.

Table 8: Explorative interviews in the wind energy industry

Type of actor	Organization	Interview partners	Sum: 13
Associations and political administrations	Provincial ministry of economic affairs	Minister, experts	2
	Federal association of renewable energies	Former president	1
	Association of the wind energy sector	Deputy managing	1
	Local network of the wind energy sector	Chairman	1
Public and private service providers	Offshore logistics service company	Managing director	1
	Wind park planning service provider	Managing director	1
	IT-consulting firm for the wind energy industry	Product manager	1
	Employee-representative department	Office manager	1
Operators of electrical plants	Utility and offshore planning for energy research	Expert quality management	1
	Large utility-based foundation	Technical secretary	1
	Operator of a network for energy research	Project manager	1
Scientific institutes	Institute of physics and wind energy research	Professor	1

Table 9: Projects of incremental innovation

(Case) technology	(Citation) Organization	Interview partners	Sum: 15
(A) Large component for wind turbines: large power train component	(Org01) Large, well-established component supplier	Strategy & marketing manager	1
		Project manager	2
		Key account manager	1
		R&D power train component	1
		Project sales	1
(B) Small component for wind turbines: rotor brake system	(Org01) Small component supplier and newcomer to the wind energy industry	Manager product department	2
		Product center manager	1
		Marketing engineer	1
		Innovation manager	1
		Construction engineer	1
		Manager manufacturing	1
		Manager quality management	1
	(Org2) Another component supplier	Marketing manager	1

Table 10: Projects of radical innovation

(Case) technology	(Citation) Organization	Interview partners	Sum: 26
(C) A radically new rotor blade coating system based on robotics	(Org01) Rotor blade manufacturing site	Factory manager	1
		Coating process engineer	1
		Production engineer	2
	(Org02) Project partner and engineering service provider	Managing director and system planner	1
		External project engineer	1
	(Org03) A sub-contractor in the project	Managing director	1
		Product managers	1
	(Org03) Firm formerly specialized in rotor blade manufacturing	CTO, member of the board	2
(D) Radically new support structure for onshore wind turbines	(Org01) Start-up firm	Senior product developer	1
		Construction manager	1
	(Org02) Material testing institute	Expert material testing	1
	(Org03) Construction approval authority	Test engineer	1
	(Org04) Certifying body	Team manager	1
	(Org05) Timber engineering service provider	Managing director	1

Table 11: Emerging technology fields

(Case) technology	(Citation) Organization	Interview partners	Sum: 26
(E) Different mitigation systems for offshore wind	(Org01) Public wind park approval authority	Approval expert (only notes allowed)	1
	(Org02) Engineering service provider and system supplier	Managing director and entrepreneur	2
		Technical assistant	1
	(Org03) Engineering service provider and system supplier	Managing director	1
	(Org04) Utility (A), wind park planning department	Offshore engineering manager	2
	(Org05) Utility (B), wind park planning department	Expert noise mitigation	1
		Expert wind park approval	2
		Expert foundation structures	1
	(Org06) Measurement stations	Measurement specialist and consultant	1
	(Org07) System supplier for offshore construction	R&D noise mitigation systems	1
	(Org08) Foundation for the offshore wind industry	Office manager	1
	(Org09) Monopile foundation supplier	R&D monopiles	1

(Case) technology	(Citation) Organization	Interview partners	Sum: 26
(F) A new foundation system turbines	(Org01) Offshore system developer	Senior manager	2
		Design engineer	1
	(Org02) Applied research institute	Research project manager	2
	(Org03) University department	Expert geotechnics	1
	(Org04) Material testing institute	Expert material testing	1
	(Org06) Utility (C)	Expert corporate communication	1
	(Org07) Offshore logistics service provider	Manager offshore logistics	1
	(Org08) Ministry for Economic	Expert	1
		Expert	1

5. Projects of incremental innovation

In *chapter 3*, it was concluded that in technology fields, the social process of establishing common working standards could explain the outcome of innovation projects. To analyze this process in empirical cases, it was proposed that in projects of incremental innovation, collaboration is based on *practices of monitoring technical standards and sanctioning nonconformity (P1)*. It was argued that in such projects, where technologies are typically developed based on technical standards, the innovation praxis tends to reproduce technical knowledge, conform to design rules, and involve familiar partners instead of innovating from scratch.

This proposition is evaluated on the basis of two examples of component development in the wind energy industry. This chapter compares the two cases. *First*, the field of component development is characterized (5.1); *second*, it is shown which practices of knowledge integration could be observed (5.2); *third*, the reader learns how collaboration was organized (5.3); fourth, it is discussed which discussed which institutional barriers occurred and what they caused. Finally, the results are summarized and preliminary conclusions are drawn.

5.1 Positions of partners in the field

This section illustrates how the two fields of incremental innovation studied were structured. Both fields of component development were organized around a large WTM collaborating with a medium-sized German component supplier. In both cases, high power asymmetries between the development partners could be observed. In both cases, the collaboration structure resembled a hierarchical innovation network with a large WTM dominating technology development.

However, the two cases differed in two respects. First, the relative position of the component suppliers vis-à-vis their customers: On the one hand, we had an established component and market leader; on the other hand, the component developer was a newcomer and niche product supplier. Second, the cases differed in the cause of the collaboration: an order development in case A and a joint R&D project that turned into a supply relationship in case B. This had direct consequences for the regulation of the collaboration.

5.1.1 Case A: An incumbent supplier and market leader

The first case of a component supply relationship developed a relatively large component that is installed in the nacelle of wind turbines. The case is a story about a supplier company that developed a new component for an existing type of wind turbine of a large European WTM. In fact, the component is part of the drive train of the wind turbine, which consists of three large components: rotor, gearbox and generator. The component thus plays a prominent role in the architecture of wind turbines.

The supplier, whose daily development and production practices were observed, is a medium-sized company based in Germany. The company is one of the pioneers in the wind energy sector and has been specializing in such technologies for more than forty years, as expressed by the strategy and marketing manager (A-Org01): "*We are one of the pioneers in the wind industry. We have been in the wind industry since the beginning. We supplied the first [major components] for wind turbines in 1977. At that time, wind turbines were still assembled in garage yards. [The company] only does wind, can only do wind, and thinks only in wind. That starts with the management and ends with the guard. We can do nothing else.*" As the interviewee points out, the company has evolved from a pioneer to a globally recognized specialist and market leader. Today, the company is an established supplier of electromechanical components for almost all leading WTMs.

5.1.2 Case B: A newcomer and niche product supplier

The second case also involves a medium-sized German supplier of wind turbine components. Compared to the first case, however, the component is part of the rotor and much smaller than in case A. In fact, the component is part of a system that stops the rotors from turning, for example, during maintenance. Therefore, compared to the first case, the second component is smaller, relies on less electromechanical engineering knowledge and plays a less prominent role in the wind turbine architecture.

The two cases also differed in terms of the social position of the component suppliers in the wind energy industry. In the first case, the company had been supplying components for decades and had become a global specialist and incumbent. In the second case, the component supplier was a newcomer to the wind energy industry. Before entering the market, the company had supplied components to the rail vehicle industry. It was only at the beginning of the 21st century that the company decided to enter the wind energy market, as the product department manager (B-Org01) recalls: "*They decided on wind power because, unlike today, it was still booming eleven years ago.*" To position itself as a newcomer, the company decided to expand its business activities into the wind energy market and developed an idea for a radically new component together with an applied research institute. The company was able to establish a joint R&D partnership with a leading WTM, which evolved into a component supply relationship.

Figure 2: Field of component development

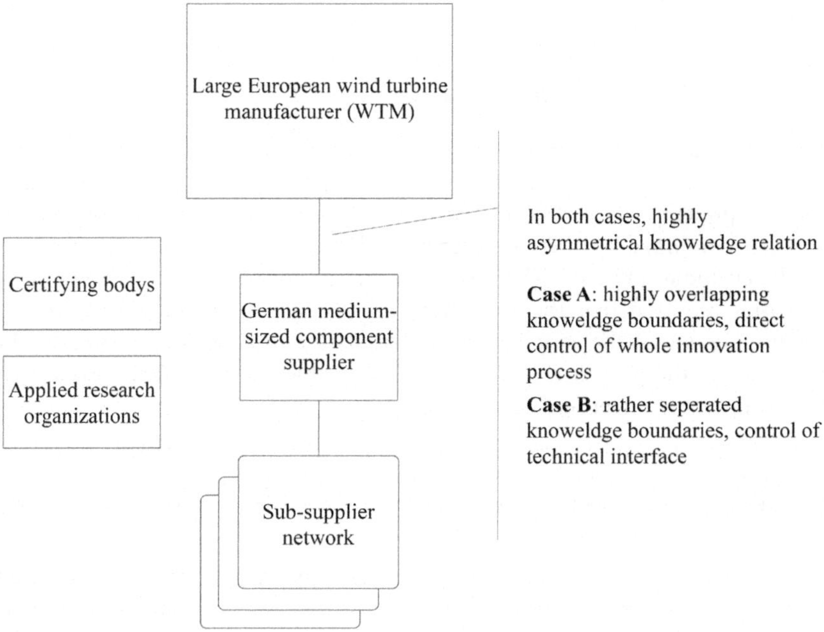

Figure 2 illustrates the field of technology development in cases A and B. The collaboration structure takes the form of a hierarchical innovation network with a large European WTM at the top. Consequently, strong power asymmetries characterize the collaboration in both cases. However, the observed supply relationships differed significantly in terms of the underlying practices of knowledge integration. In case A, these processes were highly institutionalized, while in case B, the collaborative relationship had just changed from an R&D partnership to a supply relationship.

5.2 Analysed practices of knowledge integration

After describing the two studied technology fields, this section shows which practices of knowledge integration could be observed in the two cases. In section 2.2, knowledge integration was defined as the combination of specialized and complementary knowledge to accomplish specific tasks. In both cases, a large WTM and a supplier company were the main actors that combined their knowledge to design a new product that could be integrated into wind turbines.

5.2.1 Case A: Highly regulated product development

In both cases of incremental innovation studied, knowledge integration took place in the process of designing the new component. In the first case, where the component was part of the drive train of wind turbines, a component supplier combined its internal expertise with technical specifications provided by the customer (WTM). The project manager coordinating the development activities reported that the customer provided a large amount of technical requirements that the supplier had to translate into a working prototype. In this case, as the project manager suggests, product development was more a task of reducing uncertainty than of inventing something new:

> *[W]e are now getting huge amounts of load information. In some cases, it's several gigabytes of data. We have to process it computationally. (...) The less accurate they are or the more uncertainty they contain, the more uncertainty we get [in the component]. (A-Org01, Project manager)*

Interestingly, in this case the component development was largely pre-defined by technical standards and implemented on the basis of standardized engineering procedures established in the development company. Apart from detailed technical requirements, the component design was largely based on industry standards. In addition, quality standards such as loads and performance criteria were defined in detail by the customer. The project manager (A-Org01) mentioned that his colleagues used standardized engineering procedures such as the Finite Element Method (FEM) to implement the customer's technical expectations. technical expectations:

> *We get [from the customer] so-called wind simulations for different turbine configurations and locations. These are also classified via the [industry standard]. We then run simulation calculations over the entire lifetime of about 20 years. We need the complete data for the structural-mechanical verification, e.g. FEM calculations.*

As these results show, the knowledge integration process has two characteristics. First, knowledge was easily combined across the organizational boundaries of the companies involved – WTM on the one hand and the component supplier on the other. Second, the knowledge integration process was highly regulated, based on routinized engineering procedures used to translate the customer's detailed technical expectations into a new product design. Another interviewee responsible for internal R&D added that in addition to these development routines, testing procedures were also highly regulated:

> *At the moment, it is standard practice for us to test every component we build up to its rated load. (...) This enables us to ensure that every component that leaves the yard works reliably within the requirements. (A-Org01, R&D component technologies)*

As you can see from these quotes, both the design and testing processes are highly standardized. These well-established working standards facilitate the integration of complex technical knowledge into a new component.

In fact, as the project manager (A-Org01) suggested, the component was basically defined hierarchically by the customer based on industry standards, the customer's technical standards, and the component supplier's own technical standards: "*In addition to the industry standards, there are also customer requirements that define even stricter requirements under certain circumstances. In addition, we also work with our own interpretation guidelines.*"

In conclusion, the knowledge integration process in this case was institutionalized in the form of the customer's technical standards and established working standards for how to design, build, and test new components. In essence, the development company's main task was to combine technical standards based on well-established working standards. Consequently, the project manager (A-Org01) metaphorically characterized the knowledge integration process as arranging a "large bouquet of configurations":

> *That is a large bouquet of configurations that have to be taken into account at the end of the day during development.*

5.2.2 Case B: A new component supply relation

While knowledge integration in the first case was characterized as the combination of technical standards based on well-established working standards, the second case presented a different picture. The knowledge integration process was much less institutionalized. In fact, it started as a joint R&D project. Together with an applied research institute, experts from the component supplier specialized in technologies used in the rail vehicle industry developed the "idea" of a radically new component for wind turbines in order to differentiate the company from component suppliers and competitors already well established in the wind energy industry. The product manager (B-Org01) remembers:

> *At that time, two or three people from [the rail vehicle components division] had the idea and developed it together with the Fraunhofer Institute.*

While in the first case the component supplier was an established and leading specialist in the wind energy industry, in the second case the supplier company started as a newcomer with limited experience in product development for WTM. In particular, as the design engineer (B-Org01) recalls, the company had to learn how to deal with shorter innovation cycles and increased price competition: "*[W]e were not used to very cost-oriented development here in the company. (...) This means that for many development steps in railway technology we could say that we knew roughly where we would end up (...). In retrospect, we then looked at what the fun really cost, also taking into account economies of scale.*" Compared to the first case, the supplier's engineering processes were not yet institutionalized because it was a newcomer to the wind energy industry. The company had to establish new working standards in order to be able to work with large WTMs.

It was the component supplier that, after developing a first product idea, actively initiated an R&D project together with a large European WTM to develop a working prototype and gain a first foothold in the wind energy industry, as the product department manager (B-Org01) added:

> *Once the "electric vice" was developed, a partner was sought (...) and the concept was presented to them. They were enthusiastic because this company sells its wind turbines only with a maintenance contract and maintains the turbines itself.*

After establishing this new component supply relationship with a large WTM, the component supplier took a niche position in the wind energy industry. The component was radically new because it incorporated a technological principle that deviated from the established technological paradigm used by competitors. That is, instead of using hydraulics to generate holding forces, which was the primary component technology in almost all existing supplier relationships, the newcomer introduced an innovative solution based on electronics. Thus, the company introduced an innovative component that deviated from established technologies. In doing so, the company positioned itself in a market niche.

Consequently, the component supplier not only acted as a newcomer, but more importantly for the understanding of this case, it also remained a niche product supplier for a technologically rather "simple" component, as the product department manager (B-Org01) explains below. As a result, there were few knowledge interdependencies on either side of the partnership and thus strong power imbalances in favor of the large WTM.

> *[The customer] uses them as a relatively simple component because they themselves have a very complicated control system in the tower.*

In conclusion, as Figure 5.1 shows, the practices of knowledge integration observed in the two technology fields crossed the boundaries of three actors:

(1) a large European WTM, (2) a component supplier, and (3) a network of subcomponent suppliers. In both domains, the collaborative structure took the form of a hierarchical innovation network, with the WTM at the top dominating the development activities of the component supplier.

However, the cases differ significantly in terms of the position of the component supplier in the field. These positions had a direct impact on the knowledge integration process. Case A tells the story of a supplier relationship between a component developer and an incumbent; in this case, the knowledge integration process combined technical standards based on highly regulated engineering procedures.

Case B showed the opposite. Here, the knowledge integration process, as well as the entire supplier relationship, was hardly institutionalized. Component development was initiated as a joint R&D project. In the early years, the component supplier struggled to adapt its engineering procedures to the working standards of the wind energy industry, such as short innovation cycles. Knowledge integration mainly took the form of joint R&D and creative engineering. In order to gain more customers and to expand its innovation network, the component supplier tried to "impose" product improvements on its main customer in order to broaden its product range and to leave the occupied market niche, as the product department manager (B-Org01) reflects:

> *You could say that we forced it on them a bit, but we played with open cards (...). We also said that we expected new customers with the [advanced components] and that we could sell the [component] in higher quantities so that the price would eventually become lower due to volume effects. This was also a reason why the customer agreed.*

As these findings show, in contrast to the first case, the second component supplier took a position as a newcomer and niche product developer in the field. Due to these different positions in the field (incumbent vs. newcomer), the application of standards played a different role in the two technology projects, as will be discussed below.

5.3 Realizing technology development

The previous section introduced two technology fields that were very different in terms of the supplier firm's position (an incumbent vs. a newcomer). In this section, the impact of these structural configurations on the organization of the two technology projects is shown. It will be the case that in both cases the coercive imposition of technology development was the dominant social process of technology development. WTMs imposed their standards on component suppliers due to their superior power positions.

5.3.1 Case A: Imposing technical standards

Starting with Case A, it will be shown how the collaboration has been coordinated in the case of a large component for the drive train of a wind turbine. It will be shown that the WTM was able to impose its technical standards on the engineering praxis of the component supplier, mainly due to its superior position of power in the field.

5.3.2 Contractually defined technology projects

In this case, contractual agreements were a central means of regulating the cooperation between the WTM and its supplier. As the key account manager (A-Org01) explains, customers often have a fairly elaborate idea of the design of the future technology prior to the start of the project, which includes key component suppliers. As a result, development contracts specify how the project will be structured.

> *Even before customers go public and announce that they want to install a new turbine, they often have a contract in place with key suppliers. The whole concept is already in place. (A-Org01, Key account manager)*

The investigated project was based on two contracts. First, as shown above, the supply relationship was firmly institutionalized, or as a strategy and marketing manager (A-Org01) stated: "*This is not the first project we've done with [this customer]. This is the umpteenth project, so we already know what they want.*" This particular development partnership included a framework contract that defined the basic agreements between the two partners, as explained by the key account manager (A-Org01): "*[I]n general, there is a framework agreement under which everything can be roughly handled, from deliveries to requests, etc.*". The production manager stated that some customers even limit the supplier's choice of subcomponents due to customer-specific quality requirements: "*There is one customer in particular who requires us to source 100 % of the components from our internal parts production*" (A-Org01, Manufacturing manager).

Second, in addition to framework contracts, development contracts further specify the "*rights and rules*" of technology development, such as ownership of newly developed components. In this way, customers limit the component supplier's ability to use new components in other projects, such as projects with customers producing smaller wind turbines, as the same expert points out:

> *Development agreements can be made specifically for such projects, including rights and rules. In the past, this was not done at all (...). Now, customers are increasingly demanding to secure the rights to these products. We would not push for that because the old approach suits us much better. It allows us to be more flexible and use the component for smaller customers as well. (A-Org01, Key account manager)*

These findings show that in this first case, framework agreements and development contracts limited the component supplier's choice of subcomponents or knowledge transfer. The key account manager (A-Org01) added that such contracts are used to define the project budget, technical requirements, project timelines, or technical innovations agreed upon by both partners: "*At the beginning of a project, you draw up a budget. How much is the component going to cost? What are the customer's requirements? During the course of the project, we check whether the project is still within budget or whether there are new findings that mean something cannot be technically implemented as planned and a more expensive variant has to be used*" (A-Org01, Key account manager).

Thus, contractual agreements pre-define projects and limit the possibilities for innovation. In fact, as the project manager explained, each technology development project for large customers such as General Electric, Vestas or Siemens is exclusive due to contractual obligations and "non-disclosure agreements." This expert speaks of "*separate development paths*" to illustrate that any knowledge integration between customer-specific technology projects is forbidden: "*These are necessarily separate development paths, as each manufacturer has its own requirements and philosophies. Of course, we are constantly developing our knowledge base and design guidelines (...). But it is definitely not the case that there is any internal merging in [component development] between different customers. There are contractual agreements and confidentiality agreements, some of which do not allow us to transfer the solution from one application to another*" (A-Org01, Project manager).

In summary, these results show that WTM uses contractual agreements (such as such as framework contracts, development contracts, or non-disclosure agreements) to impose technical standards (e.g., technical requirements, price expectations, and property rights) on component suppliers. They define the project setup before it starts, including project schedules, subcomponent suppliers, or technical designs. It was interesting to observe that such contracts impose legal boundaries that prohibit knowledge integration across custom technology projects, thereby limiting the component supplier's potential for innovation.

5.3.2.1 Central control of component developers

In addition to contracts, the WTM in Case A used technical standards to predefine component development. Basically, three types of technical standards could be observed, which together describe a pyramid. First, at the top of the pyramid are industry standards, such as those issued by the International Electrotechnical Commission (IEC). The project manager (A-Org01) explained that IEC standards for wind turbines contain chapters that also define the design of subcomponents:

> *For example, reliability must be demonstrated using statistical methods to ensure that only a certain failure rate can be expected for [a component] over its entire service life. Ultimately, this is broken down to each subcomponent, for which we have to provide the appropriate evidence. There are standardized standards for this.*

This quote illustrates the use of technical standards to control the development of external components. Such technical standards cannot be negotiated because they are defined in development guidelines. In addition, the component supplier relies on working standards and engineering procedures, such as statistical methods, to demonstrate compliance with technical standards – work that is controlled by certifying organizations such as Germanischer Lloyd, TÜV, or DEWI.

The second type of imposed standards refers to the technical requirements of the customer, which largely determine the design of the new component, as the manufacturing manager (A-Org01) explains: "*The projects are usually customer specific. Based on the individual turbine types defined by the customer: Does the turbine have large blades, what wind conditions will it be installed in, etc.? In the end, each project has its own specifications.*" Thus, in addition to industry standards, the customer's expectations control the development of components.

It is also interesting to note that, in addition to technical specifications, the customer imposes working standards on the project partners, including quality, reliability and safety standards. For example, the project manager (A-Org01) distinguishes two customer strategies for exercising normative control. Customers can either define high quality criteria or directly control the daily engineering praxis by "*questioning in detail*" the supplier's procedures and methods, such as statistical calculations or design simulations:

> *There are customers who think they can buy safety by entering higher safety factors into the calculation. Higher load factors are then specified, which we have to take into account in the calculation. The other strategy is to go into a lot of detail and maybe ask us to do more calculations and simulations. (A-Org01, Project manager)*

These findings point to a highly centrally controlled innovation praxis. In fact, the component supplier has organized its internal engineering processes according to the requirements of its four major customers, as the strategy and marketing manager (A-Org01) explains: "*Project management and the development team are customer specific, i.e. they only work on projects for a specific customer.*" This shows that each project partner develops technologies exclusively for one customer. Knowledge integration between these development lines is largely prohibited, which not only increases the supplier's dependency on the customer and limits the supplier's innovation potential, but also limits the customer's innovation potential.

Time frames was also highly regulated in this case of technology development. The interviewees explained that a project typically lasts 18 months. Within this timeframe, the innovation process is divided into four stages: (1) sourcing (two to three months); (2) component development (about ten months); (3) prototype testing (about three months); (4) pilot production (about one to two months). The project manager stated that after each major project step – acquisition, concept, design, prototype – the customer approves the given result. For example, "*the concept phase is completed with a milestone, also with the customer. This phase ends with a joint meeting.*" As you can see, the two organizations involved in the project partnership are linked by common working standards as well as common time concepts (milestones).

When, as in this case, the participating project organizations are structurally coupled on the basis of a common time concept, the project manager of the component supplier takes on an interesting role. He or she not only coordinates the project work and moderates the communication between the specialist departments; the project manager also maintains an exclusive communication channel with the customer (Single-Point-Of-Contact"; SPOC). Interestingly, the project manager in Case A (A-Org01) reported that he interprets his role as a "*customer's lawyer*" who ensures that the project work is in line with the customer's "*requirements*" and "*needs*":

> *Basically, I see myself here in the company as the customer's advocate, making sure that as many of the customer's needs and wants as possible are met. But we must not lose sight of our own goals in terms of deadlines, quality and costs, because at the end of the day we have to make money with the product. It is always a bit of a balancing act.*

In conclusion, these findings show how external component development is managed on the basis of common industry norms and customer technical standards. In addition, the project organizations involved share certain working standards, time frames (milestones), and exclusive communication channels between project managers (SPOC). Such a highly regulated innovation praxis makes it easier for the WTM to control external component development.

It should be noted that these findings only partially support Proposition 1. In contrast to P1, which states that in incremental innovation projects, project work is mainly organized through practices of monitoring technical standards and sanctioning nonconformity, the technology development project in Case A was organized on the basis of central control and the coercive imposition of technical standards by the customer. For the component supplier, the scope for innovation or the creation of alternative work standards was limited. However, in line with P1, practices of monitoring the customer's expectations were found in the role of the component supplier's project manager, who ensured that the customer's technical standards were met.

5.3.2.2 Working standards that control sub-component suppliers

It was shown above that, in contrast to P1, project work tends to be characterized by the coercive imposition of technical standards by the customer. This section shows that such central control is also based on work standards imposed on the entire innovation network, including subcomponent suppliers.

Sub-component suppliers tend to be preferred partners that the component supplier has "*qualified*" in the past to meet the quality standards defined by the component supplier and/or its customer, as the project sales expert (A-Org01) of the supplier organization studied points out: "*[w]e are gradually qualifying new suppliers, of course, to introduce a certain amount of competition*". Similar to the partnerships observed between the component supplier and its customer, the subcomponent supply network is controlled by centrally defined standards, such as quality standards. The component supplier not only imposes product prices on the subcomponent suppliers, but also imposes "*quality requirements*" that force the subcomponent suppliers to comply with process standards, as explained by the project sales expert (A-Org01):

> *It takes a certain amount of time for a supplier to really meet our high quality requirements. It takes time for them to reach a certain level of process capability.*

The strategy and marketing manager (A-Org01) adds that such development relationships are usually highly regulated, and knowledge integration is not a problem if the component supplier executes processes properly and defines technical requirements accurately: "*You are in a customer-supplier relationship here (...). They know the systems. You do a preliminary design and they work on it. That works quite well. It's more the emotional component that gets in the way. Otherwise, with today's methods of communication and data transfer, it's not a problem. You just have to define exactly what you want.*" The same manager concludes that a common understanding of quality standards and formal engineering procedures facilitates knowledge integration because it makes information sharing independent of the skills or idiosyncrasies of individuals:

> *Large companies are much simpler in terms of process capability. They also understand why we are implementing an automotive quality safety standard and why we want this part to be tested in the same way. A manufacturer from the Black Forest with twelve employees, but who is brilliant, says that we can't get this from him because he doesn't have the people for it (...).*

Finally, it was noted that the component supplier used working standards related to shared quality norms to control the entire innovation network, including subcomponent suppliers. This highly regulated innovation praxis facilitated knowledge integration by decoupling communication within the project from individual skills or idiosyncrasies.

5.3.2.3 Personal inspection and transparent manufacturing

The centrally controlled innovation praxis described above also extended to the manufacturing process. In addition to common engineering procedures, common time concepts, or communication channels between project managers, there were also common production standards. The manufacturing manager (A-Org01) explained how some customers personally inspect the manufacturing process: "*It is very characteristic of the wind gearbox industry that the cooperation with customers is extremely close. I can certainly say that we have, for example, 100 % inspectors employed by certain customers. They walk through the assembly lines here every day, looking for defects and wanting to rectify them quickly.*" The project sales expert (A-Org01) describes a similar practice of personal control. Together with the company's customers, the expert personally checks whether the subcomponent developers meet the mutually agreed quality standards:

> *Some of our customers demand that we visit the suppliers, so we go there together with our customers. (...) This is included in the quality plans that we have with our suppliers. (A-Org01, Project sales expert)*

The same project sales expert (A-Org01) provides further insight into this form of personal inspection. The expert reports that customers use quality standards to control the entire supply network. In particular, for so-called "*structural components*", some customers require that production processes be "*frozen*" at certain defined points in time. This means that each production step must be recorded: "*It is recorded which processing machines he uses to produce this.*" The supplier is not allowed to change the production process without the customer's approval:

> *The customer requires us to freeze these processes and only change them with our approval and that of the customer in order to guarantee the quality of the parts, i.e. that they are always produced using the same manufacturing process.*

These findings confirm the prevalence of a highly regulated innovation praxis. In the manufacturing process, standards of transparency regarding individual responsibilities and work processes facilitate direct control. For example, central monitoring takes place on the basis of a so-called "*electronic assembly and test stand protocol.*" This protocol, explains the production manager (A-Org01), "*is a document that we create for the customer. (...) With this standard, the customer can of course see exactly how we [have organized our assembly] and can establish this accordingly in his processes.*" This transparency makes it easier to control production, as the production manager points out:

> *Each assembly station has a computer operated by the workers themselves. They sign in with their own identification number so that the customer can see exactly which worker tightened which screw. Of course, this means that the worker is very concerned that the documentation he provides and the work he does are 100 % correct. (...) Ultimately, this is complete transparency.*

In this case, both WTM and the component supplier rely on well-defined working standards (such as process and quality standards) to regulate the innovation praxis and facilitate centralized control of component development. Manufacturing processes are also standardized. Production is tightly controlled through transparency standards and personal inspections. In this case, the prevailing work standards were not negotiated, but well established and used to coercively control the entire innovation network.

5.3.2.4 Homogeneous knowledge on both sides of the partnership

Achieving the centralized control of component development described above is easier when the technical knowledge on all sides of the partnership is highly homogeneous. Several interviewees stated that the partners involved have similar expertise, which enables the customer to define the component development. For example, the strategy and marketing manager (A-Org01) reported that large customers have in-depth knowledge of components and are therefore able to impose and monitor quality requirements:

> *The turbine manufacturers have built up a lot of [component] expertise. There are really [component] design engineers working there, some of whom came from [component] manufacturers and some of whom also work in quality assurance (...). Depending on the customer structure, they are more or less involved.*

Despite the high degree of specialization, no knowledge asymmetry between component suppliers and their customers was observed. Rather, as the quote above illustrates, strongly overlapping knowledge boundaries enabled the customer to maintain a power position vis-à-vis the component supplier and to "*interfere*" in the daily project work.

The key account manager (A-Org01) supported this conclusion. This expert stated that particularly large WTMs with high business volumes and market shares have in-depth component knowledge and professional competencies that enable them to define components in detail and impose their expectations on the component supplier: "*Our large customers have people on the other side of the development team who know the components in detail. They have real expertise and a very specific idea of what their components should look like.*" The project manager (A-Org01) adds that because large customers have inside knowledge of various components, they are able to impose technical designs on the component supplier:

> *A large system manufacturer has more experience with different component concepts. (...) Based on this experience, they can usually impose requirements on us that are different from our own philosophy.*

In summary, a relatively homogeneous knowledge base shared among innovation partners facilitates centralized control of component development. The experts interviewed speak of "*experiences*", "*imaginations*" or "*philosophies*" to describe how a large customer can impose its cognitive framework (e.g. technical designs, quality standards) on the component supplier, as the strategy and marketing manager (A-Org01) put it:

> *There are customers who really tell us that [the component] has to look exactly like this and that. (A-Org01, Strategy & marketing manager)*

5.3.2.5 Preliminary conclusions

Based on these findings, a number of preliminary conclusions can be drawn with respect to P1. In Chapter 3, it was argued that in *contexts of incremental innovation, technology projects are mainly organized through practices of monitoring technical standards and sanctioning nonconformity*. These assumptions are only partially supported by the empirical findings in Case A.

In fact, in this case, a large WTM at the top of a component development network mainly used contracts to predefine the development project and impose its technical standards (such as technical requirements, price expectations, property rights, or project schedules) on the studied component supplier. The coercive imposition of technical standards appeared to be the dominant social mechanism structuring the development of the new technology, as summarized in Table 13.

It was particularly interesting to observe that the entire innovation process, including the manufacturing process, was centrally controlled, not only by the imposition of technical standards, but also by the imposition of labor standards. Shared norms of efficiency, quality, reliability, safety, or transparency, but also exclusive communication channels (SPOC) between project managers on both sides of the partnership, as well as personal inspections of the manufacturing process, facilitated central control.

Thus, contrary to the expectations raised by P1, this technology project was largely organized on the basis of the coercive imposition of technical and labor standards. A collaborative innovation praxis characterized by horizontal negotiations was not found.

Table 12: Innovation praxis in established fields

Technical standards	**Working standards**
Customer's technical standards, mainly based on industry norms and development contracts	Shared conceptions of time (milestones); exclusive communication channels (SPOC) between project managers
Component supplier's internal technical guidelines	Shared engineering and manufacturing norms (regarding quality, reliability, security, transparency)
	Homogeneous knowledge on both sides and a technological frame imposed by the customer

5.3.3 Case B: Dominating a supply relation

The previous section showed that incremental innovation processes tend to be centrally controlled by the customer. The dominant praxis of technology development found was coercive imposition based on technical standards, development contracts, and homogeneous knowledge. This section discusses how collaboration was organized in the second case of a component supply relationship. Again, the results partly reject P1, because an innovation praxis hardly emerged. Instead, an initial R&D partnership was reduced to a simple market relationship.

5.3.3.1 The power to control technology development

Compared to the first case of a large powertrain component, in the second case of a small component, the technical design as well as the interface was much less complex and actively kept simple by the customer, as described by the Product Center Manager (B-Org01):

> *The external interfaces, i.e. the screwing points and also the connector, were the same as on the prototype. This means that nothing really changed with this connector. (...) We had suggested ideas on how to improve the electrical interface*

because it's very simple now, but the customer didn't want that. They didn't want to change anything. (B-Org01, Product center manager)

Having introduced a new product idea some time ago because it deviated from established component technologies, the component supplier found itself in a niche position outside of well-established supply networks. To expand its customer network and move out of this niche market, the supplier creatively improved the original product design. According to the product center manager (B-Org01), to make the product attractive to other customers, the company improved the engineering design and added electrical intelligence to improve the component's communication with neighboring components in the wind turbine. However, the main customer showed no interest in further collaborative innovation and demanded that the interface be kept simple:

[Our [component] has been further developed since then. The relatively simple vice, where you could just say 'open' and 'close', has now become a very complex and complicated device controlled by an intelligent microprocessor. (...) This could become part of the wind turbine control system, but this company has no need for it.

These quotes indicate strong power asymmetries between the two partners. It is also clear that the component supplier tried to get out of its niche position by engaging in collaborative innovation processes not only with its customers but also with other WTMs. However, the customer showed no interest and actively prohibited further innovations that would have changed the architecture of the wind turbine. In the words of the product department manager (B-Org01): "*[The customer] naturally wants to keep control of the system control as much as possible.*"

Thus, in this case, the customer coercively controlled the development of the components. The supply relationship offered few opportunities for collaborative innovation. On the contrary, the customer actively reinforced its power position and thwarted all attempts by the component supplier to introduce innovative product variants by keeping the technical interface between the component and the wind turbine simple, as the product department manager points out: "*Unfortunately, we still do by far the most sales with this company. So we are dependent on them. This is also partly due to the fact that they use our [product] as a relatively simple component because they themselves have a very complicated control system in the tower.*

Thus, although this inter-company relationship began as a collaborative R&D project, it quickly evolved into a highly asymmetrical power relationship dominated unilaterally by the customer. WTM showed no interest in establishing a praxis of collaborative innovation. It rejected all attempts by the component supplier to gain some control over the wind turbine's architecture by integrating technical intelligence into the component, which would have established certain knowledge interdependencies. Instead, the customer was primarily interested in minimizing the price of the product. as described by the product department manager (B-Org01):

> *The pressure to build this [component] and to make it cheaper came from outside.*

In conclusion, compared to the first case, a joint innovation practice was observed in Case B only at the beginning of the innovation process. However, the initial joint R&D partnership turned into a simple market relationship reduced to keeping product prices low and rejecting any further technical improvements. In fact, the customer imposed product prices and interface data on the component developer.

5.3.3.2 Technical interfaces as a power instrument

Having developed a new product and being a newcomer to the wind energy industry, the component supplier was initially a monopolist. However, a few years after the introduction of the new product, a competitor entered the market and weakened the supplier's position, as recalled by the product department manager (B-Org01): "*[Four] years ago, a large part of the team left the company and started their own business with the same product.*" The marketing engineer (B-Org01) adds: "*They had been gone for six months when they had already delivered the first component from the new position.*" The product manager points out: "*This was a real problem for us because they continued to supply this system manufacturer. Suddenly there were two suppliers, which of course meant that sales were halved.*" The monopoly turned into fierce competition between the two component suppliers. This, in turn, strengthened WTM's relative power position vis-à-vis the component supplier:

> *At that time, we were the monopolist for such components, which this wind turbine manufacturer didn't like. That's why they were happy when we split up and some employees went into business for themselves, because now they suddenly had two suppliers. (B-Org01, Product department manager)*

The emerging competition between the two component suppliers strengthened the power position of the customer. As the construction manager (B-Org01) explains, WTM usually buys components from at least two different sources (second-source strategy) and tries to impose its technical standards on each component supplier: "*[The customer] also has to realize that we are not the only supplier, that there is at least one other supplier. If one supplier changes something, the customer would also have to discuss everything technically with the other supplier.*" The emerging competition thus weakened the component supplier's monopoly position and strengthened the customer's position of technical and commercial dominance.

To regain at least some of its former monopoly power, the supplier improved its product design to differentiate its product from its competitor, as the design engineer (B-Org01) explains: "*Ultimately, it was an attempt to put together a functional package that offered good value for money and that could only be copied by our competitors with as much effort as possible.*" But once the component was improved, adds the product manager (B-Org01), the competitor quickly caught up: "*This is now new, but the competition has caught up. However, we hope to have a technological advantage.*" These findings confirm that the initial collaboration between the WTM and the component supplier, instead of establishing a joint innovation praxis, went in the opposite direction. It became a simple market relationship dominated by fierce competition.

Once again, we are faced with an incremental technology development project organized on the basis of coercion. Although the supplier company made efforts to improve its component, the WTM controlled the component supplier by simply imposing interface data and product prices, as the product department manager (B-Org01) suggests: "*Now we have the problem that although the performance characteristics of our component are well received by the customer, it is too expensive.*" A common praxis of collaborative innovation was observed only at the time of market entry, after which technology development was dominated by price competition, as the following quote shows:

> *We are currently trying to make our components cheaper. (...) This means that we already know the final price, although the product is not really ready yet. (B-Org01, Product department manager)*

In summary, despite the efforts of the component supplier, a praxis of collaborative innovation based on horizontal negotiations and knowledge interdependencies was hard to find in this case. Similar to the first case, component development was centrally controlled based on coercive power. The WTM used technical standards (e.g. a technical interface) to control its component suppliers.

5.3.3.3 Trying to leave the market niche

The previous sections have shown how a large WTM used a technical standard to control its component suppliers, reduce knowledge integration to a minimum, and minimize social interactions to simple market transactions. The innovation project was reduced to mere contract development – a situation from which the development company tried to escape.

In order to escape these dependencies and to strengthen its power position, the studied supplier tried to engage in collaborative innovation with other customers. According to the quality manager (B-Org01), only such collaborations provide the application-oriented or "*real*" knowledge needed for the development of new product variants and the expansion of the product range.

> *The know-how of a customer who is involved in the use of a product is incredibly important. (...) You also want the customer to point out weaknesses.*

> *You can do the best test in the world in your own dry dock, but you don't get the real knowledge from the field if you do it in-house. This can be simulated, but the real field tests are even more important.*

After introducing its new technology, the component supplier was initially stuck in a market niche. In order to get out of the niche, the supplier had to convince customers to "consciously" choose the niche product, as the marketing engineer (B-Org01) reports: "*The crux of the matter is to make the right decision, because in addition to the many hydraulic components, our electromechanical product is still a real niche product. The customer has to make a conscious choice.*" For an outsider to established supply networks, however, it is almost impossible to find new customers willing to engage in collaborative innovation processes, as the product department manager (B-Org01) concludes: "*[W]e hardly get any contact with them because when they hear electromechanics, most of them say they have hydraulics and that's fine.*"

These findings show that because the component supplier operated in a highly competitive environment where only product prices mattered, reducing production costs rather than collaborative innovation dominated interactions with other WTMs, as the product department manager (B-Org01) notes: "*You are invited and told that you don't talk about price because you are a designer and after an hour they just ask how much it costs because everything is about price. I've seen that everywhere. The cost pressure in this industry is very high.*" Therefore, no praxis of collaborative innovation could be observed in this case. In fact, when the interviewer specifically asked whether collaborative innovation processes had been initiated, the product department manager (B-Org01) replied

> *Unfortunately, it has to be said that there was no such thing. The most you can say is that they weren't willing to cover the costs. (B-Org01, Product manager)*

Thus, also in this case, component development was controlled on the basis of coercive power as the dominant social process of technology development, which minimizes social interactions and knowledge exchange to mere order development and thus limits the innovative potential of the development partnership as a whole.

Under these conditions, the studied component supplier relied on the goodwill of the WTM and used communication tactics to gain at least some insight into the customer's product requirements. With a kind of diplomacy, the company's experts tried to build trust on behalf of potential customers, as the manager (B-Org01) put it: *"[You] have to get them to show interest by acting skillfully. Sometimes it works that way, but it's a bit difficult."* However, the innovation manager (B-Org01) remained skeptical about these attempts and perceived the established supply network as rather "closed", with WTM showing little "interest" or "willingness" to initiate collaborative innovation processes:

> *If you are looking for other customers, of course they have to be open to implementing this with you and clarifying the interfaces. If they're not, they're not interested in the product. You just need that willingness.*

5.3.3.4 Preliminary conclusions

In contrast to the first case of an incumbent component supplier and worldwide leading specialist, the second case dealt with a newcomer and product niche supplier. The empirical findings hardly support P1, which claims that in the context of incremental innovation, technology projects are mainly organized through practices of monitoring technical standards and sanctioning nonconformity. In fact, a collaborative innovation praxis characterized by the negotiation of common working standards was hardly found in either case of incremental technology development.

Although the supply relationship in Case B started as a collaborative R&D project, the project work was characterized by practices of monitoring technical standards on behalf of the WTM, which appeared here as a top-down innovation approach. A collaborative innovation praxis would require mutual dependencies and knowledge complementarities so that neither partner could unilaterally dominate the collaboration. In this case, however, the collaboration was centrally controlled. A WTM instrumentalized a technical standard (mainly interface data) to coercively control the component developer, reduce social interactions to simple market transactions and order development, and limit the innovation potential of the partnership as a whole.

A common innovation praxis was missing. As Table 14 shows, the only working standard that became established in the development and production processes of the supplier related to delivery times, which are much shorter in the wind energy sector than in the rail vehicle industry. However, even this standard was imposed by force.

Table 13: Innovation praxis in established fields

Technical standards	Working standards
Technologically simple interface data (imposed onto the supplier)	Product delivery times (imposed by the customer)

5.4 Institutional barriers and what they caused

The previous section focused on how two cases of incremental innovation projects were organized. It was shown that in both cases the coercive imposition of technical and labor standards served as the dominant social process. However, this led to a loss of innovation capability, as will be discussed in this section.

5.4.1 Case A: Loss of innovation capabilities

It was shown above that in Case A, technology development was based on the coercive imposition of a customer's technical standards, which implied that processes of combining knowledge beyond the scope of the project were prohibited. Thus, it can be argued that strict standardization led to organizational rigidity, which in turn reduced the overall innovative capacity of the network.

During the research, it became clear that in this particular case of a well-established development project, as the production manager (A-Org01) called it, the component supplier's development options were limited by the technical expectations of the customer. The project manager further explained that the company's development options were limited by the customer's specifications on how the new component should fit into the wind turbine's architecture: "*Constructively, our scope is already defined by the fact that boundary conditions have to be met. (...) We are given relatively precise specifications regarding the connection dimensions of the [component]. This defines the installation space within which we can operate.*" In other words, technical standards primarily define the "mounting space.

In addition, technical standards also define the design of the component. The strategy and marketing manager (A-Org01) emphasized that in some projects the customer's technical standards are narrowly defined in order to meet a predefined product price: "*That means you have to somehow see where you can save money with the freedom you still have (...). Maybe you can design one or two components to be cheaper, but that is not innovation. That is design-to-cost.*"

In this way, standardization limits the development options and the "*freedom*" of the component suppliers to be creative and to experiment. As a result, suppliers rarely create new technological innovations in highly regulated technology projects. The strategy and marketing manager (A-Org01) of Organization A reasons that when innovation does occur, it often involves minor technological improvements adapted from other industries, such as the automotive industry:

> *It's usually not a breakthrough or a huge innovation, but it really happens on a small scale where you introduce simple things like new screws (...) Often it's nothing new. The car industry has been doing it for x years. (A-Org01, Strategy & marketing manager)*

In essence, technical standards provide an impetus for incremental innovation. In fact, the component supplier studied regularly introduces "simple improvements", as several interviewees stated. For example, the key account manager (A-Org01) explained that when customers' expectations cannot be met by relying on existing technological solutions, "*you are forced to think about how to do it in a slightly different way.*"

Based on these empirical findings, the following conclusion could be drawn. The forced imposition of technical standards, which excludes practices of knowledge integration beyond the scope of the project, reduces the innovative capacity of the entire component supply network. This link between a customer's strategy to control external technology development and reduced supplier creativity is also evident in the following quote from the strategy and marketing manager, who acknowledges that customers sometimes demand the creation of "new ideas":

> *Some customers push you in the direction of coming up with new ideas yourself. (...) But there are also customers who just want a proven and cost-effective transmission. That's what they specify. (...) Then there are no gimmicks and no experiments. It just has to work. And of course there are no innovations. (A-Org01, Strategy & marketing manager).*

Customers sometimes even use technical standards as an instrument to minimize creative problem solving and experimentation. As the key account manager (A-Org01) explains, the primary motivation behind this strategy is to reduce the "cost of energy": "*Ultimately, it's always about presenting something at the best possible cost. You can always improve the technology, but that doesn't necessarily make it cheaper. At the end of the day, the only thing that matters is the cost of energy. What does it cost to produce a megawatt hour of electricity?*" Thus, standardization of technology projects may increase the efficiency of components and reduce energy costs, but it also risks reducing the ability to innovate.

A key reason why the imposition of technological standards reduces the innovative capacity of innovation projects is the lack of social integration between the suppliers of the main components of the wind turbine, such as the rotor, the generator and the gearbox. The interviewees explained that both electrical and mechanical components are technologically interdependent. Therefore, the key account manager (A-Org01) argues that an "*optimized*" technical design of a wind turbine should include interactions between all components – and their suppliers, because increased social integration between component specialists could increase innovation capacity:

> *When a customer comes to us, they only ask us about the mechanics and then wonder why the component is way too expensive. They may have budgeted extra costs for one component to compensate for the other. But he won't let us talk to the manufacturer of the other components to find the optimum solution.*

As this quote suggests, customers often prohibit information sharing among the specialized manufacturers of mechanical and electrical components within the wind turbine, instead of increasing social integration among these component suppliers. During the research, the interviewees discussed the topic of increased social integration among component specialists under the keywords "system solutions", "system integration" or "system coordination." For example, the project sales expert (A-Org01) criticized poorly developed collaborative arrangements that result in "everyone doing their own thing": "*The whole issue of system coordination is going to be a huge problem because everyone is cooking their own little soup. Everyone is trying to get their partner on board as much as possible, but at the same time they are trying to share as little information as possible.*"

Due to the technological interdependencies between components, system integration is apparently an ongoing debate within engineering communities, as the sales expert adds: "*We are slowly realizing that the component manufacturers need to be brought on board because the forces coming from the rotor shaft may be significantly higher or the individual components may stimulate each other. I think people are becoming more and more aware of this.*" Another expert confirms that technological interdependencies have made the entire industry more "open" to collaborative innovation. In fact, this manager suggests that horizontal collaboration between WTMs and their component suppliers is an emerging phenomenon:

> *The industry has become more open (...) What's happening now is that people are discussing these things with us and not just focusing on our component, but also asking what can be changed. (A-Org01, Key Account Manager)*

In conclusion, this section has associated the social process of coercive control of component development with a loss of innovative capacity. Despite the technological interdependencies between the major components of a wind turbine (e.g. rotor, gearbox, generator), customers actively prohibit social integration and information exchange among the specialized suppliers of all major mechanical and electrical components of a wind turbine. This strategy leads to organizational rigidity, which reduces the innovative capacity of the entire network.

In mature technology fields, innovation tends to take the form of small technical improvements resulting from incremental adaptation of technical standards, including standards used in complementary industries such as automotive or aerospace. For "*big technological steps*" or radical innovations, on the other hand, suppliers depend on their customers, who have the application knowledge as well as the infrastructure needed to test new components under "real conditions," leading the key account manager (A-Orgl) to conclude: "*We can only advance technologies internally, and then we are dependent on customers. The really big steps are usually driven internally [by the component manufacturer].*"

It turns out that a fairly mature field of onshore wind energy technologies is not doomed to reproduce existing technologies. As new generations of wind turbines become larger and heavier, component suppliers are being "pushed" into new technology areas such as lightweight construction, as the R&D expert (A-Org01) explained: "*The fact that the power classes are increasing has a positive effect. The larger systems are getting heavier and heavier, but they are also being designed more and more in the direction of lightweight construction.*" The interviewees stressed that the continuous growth of wind turbines is driving technological innovation, which could even lead to radically new technologies, as the strategy and marketing manager (A-Org01) concludes:

> *[As we move further into the offshore market and into the eight megawatt range, we will also look again at the space standard. We have just launched an initiative in this area. Imagine you are in a space capsule and we want to be 100 % sure that we come back to earth safely. We will certainly go beyond the automotive standard.*

5.4.2 Case B: Remaining trapped in a market niche

The second case told the story of a newcomer to the wind energy industry. It introduced a new technical standard, but was unable to break out of its market niche. The product idea was supported by the top management and mainly driven by the head of the product department. He initiated product improvements, brought internal departments such as manufacturing and engineering together to solve technical problems, and tried to expand customer relationships around the world, he recalls: "*I have now visited [major customers] in and around Germany myself. I've also been to China six or seven times, and we're still trying, but I'd say we haven't really made a breakthrough yet*" (B-Org01, Product Department Manager). Up to the time of the study, the company had not succeeded in establishing further cooperation, although it had tried to set up a new supply network, as the design engineer (B-Org01) explains:

> *The feedback was that they all thought the features were great, but they weren't using them at the moment. (...) You can then deduce where the shoe pinches and where it doesn't.*

From its position outside the established supply networks, the component supplier relied on "*reading between the lines*" to identify customer needs. However, until the time of the investigation, the supplier had no additional supply relationships with large WTMs. The product center manager (B-Org01) attributed this to increased market competition and customers' unwillingness to test uncertain, potentially less reliable technologies: "*They are all under a lot of cost pressure and also under pressure that all their systems have to work. Availability has to be very high, and as a result, they are all now very afraid to embrace technological innovation.*" The same manager concludes that when WTMs introduce radically new technologies, they tend to do so alone or with trusted partners:

> *When [wind turbine manufacturers] innovate or improve something technically, they do it internally. No information about what they are doing is shared with the outside world. They may also improve certain components, but they do it with the existing suppliers.*

In conclusion, in this case, the component supplier were unable to act as an institutional entrepreneur and break out of the market niche. The customer's strategy of controlling component development created a barrier to further technological innovation. In addition, the component supplier failed to initiate additional innovation projects with other large WTMs. As a result, the company remained an outsider to established supply networks. The company remained structurally excluded from innovation projects through a "*cloak of silence*", as the product center manager (B-Org01) pointed out:

> *[T]his is all done under a cloak of silence from the public.*

5.5 Interim conclusions

This book examines the institutional barriers to collaborative innovation. This chapter discusses the extent to which incremental innovation processes are organized through practices of monitoring technical standards and sanctioning nonconformity (Proposition 1). For this purpose, two empirical examples of component supply relationships between a medium-sized German component supplier and a large European WTM were presented.

The empirical evaluation was divided into four sections: first, the positions of the relevant actors in the field were characterized; second, the practices of knowledge integration involved were described; third, it was shown how the cooperation was organized; and fourth, the observed outcomes were discussed. This section provides a preliminary summary of the empirical findings (cf. Table 15 and draws conclusions regarding the research question.

In both cases, it was observed that the respective WTMs imposed their technical expectations on the component suppliers due to strong power asymmetries. In case A, the customer instrumentally used development contracts to pre-define the technology development. In addition, the WTM centrally controlled the technology project based on common work standards such as time frames (milestones), exclusive communication channels (SPOC) between project managers, and personal inspection of manufacturing processes. Based on these findings, coercive power was identified as the dominant mechanism of technology development.

Table 14: Fields of incremental innovation

	Case A: Large component	**Case B: Small component**
Knowledge Integration	Based on highly standardized working procedures, a component supplier combined technical standards to design a new prototype	Through a joint R&D project, a component supplier collaboratively developed an innovative product
Realizing technology development	The WTM uses development contracts, technical standards as well as shared working standards (e.g. shared milestones) to coercively control technology development	The WTM coercively controls component development based on a technologically simple technical standard as well as fierce market competition between its suppliers
Institutional barriers	Rigid standardization of component development (e.g. prohibiting knowledge integration between component specialists) reduces the innovative potential of the whole supply network	The lack of collaborative innovation processes involving a large WTM caused the component supplier to remain trapped in a market niche

The second example of a small component (Case B) was also dominated by hierarchical control and the imposition of standards. In this case, however, the WTM simply used technical standards to coercively control the component supplier. An initial collaborative R&D project turned into a simple market relationship without collaborative innovation.

Consequently, the findings partially support the assumptions of P1, which postulated that incremental innovation projects are mainly organized through practices of monitoring technical standards and sanctioning nonconformity. Initially, it was expected that technical standards would play a central role in incremental innovation projects, but that coercive power would be irrelevant due to interdependencies and knowledge complementarities. However, the empirical cases revealed that coercion, central control, and hierarchical dominance characterize technology development in areas of incremental innovation.

This lack of collaborative innovation could also be associated with institutional barriers. In Case A, rigid standardization implied that learning and knowledge integration between component specialists could not take place, although due to the technological interdependencies between the rotor, gearbox and generator of wind turbines, knowledge integration would be required to optimize the overall system architecture.

In Case B, the customer explicitly prohibited further innovation. At the same time, the component supplier failed to engage in innovation projects with other WTMs to broaden its product range. Due to this lack of collaborative innovation, the company remained trapped in a market niche.

Thus, both cases showed that coercive control based on rigid standardization reduces the innovation capability of the entire component supply network. Wind turbines are complex technologies with many technical interdependencies between components. Since coercive control prevents component suppliers from collaborating on the further development of components and system architecture, coercive power jeopardizes the optimal performance of wind energy technologies and reduced the innovation capabilities.

6. Projects of radical innovation

The previous chapter showed that coercive power dominates incremental technology development. This finding only partially supports P1, which predicted a more horizontal approach due to technological interdependencies.

This chapter contrasts the results of the last chapter with two examples of radical innovation. Since in such contexts innovation projects deviate from existing technical standards and firms collaborate with new partners, it was assumed in Chapter 3 that radical innovation projects are organized on the basis of newly created procedures and methods of collaborative problem solving (P2). This proposition is evaluated below based on two cases of radical innovation, a robotics-based rotor blade coating system (Case C) and a prototype of a 'wooden wind turbine' (Case D).

The chapter is structured as the previous one. First, the two technology fields are characterized (6.1); second, it is discussed which practices of knowledge integration were observed (6.2); third, it is shown how collaboration was organized in each case (6.3); and fourth, it is discussed which institutional barriers occurred and what they caused. Finally, the findings are summarized and some preliminary conclusions are drawn.

6.1 Positions of partners in the field

This section describes the two fields of radical innovation. In contrast to the component development fields analyzed in the previous chapter, these fields were characterized by more horizontal collaboration, organized around a focal firm that initiated the innovation process and collaborated with heterogeneous partners.

6.1.1 Case C: The three major players

This case deals with the introduction of radically new robotic-based processes for coating rotor blades at a manufacturing site of a large European WTM. The innovation project involved three main partners.

The focal company, which initiated the innovation project, is a rotor blade factory of a large European WTM located in Germany. In the mid-2000s, the rotor blade manufacturer pursued the idea of using robotics to automate its coating processes, as the factory manager (C-Org01) recalls: "*The automatic coating system was actually developed in our factory. (...) It was a complete change of processes that was done with relatively little support from the devel-*

opment departments and was initiated by a team in my plant." To specify the project idea, the plant set up a project team that integrated heterogeneous knowledge provided mainly by experts in coating processes, logistics and sales, as well as external production specialists, as the plant manager (C-Org01) adds:

> *Of course [you] need people who can immediately assess the consequences of making the booth twice as big; what filter systems they need; someone has to take into account the environmental protection requirements (...).*

The innovation project had to specify the project idea and select a system supplier capable of designing and building such a radically new technology. As the plant manager explained, the project chose a partner that specialized in process automation for the automotive industry:

> *In collaboration with an automotive supplier, we have developed a system specifically [designed] for these very demanding conditions, i.e. painting 50-meter-long parts (...) in two colors.*

6.1.1.1 An engineering service provider as "boundary spanner"

The innovation project worked closely with an external engineering service provider. This consulting firm specializes in robotics-based automation technologies and brought in-depth technological experience from the automotive industry to the project, as the company's project engineer (C-Org02) explains:

> *We ourselves are suppliers to the automotive industry when it comes to paint shops. (...) We ourselves (...) have already carried out the programming of painting systems on the robot side. We have programmed the control systems for the painting processes, i.e. the paint booths themselves. (...) We had not yet taken over the robots at that time.*

Before the project started, the consulting firm was already a maintenance provider and a trusted technology partner of the rotor blade factory and the focal company. In fact, the managing director of the consulting firm was involved in initiating the innovation project, he recalls: "*I had just returned from DaimlerChrysler in Sindelfingen, where I had been given the task of designing and building a painting system, and I asked myself why they did not have a painting robot. That was how the project started for us*" (C-Org02, Managing director). The consulting firm's experts brought project experience, personal contacts, and references to the project, which made them important and trusted partners for the focal company's plant management, as the project engineer (C-Org02) recalls:

> *[Because of our reference in the automotive painting sector from our own projects, we were asked if we would like to accompany them.*

Together with this consulting firm, the plant's specialists specified the system idea ("Lastenheft"), as the plant's coating process engineer (C-Org01) points out: "In terms of knowledge and experience, he at least had more experience with the systems than we did when it came to the specification. Of course, we took advantage of that and bought the service to help us write the specifications, select a suitable vendor, and [support] the implementation.

The consulting firm became a key player in the innovation project. With its technological expertise and practical experience from previous projects in the automotive industry, the consulting firm was able to 'bridge' gaps in the factory's process requirements with external knowledge of how to automate production processes. The consulting firm thus acted as a "boundary spanner" between the technologies used in the automotive industry and the technical requirements of the wind energy industry (Tushman, 1977). It helped the factory translate its process requirements into a technical specification, as the consulting firm's project engineer (C-Org02) points out:

> *[We have the intellectual know-how of how such a paint booth works. For example, what are the technical framework parameters for such a painting system, because as programmers we need to know that. (...) We also know what a paint job has to look like, because we know all that from our own work in paint booths, because we have often been on the other side of the table. We were used on the customer side [in this project] and were able to contribute our knowledge.*

As these findings show, in this innovation project, collaboration with a trusted external specialist enabled the factory to specify the idea of a radically new technological architecture. In the day-to-day project work, the external technology specialists acted as boundary spanners between the expertise areas of rotor blade manufacturing on the one hand and process automation on the other.

6.1.1.2 The general contractor and project coordinator

Apart from the factory's internal specialists and an external consulting firm, a third major player was a system developer specialized in coating process technologies for the automobile industry. The coating process engineer (C-Org01) explains that this firm coordinated the innovation project as a general contractor. The expert further points out that this firm was specialized in the automotive industry, but inexperienced in the wind energy industry: "*For him, rotor blade painting, or being in the wind industry at all, was absolutely new. The manufacturer is a general contractor in the sense that it usually sells painting systems to the automotive industry to paint parts such as car bodies and bumpers. (...) He actually makes complete packages and then has his partners for the individual items.*"

These quotes show that the project integrated knowledge from new areas of expertise and brought together formerly unfamiliar partners. For the system supplier, the innovation project offered an opportunity to gain a foothold in the wind energy industry, as the external consultant adds:

> *At the time, companies were very keen to have such a reference for painting large parts. (C-Org02, External project engineer)*

The system supplier acted as a general contractor and enlarged the innovation network by bringing additional specialists (sub-contractors) into the project. In fact, as one of the factory's rotor production process engineers stresses, such sub-contractors play a major role in technical problem-solving because they provide additional expertise, for example of application technologies and coating materials: "*Our painting technology involves robotics and the suppliers of the materials or paints were also involved in the project. They can often give a lot of tips*" *(C-Org01, Production process engineer).*

Consequently, as Figure 3 illustrates, the collaboration structure in case C was far more distributed over several different actors than the cases of incremental innovation presented in the previous chapter, with several heterogeneous specialists being involved in the innovation process.

Figure 3: Field of introducing robotics-based production processes

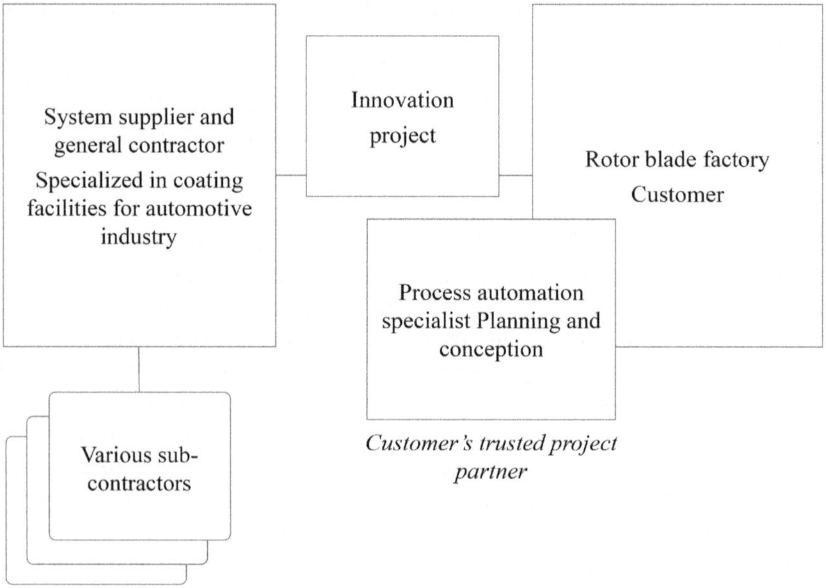

In summary, in this example of a new technological architecture, the project team involved three key players: First, a rotor blade factory that initiated the innovation process; second, an engineering service provider and technology specialist that acted as a boundary spanner; and third, a system developer. The latter coordinated the project work as general contractor, collaborating with various subcontractors, such as production logistics, application technologies, or paints. The boundary spanner played a central role in the knowledge integration process observed in this case, as will be illustrated below.

6.1.2 Case D: A newly established innovation network

Case D deals with a start-up company that has introduced a radically new support structure for onshore wind turbines. Unlike the established designs, this support structure uses wood instead of steel or concrete as a construction material. The concept of a 'wooden wind turbine' was radically new at the time, as the managing director (D-Org05) of a timber engineering service provider explains:

> *Never before has a wooden structure been built 100 meters high. On top of the 100 meters there is a generator house, which has a weight of 10 to 15 tons. If there is a storm or a hurricane, this whole structure has to withstand the strain. This means that this wooden tower is exposed to enormous dynamic loads. (D-Org05, Managing director)*

The start-up company that initiated the innovation process is a German company founded in 2008. Its founder had the vision to introduce the innovative idea of a 'wooden wind turbine', as one of his employees reports: "*[The managing director] had the idea that wood could also be used, because he knew from the history of wood that it was used a lot in radio masts at the beginning of the 19th century. (...) He then started his own business in 2008 with the idea of building wooden support structures for wind turbines*" (D-Org01, Construction manager). At that time, the start-up company had the position of a newcomer in the wind energy industry and wanted to establish itself as a new component supplier for wind turbine manufacturers (WTM), as the same expert points out:

> *Our real business goal is to be a supplier of a major component for wind turbines. That is why we try to describe our product as well as possible, so that (...) the tower can be assembled with the help of work instructions, execution plans, assembly instructions and our manual.*

In a first step, the start-up company developed a prototype of a 'wooden wind turbine'." In this phase, an internationally operating WTM acted as an important development partner. As the construction manager (D-Org01) recalls, this company was less involved in the product development because it mainly provided technical data (e.g. loads), which the start-up company used to adapt the support structure: "*They had developed the first prototype together with a wind turbine manufacturer (...) [This manufacturer] was the only one who was open and gave us a chance. For them it was more of a side project. They didn't really throw themselves into it and didn't give us as much support with our technical questions. The support was in the form of at least providing us with loads.*" With regard to this particular collaboration, the construction manager of the start-up company (D-Org01) describes the interaction with the WTM as "minimal effort", based on iterations of technical information exchange:

> *This is minimal effort. But [this partner] was actually the only turbine manufacturer that ever did this with us. It's an iterative process, because the way it works is we give the turbine manufacturer our tower geometry, and they put it into their load program. Then they do a load calculation. That goes back to our tower. (...) This goes on until the geometry does not change.*

In addition to the WTM, the start-up company established relationships with various other specialists to develop the prototype. These partners were private and academic experts in wood engineering, materials, adhesives or steel components, among others. For example, to further improve the design, the company relied on the knowledge of adhesive suppliers, as the construction manager (D-Org01) outlines: "We had to rely on fasteners or products that came from outside or were developed there. For example, we would never have been able to develop an adhesive ourselves.

These collaborations were the source of a large number of innovations, such as joining techniques for assembling the components, a foundation for the tower or an adapter to connect the tower to the wind turbine, as the managing director (D-Org05) of a timber construction company explains:

> *Together with the professors, we developed the optimal gluing technology. The glue manufacturer also designed a machine (...) so that there was almost one hundred percent certainty about the quality of the glued joints. (D-Org05, Managing director of an engineering company)*

In addition to private companies and scientific partners, the start-up also worked with representatives of public authorities, in particular approval and testing bodies. In fact, to improve the prototype and get the new design approved, the startup gathered additional expertise and technical solutions from material testing institutes. In addition, during the approval process, publicly accredited testing organizations such as TÜV certified the new wind turbine and required some minor improvements, such as additional instruments to monitor the stability of the design. The team leader of one certification body (D-Org02) specified his responsibilities as follows

> *When we inspect, we inspect for conformance and sign off that the evidence is complete and correct. At the same time, we also signify that we have no objections to the way the tower is listed.*

Thus, after completing the design of the prototype, the start-up company further extended its innovation network and, as shown in Figure 6.2, collaborated with heterogeneous partners (e.g., various suppliers, product certification bodies, material testing institutes, and scientific institutes) to get its prototype approved for construction. An expert from a materials testing institute (D-Org02) adds that technical reviewers from different universities were important players in the approval process:

> *There is an expert committee for timber construction that also has to approve. Of course there are also testing engineers. (...) It also included the experts [from various universities].*

All in all, in the example of a 'wooden wind turbine', a small German start-up company initiated the innovation process and established an innovation network that included specialists from industry, science and regulatory authorities. As will be shown below, through these network connections, the start-up also gained access to new ideas, expertise and solutions to get its first prototype approved for construction.

6.2 Analysed practices of knowledge integration

The previous section introduced two fields of radical innovation. This section describes the practices of knowledge integration that were observed. In Chapter 2, knowledge integration was defined as the combination of specialized and complementary knowledge to accomplish specific tasks (Berggren et al., 2011b, p. 7). In the empirical cases of radical innovation, two different focal firms – a rotor blade factory and an innovative start-up company – combined their own competencies with knowledge from new fields of expertise.

Figure 4: The field of introducing a 'wooden wind turbine'

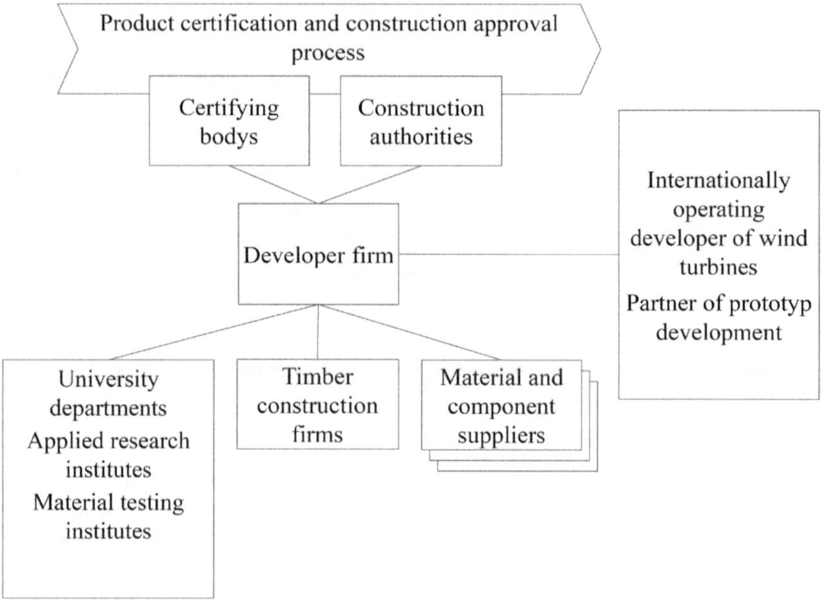

6.2.1 Case C: Specifying a radical innovation

Compared to the component development cases, the collaboration structure for the rotor blade coating system was much more distributed across different actors. Here, the practices of knowledge integration involved three major actors: the customer organization (rotor blade factory), an external engineering service provider, and a system supplier. The latter coordinated the innovation project as a general contractor and integrated additional subcontractors. The project idea of automatically coating rotor blades was radically new, as the coating process engineer (C- Org01) explains:

> *Many other industries still do this manually. Even the wind industry as a whole used to do most of its work manually, and there is very little automated coating in the aerospace industry.*

Due to the radical nature of the new technology, it was not an option to purchase an off-the-shelf coating system or to adopt the technical solutions used by competitors. As a result, the plant created a project team to develop a technical design from scratch, as the following quote illustrates: "*We first held a workshop to develop the painting concept. How do we want to paint? (...) The workflow had to be defined first. Then the system concept is worked out and the costs are always looked at to see if we can afford it. (...) [T]his tool for finding a solution, which is quite complex, is of course only put together when necessary*“ (C-Org01, Factory manager).

As the above quote illustrates, in the knowledge integration process observed in this case, the project team combined knowledge of manual rotor blade coating with expertise in robotics-based process automation. One of the first objectives of the project was to specify the system idea, as the coating process engineer (C-Org01) points out: “*The first [step] was to draw up a specification sheet with the local engineering office, i.e. a requirements specification: what the automated painting system should be able to do in practice in the end. This was, of course, a huge document of several hundred pages describing the requirements and what it had to be able to do.*” Far from being a standardized task, it was characterized by personal interaction and various meetings, as the external consultant recalls:

> *It was really always meetings around a table. We got everyone involved [at the customer] on board and then wrote down on a big board everything that needed to be considered and what was required for a paint shop. Of course, the first discussions with the suppliers took place at that time. (C-Org02, Technical manager)*

The process engineer (C-Org01) further illustrates how the project team defined the new coating process, which had been performed manually prior to the innovation project: “*As you can imagine, there are specifications for what the wing surface should look like. There are certain specifications that are checked on the result of this painting and that must be adhered to. (...) In this case, it is a set of instructions to the painter who is painting the wing with his spray gun. (...) In other words, we had to work with the manufacturer of the system to define specifications that describe this process in order to achieve the same result as before.*“ In the next steps, the project team had to define technical standards from scratch, such as process speed, coating quality or materials, as the quote below illustrates:

> *A lot is expected from the manufacturer in terms of exactly how you want to do it, and on the other hand, the manufacturer will always offer several options. So we set certain requirements and conditions, such as that the sheet must be painted at a certain speed. (...) This results in certain processes that are used. (C-Org01, Coating process engineer)*

It is interesting to observe that during the innovation process, the technical specification sheet not only functioned as a knowledge reservoir, but also as a tool to gain some control over the innovation project. The technical specification sheet enabled the factory to negotiate prices, select a system developer, and control project outcomes, as the managing director (C-Org02) of the external engineering service provider recalls: “*In the end, we decided on the solution we thought would work best and put it on paper in the specifications. Based on that, a price was set.*" However, as the coating process engineer admits, the document left a number of questions unanswered:

> *We also approved the specifications and read through them and found them reasonable. It has everything we want. It also includes everything we didn't know.*

These results show that the project team encountered significant knowledge gaps in the example of a robot-based coating system. To fill some of these knowledge gaps, the project team integrated specialists from different areas of expertise and created a technical specification sheet that functioned as a boundary object (Star & Griesemer, 1989). The specification sheet also gave the customer some contractual control over external system development, as the coating process engineer (C-Org01) claims:

> *I can only do this acceptance test on the basis of a guideline. (...) If it's OK, then the supplier has done his job, gets his money and ticks the box. Whether I solve my process with it or not is of no interest to the manufacturer. All that matters is how well I wrote my specification.*

In conclusion, in this case the project team established a collaborative innovation praxis and creatively combined knowledge from different areas of expertise (e.g. process automation, robotics and rotor blade coating processes). In the context of developing a radically new technological architecture, the requirement specification acted as a boundary object. It gave the customer some control over the development of the system by defining technical standards. The collaborative innovation praxis was supported by an external technology specialist and boundary spanner who moderated the technical problem solving.

6.2.2 Case D: Establishing an innovation network

In the case of a 'wooden wind turbine', a start-up company established an innovation network to combine its own competencies with knowledge from different areas of expertise in wood engineering. In the knowledge integration process, a collaborative innovation praxis enabled the creation of additional knowledge to get the prototype approved for construction.

The investigated knowledge integration process was aimed at optimizing the statics of the 'wooden wind turbine', as the responsible test engineer (D-Org03) explains: "*The static calculation has to be checked as part of the building permit.*" *Since the radically new technology of the start-up company could hardly rely on technical standards and was operating on "new ground"*, as the expert from a materials testing institute (D-Org02) described it, the company collected additional technical evidence from "individual experts" in order to prove the reliability of the new construction, as the interview partner points out:

> *A modular tower concept with a height of 100 meters is new territory. The connection technology is also new territory. Bonding technology is new territory. This is all largely without standards. There are always standards when it comes to proven technologies that have been tried and tested over many years. This was not the case here, so experts had to look at the results and evaluate them. It was certainly a multi-stage process in which many timber construction experts gave their opinions.*

By combining the technological know-how of timber construction with the technical requirements of wind turbine construction, the start-up company was operating in "uncharted territory." It raised technological questions that could not be solved by relying on technical standards, as the structural engineer (D-Org01) points out: "*That's the technology behind it, so to speak. It's actually quite simple. But it's very difficult to implement, because German standardization is not designed for the use of wood in wind turbines or for such high dynamic loads.*" The innovation network has created a structure whose "safety" cannot be assessed on the basis of standardized approval procedures, as the same expert points out:

> *In the end, we end up with fundamental questions because no one has used this material to its full potential. (...) [W]e have reckoned with the regulations that exist in the standards. But we also say that what is in them is not correct and even wrong. (D-Org01, Civil engineer)*

To get the design approved, the start-up company mainly relied on the expertise of various university departments, applied research centers or material testing institutes, as the same expert points out: "*The approval process for the connectors in the tower (...) was relatively complicated and lengthy. [We worked a lot with external parties because it was a completely innovative joint that was not generally approved. We had to get approval on a case-by-case basis. Then I communicated with many different authorities, different professors, different material testing institutes and so on.*

In this case of a radically new design, using innovative "joining techniques," as the expert put it, the responsible authority could not approve the new design on the basis of established approval procedures. To get the 'wooden wind turbine' approved, the start-up company integrated additional ideas, expertise, and technical solutions from university departments, material testing institutes, and various suppliers. As a result, the start-up company expanded its network. However, the product design itself remained the proprietary knowledge of the start-up company, as the structural engineer points out:

> *The design of the tower is the core competence of the company, so we do not rely on external services. (D-Org01, Structural engineer)*

In conclusion, in this knowledge integration process, a German start-up established an innovation network and used its network connections to university departments and material testing institutes to prove the reliability of a 'wooden wind turbine' and get the prototype approved for construction.

6.3 Realizing technology development

As shown above, in both contexts of radical innovation, the focal firm – a rotor blade manufacturing site (Case C) and a start-up firm (Case D) – collaborated with new partners from previously unfamiliar fields of expertise. In sect. 3.3 suggested that when a radically new technology is developed, the project is likely to be organized around newly created procedures and methods of collaborative problem solving (P2). Contrary to this assumption, this section will show that in both cases of radical innovation, the focal firm relied on personal trust to gain some control over the innovation process. A strategic approach to establish a common innovation praxis was hardly found.

The strategy of relying on individual experts is criticized here as a fallback strategy. Relying on personal trust means believing in the sayings and doings of individual experts instead of institutionalizing an innovation praxis that defines collective norms of technology development.

6.4 Case C: Working together with experts

This sub-section discusses how the project to introduce a robotic blade coating system was organized. It will be shown that personal trust between the factory management and the external technology specialist enabled the project team to exert some control over the system developer.

6.4.1 Relying on a boundary spanner

In this case, the collaboration between the rotor blade factory and a trusted local technology specialist enabled the project team to specify the product idea and gain some control over the technology development. Based on previous experience, the external specialist brought expertise in robot-based coating processes to the project, as the consulting firm's project engineer (C-Org02) explains:

> *We were allowed to take over the whole thing as consultants because there was no one at [the customer] who was technically familiar with it. (...) We were brought in as an external consultant to replace that painting expertise.*

In addition to the technological expertise needed to implement such a project, the external technology specialist also provided personal contacts, for example to system suppliers and competitors (i.e. other WTMs), some of whom were experimenting with similar concepts, as the technical manager (C-Org02) reports: "*At the time, there was only [a second major wind turbine manufacturer] that had a comparable turbine, but to put it bluntly, they were unhappy with it because it did not work technologically.*" Through these personal contacts, the project team was able to discuss the system idea and gain a better understanding of what needed to be done, adds the technical manager:

> *Thanks to our automotive experience and many years of working together, we know the people and the individuals and were able to have a one-on-one conversation with them and say this is how it looks. Then we asked them how it worked and what they would do differently now.*

These findings are similar to those in Case C. The external technology specialist acted as a bridge builder, 'bridging' areas of expertise and bringing together previously unfamiliar experts. Even before the project began, the technology specialist had become a trusted partner in the eyes of plant management, as the technical manager points out: "*Because we were a system supplier. We already had a maintenance contract for [the customer]. We performed various automation tasks in the factory and had a maintenance contract to start production*" (C-Org02, Technical Manager). The consulting firm's technological expertise and geographical proximity also contributed to its status as a trusted partner at the start of the project, as the external project engineer (C-Org02) explains:

> *We provided local support there because [the customer's] support would otherwise come from [abroad]. These distances were just too far. (...) So they turned to an engineering company around the corner like us. Especially with the background that we are familiar with the subject of painting a car.*

During interviews at the top management level, both partners expressed their mutual support for each other. For example, in the following quote, the managing director (C-Org02) of the external consulting firm explains his loyalty to the plant management: "*I feel more committed to the [customer's] side than to [the system supplier's] side, because they haven't given us any orders.*" In fact, it was the managing director of the technology specialist who came up with the project idea in the first place. By providing recognized references, the manager was also able to strengthen the customer's belief in the feasibility of the project, he recalls:

> *[The [factory manager] and his technical employee at the time insisted and said that if I could manage to show references, that would be good (...). We went to the various manufacturers of such painting robots and had them make a 3D simulation for us. (C-Org02, General manager)*

In conclusion, the external technology specialist acted as a boundary spanner and a trusted partner. Personal trust is defined here as one party's belief that the other party has an incentive to act in the first party's interest or to have the first party's interest at heart. In this case, personal trust 'bridged' different bodies of knowledge from different areas of expertise and even brought together experts from competing firms to specify the project idea and strengthen the client's belief in the feasibility of the new production facility.

In this way, the personal trust between the managing director of the consulting firm and the plant manager facilitated the specification of a radically new architecture. However, a strategic approach to establishing an innovation praxis that integrated all three key players – the client, the consulting firm, and the system developer – into technology development was not found.

6.4.1.1 Using a boundary object

In the example of a new rotor blade coating plant, the experts had searched in vain for ready-made technologies. The plant manager (C-Org01) explained that due to the large size of rotor blades and their small scale of production, direct technology transfer from other industries, such as the automotive industry, was not a viable option: "*When you know that something like this is automated in the automotive industry, you get the idea to do the same. The next thing you run into are the specific difficulties, because it is not directly transferable. The automotive industry uses water-based paints and has much higher volumes and much smaller piece counts. These are all requirements that you have to find solutions for.*" Against this background, the customer's main challenge was to specify the new system, as the external project engineer (C-Org02) recalls:

> *The biggest challenge was actually whether it was technically feasible to paint such a huge part or wing automatically. (...) Because nobody really had any experience with it. There was no experience! There was only experience with manual painting. (C- Org02, Technical manager)*

The rotor blade coating system was built in the form of a large cabin in which rotor blades can be coated in an assembly line-like fashion, as the plant manager (C-Org01) explains: "*We paint in product flow. This means that we pull the workpiece through a small paint booth (...) Right from the start, this was a different concept than what was common at the time. That was the innovation. And it paid off. We were the first fully serial rotor blade paint shop.*"

With this in mind, the project team developed a technical specification sheet. As the process engineer (C-Org01) points out, this technical specification sheet acted as a boundary object, but was also used to exert a certain amount of power over the external system supplier:

> *The challenge is to provide the manufacturer of such systems with a reasonable specification sheet and reasonable 'tooling requirement specifications', i.e. specifications on the basis of which they can design their requirements specification or the layout of the machine. (...) The better we can specify it, the less he has to find out and develop himself.*

To sum up, the project team had to develop the new technological architecture from scratch because the required technical solutions were not available either in the wind energy industry or in the technology markets for the automotive or aerospace industries. The experts developed a technical specification and used this boundary object to gain some control over external technology development. However, as discussed below, relying on boundary spanners and boundary objects is not sufficient to develop a complex technology.

6.4.1.2 No common interest in "knowledge transfer"

Above, it was shown that a relationship of trust with an external technology specialist allowed the customer to believe in the feasibility of the new project and to gain some control over the system developer. Personal trust was defined above as one party's belief that the other party has an incentive to act in the first party's interest or to have the first party's interest at heart. Thus, personal trust is based on the belief that another actor will act in one's own interest, which is a risky strategy for implementing radical innovation in the context of uncertain, long-term, and expensive innovation projects. Indeed, in this case, the interviews revealed that there was no common interest in "knowledge transfer" or collaborative innovation processes.

Over the course of the technology development, the collaboration with the external technology specialist allowed the factory to monitor the technical details and control the external technology development, as the following quotes show:

> *We should accompany the technical details in order to be a company on site during the implementation, which would continue to manage, configure and convert the technology installed in it as far as possible. (C-Org02, Managing director)*

> *I practically did the technical control on the [customer's] side. It's about making sure that everything is built correctly and that the software is logical. (C-Org02, Project engineer)*

The project engineer (C-Org02) recalls that the technology specialist acted as a boundary spanner, facilitating technical discussions between the factory and the system supplier: "*Then we formed an interface to establish communication so that one person is talking to the other properly and speaking the same language. Sometimes it's a problem that some people insist on their point of view and others insist on the other point of view. Sometimes we played a mediating role.*

These findings suggest that intensive technical discussions and conflicting interpretations had to be moderated in the course of technology development. For example, according to the project engineer (C-Org02), discussions were quite intense during the phase of developing the technical specifications. For example, the project team invited several different system suppliers to negotiate technical solutions, the consultant recalls:

> *Discussions were held with different manufacturers (...). This was a separate process of finding a solution, where we sat down together again and again (...). At this point, the supplier had already been chosen, but it's worth noting that the various suppliers were brought together again and again to discuss the same problem with each of them and ultimately decide on the best solution.*

This shows that technical discussions and solution negotiations with system suppliers characterized the project work during the preparation of the technical specifications. This situation is completely different from that of the component development project in Case A. In the case of the development of a powertrain component, the development project was largely predefined by contracts and technical standards. In contrast, in the current case of the rotor blade coating system, the project team created procedures and methods for collaborative specification of the system idea, as predicted by P2. It was only in this early stage of the innovation process that collaboration was found.

However, when it came to actually building the new technology, neither the customer nor the trusted technology specialist worked closely with the system developer and thus had little control over the system development. Technology development and manufacturing took place within the organizational boundaries of the system supplier, as will be seen below:

> *We had no influence on the technical design itself. [The customer] had very little influence on that. We chose the technology in advance. We said what it was going to look like. The supplier was responsible for implementing how it should and must work in the end. (...) We could only put our finger on the wound when they said they weren't making any progress. (C-Org02, Project engineer)*

Unfortunately, experts from the system supplier could not be included in the research. However, based on the interviews conducted, a collaborative innovation praxis that would have included all relevant actors was not observed. On the contrary, the project work in the development phase was characterized by mistrust and tactics of keeping proprietary knowledge secret, as the managing director (C-Org02) points out:

> *[I always had to fight with these non-disclosure agreements. To what extent can I, as a customer insider, explain to the system vendor what they want? Again and again, I was told by the system supplier not to tell the customer too many details about the type of programming, pricing, sensors, measurement and control technology. They did not want to reveal their know-how to the customer.*

Thus, instead of establishing a shared innovation praxis, the second phase of the project, in which the new system was developed, was characterized by mistrust and tactics to exclude project partners from sharing proprietary knowledge. As a result, the managing director of the consulting firm (C-Org02), who had access to both the factory and the system supplier, had to act prudently and diplomatically to protect the client's interests. "Knowledge transfer", as he puts it, was not a common interest in this project:

> *As a designer, I told the customer that if they don't watch out, some competent painting company will come along and install a control technology where you can't even begin to read the source code. Then they have a problem. Then they charge per day, per job, per incident, and it is always in increments of $5,000. (...) You always have to be damn diplomatic. Knowledge transfer is not really desired.*

6.4.1.3 Preliminary conclusions

Based on these findings, some initial conclusions can be drawn. In Sect. 3.3 it was argued that radical innovation projects are organized on the basis of newly created procedures and methods of collaborative problem solving (P2). Experts from previously unknown fields of expertise must be brought together and integrated by establishing a common innovation praxis.

In fact, in this example of a radically new robot-based coating system, a rotor blade factory initiated the innovation process and established collaboration with specialists from new fields of expertise. However, a collaborative innovation praxis was only found in the early stages of system specification. The factory worked with an external, trusted technology specialist who negotiated the process of specifying the system idea. Based on these negotiations, the project team developed a technical specification that was used to gain some control over the system developer.

During the system development phase, however, no collaborative innovation practice was observed. A German system developer specializing in process automation technologies for the automotive industry acted as the general contractor and maintained control over technology development. The project work was characterized by large geographical distances, mistrust, and tactics of keeping proprietary knowledge secret. Therefore, the assumption underlying P2 must be rejected for this stage. A collaborative innovation praxis based on common working standards was not found.

Reliance on personal trust could be identified as the main mechanism of technology development in case C. However, as will be argued below, the lack of a collaborative innovation praxis that would have included the system developer made the project suffer from 'blind spots' and significant quality defects.

Table 15: Innovation praxis in fields of radical innovation

Technical standards	Working standards
No technical standard for such a radically new architecture was available (neither in the wind energy industry, nor in complementary sectors)	During the early stages of project work, a praxis of collaboratively specifying a radically new architecture was found
	During the stage of system development, no innovation praxis was found (project work characterized by large geographical distances, distrust and tactics of keeping knowledge secret)

6.4.2 Case D: Relying on personal trust

While in Case C the practices of knowledge integration and collaborative innovation were observed in the early stage of the technical conception, knowledge integration in the case of the 'wooden wind turbine' took place during the approval process. Here, in line with P2, it was observed that the start-up company established a praxis of collaborative experimentation and material testing in order to provide additional proof of the design's functionality and to make the authorities "believe" that the new design was safe, as the design engineer (D-Org01) recalls:

> *The biggest challenge was actually to convince the German authorities that the design we had come up with, which had been tested by TÜV, was so safe that we could build the tower without hesitation.*

Similar to case C, however, a collaborative innovation praxis that would have included all relevant actors, including public approval authorities, was not observed. Instead, the public approval authorities controlled the innovation process rather centrally.

6.4.2.1 A praxis of collaborative material testing

The start-up company created the 'wooden wind turbine' from scratch. Since the material used (wood) differed from the existing materials of steel and concrete, the responsible public authorities could not easily assess the safety of the new construction on the basis of standardized approval procedures, as the engineer of the start-up company (D-Org01) points out:

> *Most of the time it was a question of ensuring the stability of the tower.*

Certification bodies and public approval authorities play a key role in the approval process. The test engineer (D-Org03) who worked on the 'wooden wind turbine' explained that in the building industry, the approval procedures for which he is responsible are standardized in the Eurocodes: "*I have to make sure that the rules are followed, because everything is laid down in rules. Today, this is done in European standards. In civil engineering, it is the Eurocodes. (...) Unlike in the legal profession, I have no room for interpretation. We don't have that. There is a number and it is bigger or smaller than another. That determines whether it can be done or not.*" Normally, he adds, approval decisions are made on the basis of probabilities and standardized statistical calculations:

> *In the construction industry, we have what is called a semi-probabilistic safety concept. This is defined in Eurocode Zero. This is how safety is determined. As a rule, this is done in such a way that the probability of collapse is one in a million. (...) Safety factors are then derived from this, which must be adhered to.*

In the case of the 'wooden wind turbine', however, the approval process could not rely on these standardized approval procedures. Using wood as the main construction material and innovative joining techniques to assemble the components, the start-up company had created a radically new design. Nor could standards for the construction of wind turbines be applied, as the test engineer (D-Org03) points out: "*What was absolutely new was that nothing like this had ever been built in wood before. It has often been built with steel, reinforced concrete and concrete, but never with wood. (...) There is a guideline for wind turbines that also includes actions and stability proofs for the tower and the foundation. (...) The only difference is that wood is not mentioned in this guideline.*

Another expert from a certification body (D-Org02) added that although the start-up company adapted technical standards from complementary fields of expertise, it created radically new solutions such as innovative joining techniques:

> *The [wooden tower] was calculated according to the principle of a wooden bridge because there are no standards for such an application. There are no standards for perforated plate. So how should it be glued in order to join two wooden sections? There is no answer and no standard.*

In this case, the knowledge needed to certify and approve the structure had to be created from scratch. Instead of using standard calculations, the approval decision had to be based on additional "technical experiments." The experiments had to prove that the radically new design met safety standards ("operational strength"), as the same expert explains:

> *[It is] a type of construction that has never existed before. The applicability of this type of construction must be proven. By what is known in engineering. Either it has to be proved by calculation, because today we have many numerical methods that can be used to prove it if necessary, or it has to be proved experimentally. Experiments played an important role in the compounds.*

To get the prototype approved, the focal company expanded its innovation network and established a praxis of collaborative experimentation and material testing with experts from various universities and material testing institutes, as the structural engineer (D-Org01) recalls: "*That was one of the biggest challenges for this fastener because it didn't have a building authority approval where the inspector could say it was a regulated construction product and just check the box. You had to think about it, for example, on the basis of tests that were done, or on the basis of different calculations and a lot of statements and opinions from experts or a lot of different people, all of whom were experts in timber construction.*

This innovation network gave the start-up company access to testing laboratories and expert opinions that were used to improve the safety of the 'wooden wind turbine' and get the prototype approved for construction, as the test engineer (D- Org03) explains:

> *You have to have the right material properties and then you can calculate if necessary and these material properties have to be measured first. (...) Then you get an expert opinion. They are in there. (...) These measurement results are evaluated and then an expert opinion is written saying that the material behaves in such and such a way.*

In conclusion, the approval procedure for the 'wooden wind turbine' could not be based on common working standards. Therefore, in line with P2, the start-up company relied on establishing a praxis of collaborative material testing with partners from various scientific institutes to get its prototype approved, as the design engineer (D-Org01) summarizes:

> *But at that time we were really dependent on external opinions and experience. Not for the development of the product, but for the verification of the details of what we were building.*

6.4.2.2 No power to socially close the approval procedure

To get the prototype approved, the start-up company had to gather additional technical proof of the safety of the 'wooden wind turbine', as the civil engineer (D- Org01) summarizes: "*[The authority] said it needed this and that expert opinion.*" In order to obtain this evidence, the company's engineers collaborated with experts from various material testing institutes and university departments.

However, the approval process almost got bogged down in time-consuming code inspections, as the civil engineer (D-Org01) explains: "*This means that there are special procedures for calculating this cross-laminated timber. There is also a standard for this, but it is really about the interpretation of the standard.*" In fact, despite the newly established praxis of collaborative material testing, the approval procedures remained open and the start-up company had no power to speed up or influence the approval decision, as is evident from the following quote:

> *But then you are bound to such a procedure and as a small company you get the short end of the stick. (D-Org01, Civil engineer)*

The approval process remained under the control of the public authorities. In addition, the position of the start-up company as a newcomer seemed to have direct consequences for the approval procedure. As the civil engineer (D-Org01) suggests, the timber engineering experts had little confidence in this new company and its construction idea: "*[There weren't] that many experts who had agreed to [check] it. They were also concerned about what would happen if it didn't work. We are not a company that has ever done carpentry or built a wooden house, but we wanted to build a 100-meter wooden structure directly, without having any idea about the material.*

Another challenge was that the start-up was dependent on a small number of people. For example, expertise in the technical evaluation of timber structures is highly concentrated in a few scientific departments, as the test engineer (D-Org03) explains:

> *[T]here is a colleague in [a southern German city] who deals specifically with these issues of the serviceability of wood. (...) I wouldn't know who to recommend, because this plays a certain role in the bridge sector, but not a major one.*

It plays a certain role, but not a central one, because today we don't build bridges out of wood for road traffic or, in the broadest sense, for cars. That is automatically done in steel or reinforced concrete. That's why not so many people are involved.

In this case, the company's dependence on individual experts was a recurring pattern. For example, in addition to the scientific departments, the start-up company also worked with material testing institutes specializing in timber structures during the approval phase. One of these institutes is affiliated with a university department. Its professor invented joining techniques for timber structures. The institute provided experience-based knowledge and was able to propose "*alternative solutions*" for the 'wooden wind turbine', as the expert from the materials testing institute (Org02) points out:

> *At that time, the company had a concept. They contacted [our] university with this concept. The intention was to test this joint technology, and we had been working on the joint technology for a long time. In principle, we had submitted an alternative proposal that was eventually pursued.*

This materials testing institute played an important role in the innovation network. It gave the start-up company access to laboratories and testing equipment, the same expert adds: "*That was certainly one of the reasons why all these tests could be done here [at the institute], because there is a testing machine that covers exactly this load range. It must be possible to apply relatively high loads. We can handle that.*" However, the expert also mentions that due to the non-standardized approval procedure, the network has established an "*individual*" testing procedure:

> *[Not] everyone can test the way they want. There are standards for testing. (...) We couldn't fall back on that here, because it was all new territory. That's why they were individual tests, but they also had to be coordinated with the experts, the assessors, the specialists, so that they would be accepted. This is different with standardized tests.*

These findings support the assumptions made in P2. The start-up company established a common praxis of material testing and scientific experimentation. However, it was also interesting to observe that during the approval process, the start-up firm was not able to complete the innovation process by proving the norm conformity of its design. During the approval process, the authorities kept raising "*new questions*" that reopened the innovation process, as the same expert from the material testing institute (Org02) points out:

> *Our role was really to obtain experimental results as a basis for the later project. There was certainly a peculiarity in the whole process. During the process, more and more tests were requested. The tests carried out at the beginning of the project were not sufficient, as the building authorities and the relevant experts and surveyors raised new questions during the course of the project, which then had to be answered. This was certainly a peculiarity in the development of the wooden tower.*

In conclusion, despite the newly established praxis of material testing and scientific experimentation, the innovation network and its coordinator, the start-up company, did not have the power to socially close the innovation process. Ongoing interpretations of the standards constantly reopened the approval process and caused significant delays in the project.

6.4.2.3 Depending on a small number of experts

Interestingly, it was the reputation of a few experts that finally enabled the start-up company to socially complete the innovation process and get its prototype approved for construction. In fact, personal trust provided a "*shared belief*" in the safety of the 'wooden wind turbine', as will be shown below.

The start-up company worked with several renowned experts in wood engineering, as the construction manager (D-Org01) points out: "*There are also many individuals who have supported us. (...) For example, there is Professor [name anonymized]. (...) He is always called in when there is no one available. He is so experienced that they always value his opinion and call him in.*"

The interviews revealed that the reliance on individual expertise and reputation is a typical pattern in timber construction. For example, several interviewees described the approval process in timber engineering as being based on a few experts. The representative of the material testing institute (D-Org02) mentions a renowned scientist "*who (...) has dealt with fatigue and developed the design approaches for timber bridges under fatigue relevant loads in Germany. For example, for road bridges in timber construction. That was one of his topics, and he was basically the only one who knew about fatigue.*" In the timber construction industry, the expertise required for the approval of new buildings is highly individualized and distributed among only a few scientific institutes.

In the case of the 'wooden wind turbine', individual expertise and the reputation of individual scientists had a strong influence on the interpretation of the standard and the approval decision, as the following quote shows:

> *There are different views [on the interpretation of the standard]. The professor we chose had agreed to do this, and he also enjoys a high reputation. In the end, it was good for us that he signed it, because we could say that this professor had done it, and [the admissions office] replied that it was all right. In addition, we could say that another professor had said that it would hold, so [the authority] said again that it was in order. (D-Org01, Civil engineer)*

In effect, the start-up company relied on the reputation of a single expert to get its prototype approved. For the building authority, it was this individual's expertise that provided sufficiently reliable evidence of the wood wind turbine's compliance with existing standards, as the test engineer (D-Org03) recalls: "*[For this] connection there was nothing before. Except what Professor [name anonymized] had developed. Because this development, which was used in the tower, came from [him]. I think that this is something that is very important here. It also makes it clear who came up with what idea. This was the idea of [this professor].*"

As these findings show, the start-up's innovation network provided access to technical solutions, but, more importantly, it increased the legitimacy of the prototype by including reputable individuals. The expert from the material testing institute (D-Org02) confirms that "*this idea of Mr. Professor [name anonymized] was new. The idea of embedding a piece of metal in wood was his idea many years ago.*" In fact, based on a new technical solution and the reputation of a professor, the start-up company was able to create a "common belief" in the safety of its innovation:

> *The [professor's name] was the originator of the idea, and he is the central figure. He did the experimental research and documented it. In addition, comparative studies were carried out at the Technical University [of a southern German city] as part of the application for funding. (Case-D-Org03, Test engineer)*

> *[W]hen this connector was used for the first time by Professor [name withheld], he already knew how it was to be done and what you could really expect from the wood, but also how the machine configurations had to look like. (Org01, Design engineer).*

As these quotes show, the start-up company relied on the expertise and reputation of a few experts to get its innovation accepted. The reputation and trustworthiness of one expert in particular strengthened the "belief" of the public approval authorities that the new design was safe. However, as these findings also show, personal trust is a risky innovation strategy when radically new technologies are being developed, which means that innovation projects are long-term, expensive, uncertain, and dependent on collaboration with experts from different fields of expertise.

6.4.2.4 Preliminary conclusions

Similar to the case of a robotic rotor blade coating system, the case of the 'wooden wind turbine' tells the story of the development of a radically new technology. Under such conditions, an innovation project is likely to be organized based on newly created procedures and methods of collaborative problem solving (P2). However, the case of the 'wooden wind turbine' only partially supports this thesis.

It was found that a German start-up company successfully established an innovation network to design the prototype of a 'wooden wind turbine'. In later stages of technology development, it also established an innovation praxis of collaborative material testing and scientific experimentation to prepare the prototype for construction. In line with P2, the focal firm continued to invent additional technical solutions and improve its prototype based on this collaborative innovation praxis.

However, the established innovation praxis was not sufficient to socially complete the innovation process. Because the approval process was not based on established technical standards, it took time for the development partners (mainly the focal firm and an approval authority) to agree on a technical design and socially close the innovation process. In the end, the mechanism for developing – and approving – a new technology was the personal trust that representatives of the approval authorities placed in a few wood engineering experts.

Table 16: Innovation praxis in fields of radical innovation

Technical standards	Working standards
No technical standard for such a radically new architecture was available (a new technical standard was invented based on solutions from another sector)	A praxis of collaborative innovation as well as collaborative material testing and scientific experimentation was established
	The lack of standardized approval praxis delayed the innovation process

6.5 Institutional barriers and what they caused

The empirical findings in this chapter partially support P2. A strategic approach to establishing a practice of collaborative innovation was observed only in the early stages of the innovation process in the case of radical innovation projects. In the case of the robotic rotor blade coating system, the system idea was specified collaboratively. In the case of the 'wooden wind turbine', a collaborative praxis of material testing and experimentation was observed.

In both cases, however, significant unintended outcomes occurred, such as quality defects and project delays. This section argues that these outcomes were caused by the lack of a shared innovation praxis that would have integrated all relevant actors. In case C, the system developer was not part of the innovation praxis; in case D, the licensing authority was not part of the innovation praxis. In both cases, a strategic approach to establishing common working standards was not found. The innovation projects relied on personal trust to specify the new system architecture or to get the innovation approved.

6.5.1 Case C: 'Blind spots' of technology development

The case of a robotic coating system was characterized by a high degree of uncertainty and technological complexity, as the coating process engineer (C-Org01) explains: "*There are comparatively few robotic processes that take more than two hours. The [system manufacturer] had no experience with this before. (...) [W]hen I make changes to a program that takes two hours instead of half an hour, then I have a completely different level of complexity.*"

This chapter has shown that a common innovation praxis was not found in Case C. Instead, the project work was characterized by long geographical distances, mistrust, and tactics of keeping one's own knowledge secret. At the same time, the interviews revealed that the project suffered from technical shortcomings: Once implemented, the system did not work properly; rotor blades were not coated as expected. The author of this book that these quality defects were caused by the lack of a common development practice.

This assumption is supported by the empirical evidence presented. In fact, as the coating process engineer (C-Org01) suggests, a shared praxis of technical problem solving emerged only after the system was introduced:

> *[After the implementation], the problem solving mode actually started. In December, with the acceptance of the painting, it was clear that this was an important milestone. The deadline has been reached and you are now painting. It looked terrible. (...) It was clear to everyone that this could not be the final result.*

As this quote illustrates, the innovation project suffered from serious quality defects that delayed the launch of the new system, which is interpreted here as significant unintended outcomes. Interestingly, the coating process engineer (C-Org01), who was directly involved in the implementation process, states that this outcome occurred because no praxis of joint technical problem solving was established during the technology development phase:

> *If you want high accuracy, the process has to take longer (...). Somewhere you have to decide. Ideally, the decision should be given back to the customer at some point before the whole thing is set up. This was not done. The system was built and the problems were seen later.*

Apart from the communication problems mentioned above, another reason why the innovation partners did not establish a praxis of collaborative problem solving during the system development phase may have been that they were separated by large geographical distances. The system was designed, built, and tested by a German company that specializes in such technologies for the automotive industry, as the technical manager (C-Org02) points out: "*The pre-assembly [of the system] was done by [the system supplier] itself in [a large city in southern Germany]. Test runs were then carried out there.*" Unfortunately, the system supplier could not be interviewed. However, the other interviewees stated that the customer and the system supplier were located about one hundred kilometers apart.

The interviews also revealed that technical problem solving during system development took place mainly within the organizational boundaries of the system supplier, although no expert staff of the system supplier could be interviewed to verify these statements. This created 'blind spots' in technology development, as the following quote illustrates:

> *In the end, our go-live took much longer than planned. There were just new problems that were not on the radar screen. (C-Org01, Coating process engineer)*

As soon as the project partners became aware of the quality defects, the project had to reopen the innovation process. The partners engaged in a blame game instead of solving the problem together. The coating process engineer (C-Org01) describes this situation as "finger pointing": "*It was a bit of finger-pointing, with the equipment manufacturer saying that the color was not consistent enough and the color mixer saying that the equipment was not good enough to work with. As a customer, you have no interest in getting involved in that discussion. Just find a solution. In the end, the ball was in the equipment manufacturer's court.*"

These technical discussions further delayed the introduction of a functional system. In fact, as the same expert adds, system development was socially reopened by "questioning everything" without knowing the reasons for the quality defects:

> *Everything was questioned. Have they got the right overlap, the right speed, the right nozzles? A lot of dummy work went into this. They were looking at things that were not the decisive factor.*

In this situation where "blind spots" were revealed and blame games delayed the project work, the focal company used the requirement specification to impose its expectations on the system supplier, according to the coating process engineer (C-Org01): "*The exact specification in the requirement specification has always been used as a lever for the equipment manufacturer to solve. That is the point. At first you are not satisfied. Why are you not satisfied? Because it says in the specification that it should look like this and that, but it does not look like that. You still have to do something.*" The expert goes on to explain that, based on the technical specifications, the customer was trying to exert contractual pressure to close the innovation process socially: "*You can make better specifications in it, or you can also better question the manufacturer's offers.*"

However, this form of contractual control over the development of the system was not sufficient to socially close the innovation process. On the contrary, the specification sheet to which the system developer was bound did not prevent "blind spots," as the coating process engineer (C-Org01) explains:

> *The expectation was that the layer thickness would vary much less with an automatic coating system than with a manual one. (...) This was previously described in the performance specification in relatively precise terms. What I found odd from*

> *my point of view was that the customer signed and confirmed this. He signed it retrospectively at that point in time without knowing whether this was possible or having any knowledge of the material.*

The 'blind spots' of technology development described above are interpreted here as the result of a poorly established innovation praxis. A "*problem-solving mode*", as one expert put it, emerged only after the system was implemented. During the technology development phase, there was no shared praxis of designing, building, and testing the new technology.

The case provides empirical evidence that in radical innovation projects, a lack of innovation praxis based on shared work norms that normatively 'ground' the design, construction and testing of the new technology can lead to 'blind spots' in technology development. As a direct result, knowledge integration in this case was very much "*concentrated*" in a few individuals, as the coating process engineer (C-Org01) put it:

> *I think that with every customization of the program that we now do almost entirely ourselves and that [the system manufacturer] did for a long time, they built up know-how. It was concentrated on a few people. The programmer who started to build up the automatic painting was there until the end. The last time we had contact with him was in the summer, when we had to make some adjustments. It was always the same person.*

In conclusion, the rotor blade coating system was plagued by quality defects in the finishing of rotor blades, which are interpreted here as the result of a poorly established innovation praxis. Based on the empirical evidence presented, the lack of praxis in collaboratively designing, building, and testing a radically new technology caused '*blind spots*' in technology development. Instead of establishing practices of knowledge integration across all relevant innovation partners (here: the customer, the general contractor, and the technology specialist), the project partners were separated by large geographical distances, mistrust, tactics of keeping proprietary knowledge secret, and blame games.

These conclusions are supported by the empirical findings in Case C. For example, the process engineer (C-Org01) pointed out that the factory usually prefers to collaborate with trusted partners, even if they are not specialized in a particular technology. Apparently, this is because collaborative relationships with such partners are stabilized by a system of norms and standards of behavior (such as trustworthiness, mutually shared references, etc.) – a conclusion that should be tested in future research. In the words of the process engineer (C-Org01):

> *In reality, it is often the case that we use suppliers that we already know and where we already know that there is experience. They have already implemented other systems with us. Of course, there are preferred suppliers who then suddenly develop other systems that they did not originally build, just because we know them.*

6.5.2 Case D: Institutional concentration of expertise

While in the case of a robot-based coating plant, quality defects were identified as significant unintended outcomes, in the case of a 'wooden wind turbine', a significant project delay of over ten months was observed. It will be shown below that this was caused by the fact that the approval process could not rely on existing technical standards and that the innovation partners failed to establish a praxis of collaborative material testing and scientific experimentation.

In order to get its prototype 'wooden wind turbine' approved for construction, the start-up company had to prove that its innovation met public safety standards. The relevant public approval authorities demanded additional material tests to provide experimental data on the safety of the new design, which significantly delayed the construction of the wind turbine, as the construction engineer (D-Org01) explains: "*They always wanted to be 200 percent sure. Everything we did and calculated was never enough – it always had to be checked by an expert. And as is always the case with hired experts, they never just say it's okay; they always find something. As a result, there was always a chain reaction that raised at least two more questions that had to be addressed. In the end, this cost us the time we actually needed for development.*" As a result, the project was more than ten months behind schedule. Tedious technical discussions and norm interpretations within the network kept the innovation process socially open.

It is argued here that this project delay was caused by a lack of "shared belief" between the start-up company and the approval authorities that the new design was safe. Typically, such beliefs arise on the basis of standardized material testing and approval procedures, as a manager of a timber engineering firm (D-Org05) explains: "*Our construction projects are organized differently because science is always involved in this case-by-case approval process. Otherwise, in construction projects, science is usually left out because we work according to DIN regulations and standards that have already been tested, approved, and authorized.*" In the case of the 'wooden wind turbine', however, because no technical standards were applicable, the authorities imposed additional tests on the project again and again, as the site manager (D-Org01) recalls:

> *The whole process was perhaps not marked by problems, but rather by regulatory requirements. We had a lot of measuring technology that we had to integrate into our tower. (...) There were repeated inspections – at 30, 60 and 90 meters. Then again after the tower was completed and after the system was installed on top. There were many authorities involved, which was not normal (...). It was not a continuous construction process. (D-Org01, Construction manager)*

These findings do not place blame on the permitting authorities, but support P2's assumption that radical innovation projects rely on shared innovation praxis – in this case, working standards for material testing and scientific experimentation. Despite a collaborative testing process involving the start-up company, material testing institutes, and scientific experts, the project was delayed because the lack of standardized approval procedures kept the innovation process socially open, with processes of norm interpretation continuing even during the construction of the prototype. The approval authority remained outside of this innovation praxis, demanding only additional evidence.

Instead of establishing a common innovation praxis, the start-up firm on the one hand and the approval authority on the other advocated different technological frameworks, which referred "*not only to the nature and role of the technology itself, but also to the specific conditions, applications, and consequences of that technology in a particular context*" (Orlikowski & Gash, 1994, p. 178). The author of this book argues that only the establishment of new approval procedures shared by the most powerful actor in the field – here, the approval authority – can 'bridge' such conflicting frames.

This conclusion is supported by field theory. The small start-up firm was in an inferior power position in the field due to its limited R&D capacities, few recognized references of its technological competencies, and a product idea that deviated from established paradigms. The company actively tried to improve its position in the field, as the design engineer (D-Org01) points out: "*Of course we are also trying to get our own approvals for the material itself. We want to take care of this ourselves, so that we can say that we no longer rely on these standards, but use our own tested values.*" However, as the managing director of another timber engineering company (D-Org05) notes, it is "almost pointless" for small companies to define their own new technical standards:

> *The effort required to get [a screw or fastener] approved, along with the series of tests that need to be conducted, is so financially demanding that only large companies with substantial development budgets can afford it. But for companies like ours, getting approval is almost hopeless.*

In addition to the inferior position in the field, the institutionalized approval procedures in the timber construction industry represent an innovation barrier for the focal company. For example, the structural engineer (D-Org01) criticizes the approval procedures for relying on a limited number of authorities: "[In timber construction] they have created a structure in which a small number of people have such great influence that they can make a considerable number of decisions. For example, in Germany there are only two testing agencies for the approval of adhesives. Similarly, there are only two testing agencies that can give a company permission to bond steel and wood components together.

Other interviewees speak of a high concentration of wood engineering experts and R&D organizations. The expert from the materials testing institute (D-Org02), for example, claims that innovations in wood engineering have traditionally been "individual":

> *Carpenters have always been very individualistic. Everyone has their own ideas, which they pass on from guild to guild within the trade. This knowledge is passed on within the guilds from one generation to the next. As a result, many carpenters develop their own unique concepts, which they then implement and refine independently. This has resulted in a wide variety of joinery techniques.*

Because of this institutional concentration of expertise and certifying bodies, the start-up company had to rely on a few actors to get its innovation approved. A strategy of defining the 'wooden wind turbine' as a new technical standard would have been "utopian", as the expert from the Materials Testing Institute (Org02) points out. This would have required the coordination of technical discussions and compromises between standardization bodies throughout the European Union:

> *Developing a timber construction standard for wooden wind turbine towers would be utopian. There would be numerous interest groups that could actively participate in the creation of such a standard. First of all, they would all have to be brought to the table. In addition, standardization has now been harmonized at the European level. This means that not only German interests would have to be represented, but also those from all over Europe.*

From its inferior position, the start-up company had no power to define a new technical standard. Instead, it tried to "find its way" through the existing standards and adapt technical solutions, as the civil engineer (D-Org01) puts it: "This means that if we want to be innovative, our goal must be to navigate along the existing regulatory framework and standards." In addition, the start-up company was dependent on building up "trust" and reputation by collecting references, as the site manager (D-Org01) concludes:

> *There is no universal formula for this. I would say that building our tower builds trust. This means that we always have to build a new tower, and then it has to stand, it has to work, it has to be accessible for visits, and it has to be seen to work – over a long period of time.*

In conclusion, the project of a 'wooden wind turbine' suffered from significant time delay of more than ten mounts. It was shown above that this was caused by the fact that the small start-up company had little influence on the approval process, and that the approval authority kept standard interpretations open for a long time. A common praxis of collaborative material testing and experimentation was not observed. Instead, personal trust attributed to a few reputable experts functioned as a mechanism to complete the approval process and introduce the innovation into the field.

6.6 Interim conclusions

In order to understand the institutional barriers to collaborative innovation, two examples of radical innovation projects were presented in this chapter. The cases of a robotics-based rotor blade coating facility (Case C) and a 'wooden wind turbine' (Case D) were used to evaluate the proposition that in radical innovation projects, a radical innovation project is likely to be organized based on newly created procedures and methods of collaborative problem solving (P2). However, a strategic approach to establishing such a shared innovation praxis was hard to find.

The empirical evaluation was structured as in the previous chapter: first, the two innovation networks were described (6.1); second, the observed practices of knowledge integration were characterized (6.2); third, it was shown how collaboration was organized in each case (6.3); and fourth, the observed institutional barriers were discussed (6.4). This section summarizes the empirical findings of this chapter.

In both cases it was found that the focal firm, a rotor blade factory on the one hand and a start-up firm on the other hand, established an innovation network that integrated specialists from new fields of expertise. However, the power structures differed significantly between the two cases.

Table 17: Fields of radical innovations

	Case C: Rotor blade coating system	**Case D: 'Wooden wind turbine'**
Knowledge Integration	A rotor blade factory collaborated with a local, trusted technology specialist to elaborate a technical specification sheet (boundary object)	A start-up firm established an innovation network and used ties with various scientific partners to get the prototype of a 'wooden wind turbine' approved for construction
Realizing technology development	Drawing on a personal trust-relation, the focal firm gained some contractual control over external system development (with the technical specification sheet as a power source)	Integrating material testing institutes and well-reputed experts into the innovation network, the focal firm tried to gain control over the approval procedure

	Case C: Rotor blade coating system	Case D: 'Wooden wind turbine'
Institutional barriers	Reliance on technical specification sheet for controlling system development turned out to be an inferior strategy (resulting in "blind spots" and severe quality defects)	Relying on the expertise and solutions of one well-reputed expert functioned as a fallback strategy for socially closing the approval procedure (with the drawback of project delays)

In Case C, the rotor blade factory was part of a large European WTM and acted as the focal company that initiated the innovation process. It set up a project team and collaborated with various specialists from previously unfamiliar fields of expertise. In particular, it worked with an external, trusted technology specialist located in close proximity to the manufacturing site. This technology specialist acted as a bridge between the expertise in robotics-based process automation and the requirements of rotor blade coating. In addition, during the system specification phase, the relationship of trust between the plant manager and the managing director of the consulting firm enabled the innovation project to use technical specifications to guide system development. The technical specification served as a boundary object, but also as a power resource vis-à-vis the system supplier.

In Case D, a German start-up company initiated the innovation process and established an innovation network to develop a radically new technology by combining knowledge from wood engineering with the technical requirements of wind turbines. During the approval process, the company expanded its innovation network and integrated experts from material testing institutes to get the prototype approved for construction. However, due to the development of a non-standardized technology, the start-up firm had little power to socially complete the innovation process.

These findings only partially support the assumptions outlined in P2. In both cases, *newly created procedures and methods of collaborative problem solving* were only observed in selected stages of the innovation process, namely the stage of technical conception in case C and the stage of material testing and scientific experimentation in case D. At the same time, unintended outcomes, such as serious quality defects in the case of the rotor blade coating system and significant project delays in the case of the 'wooden wind turbine', could be observed and attributed to the lack of a collaborative innovation praxis.

A strategic approach to establishing such a praxis of radical innovation requires the *early involvement of all relevant partners in technical problem-solving processes,* including regulatory agencies, which – according to the linear model of innovation – are usually involved only towards the end of the development process. The author of this book argues that an integrated innovation praxis would endow the innovation network with the normative authority needed to develop and introduce a radically new technology from the ground up.

7. Emerging technology fields

The previous two chapters analyzed institutional barriers in the areas of incremental and radical innovation. It turned out that a strategic approach to collaborative innovation was rarely pursued. Only at certain stages of technology development, such as joint R&D, technical specification or material testing, could an innovation praxis characterized by horizontal negotiations and knowledge interdependencies be observed. Thus, contrary to the assumption that complex technologies are developed either on the basis of technical standards (incremental innovation; P1) or on the basis of processes for establishing common working standards (radical innovation; P2), the strategic institutionalization of a collaborative innovation praxis is a rare occurrence.

The observed quality deficits and significant time delays could support the author's main argument: A collaborative innovation praxis is based on shared working standards because it integrates all relevant partners, including certification and approval authorities, which – according to linear models of innovation – are usually not integrated until the end of the innovation process. However, it is the involvement of all relevant actors and the provision and promotion of knowledge integration between them that gives the innovation partnership the normative power needed to define and develop a radically new technology from scratch.

To further substantiate this argument, this chapter presents two final cases of technology development that were studied in the emerging field of the German offshore wind energy industry. Chapter 3 argued that in emerging fields where neither technical standards nor innovation networks are established, innovation projects are likely to adapt technical solutions from adjacent fields. This chapter argues that, even under such conditions, the development of new technologies is likely to be successful.

7.1 An emerging field of technology development

This section analyzes the organization of technology development in the emerging field of offshore wind. A new field usually emerges around a new issue. In the offshore wind industry, environmental regulations provided such an issue. Regulations have been put in place to protect marine life, particularly marine mammals such as porpoises, from noise emissions from construction. These regulations require wind farm developers to find technical solutions that meet the regulatory requirements and get their wind farm projects approved for construction.

In this field, four major players were involved in the technology development. First, an offshore engineering specialist and system developer; second, large utilities specializing in the construction of wind farms that were looking for technical solutions to meet environmental regulations; third, a public authority that checked the compliance of offshore constructions with these regulations; and fourth, a measurement body that was officially certified to monitor the performance of the systems at sea. This area is described in more detail below.

7.1.1 New environmental regulations

Since 2001, a public authority has been responsible for approving the construction of offshore wind parks in the German Exclusive Economic Zone (EEZ). In close coordination with federal environmental agencies, this public authority monitors legally defined limits of noise emissions caused by the installation of offshore wind turbines. As an R&D expert of a system supplier (E-Org07) points out, these regulations have induced a new field of technology development:

> *In this context, one thing is very important to understand, namely that this is not a pure market process, but that there are also authorities in the background. They also have to approve certain concepts. They can say that you can't use this system because they don't believe it will work.*

At the time of the empirical investigation, offshore structures such as wind turbines or accommodation platforms were installed using the impact driving method[36] (von Estorff et al., 2013). In this method, large steel pipes, approximately 80 meters long and up to 10 meters in diameter, are driven into the seabed.[37] In the early years of the offshore wind energy sector, there were no standards to protect the offshore environment, as a scientist and consultant to the offshore wind energy industry (E-Org06) recalls:

It was quickly apparent that there were no national or international standards or norms to support this. They didn't even know how to do it. The second

36 Impact drive is an installation procedure that rams steel pipes which measure over 6.5 meters in diameter and up to 80 meters in height into the sea bed. One expert specified this problem as follows: "*Now this becomes relevant for the acoustics. If you take a monopile, it has a large surface area. If you hit it, you firstly need more energy to overcome the frictional resistance in the floor. Secondly, this higher energy and the large surface area then lead to a high level of sound radiation. This means that a system must actually generate a high reduction. Roughly in the order of 20 decibels*" (E-Org07, R&D noise mitigation systems).

37 Those so-called "XL-monopiles" are designed for deep-water foundations installed over 40 meters below sea-level (E-Org09, Monopile foundation supplier).

*thing that was discovered was that the measurement technology was not even available to monitor the environment, for example. So how can you determine the noise level under water with certain foundation methods?*Over the years and in close coordination with other authorities such as federal ministries or environmental associations, the public authority responsible for con- trolling offshore constructions strengthened environmental protection. Since the 1st of March 2010, new regulations strictly prohibit the killing, injury or disturbance of animals (E-Org01, Approval expert). Therefore, to get the installation of wind tur- bines approved, construction firms must now prove that noise emissions are reduced or sufficiently mitigated, as the office manager of an offshore industry foundation (E-Org08) points out:

> *[Wind farms] may not be built if these requirements cannot be met. The industry therefore has a great interest in being able to fulfil these requirements.*

When the first regulations were introduced, the offshore wind industry seemed divided over how to deal with the new environmental rules. As a result, utilities discussed the idea of a joint R&D project to kick-start technology development in this area. A representative of a major utility recalls: "*[A]t that time, I was of the opinion that they all wanted to carry out a research project on noise mitigation, but not everyone had the same interest. (...) Everyone had always believed that other problems were more important and that they would take care of environmental protection*" (E-Org05, Expert noise mitigation). Today, the offshore wind industry is working closely with authorities and technology companies to meet environmental standards and get offshore wind farms approved, he says:

> *[The individual companies report [to the authority] which noise protection measures are planned and how they can better fulfil [the public requirements] as a result. They report that they are configuring [their systems] in such and such a way and are then commissioned to do so. They then receive an addendum to the planning permission. It then states that they have to do this and that for the next eight, nine, ten piles.*

In summary, following the introduction of new environmental regulations for offshore construction, a new field of technology development has emerged around the question of how to reduce noise emissions from offshore construction. In this field, the following four main actors were involved: (1) a public authority; (2) a certified measuring body; (3) utilities and wind farm planning companies; and (4) offshore engineering specialists and system developers. The next section shows how these actors formed a new field of technology development.

7.1.2 The major players

In addition to the regulatory authority mentioned above, the other major players in the new field of technology development were large utilities that plan and operate offshore wind farms, such as RWE, E.On, EnBW, EWE, EnBW, Vattenfall or Ørsted (formerly Dong Energy). The top management of these utilities perceived the new regulations as an economic risk and decided to look for technical solutions to reduce or mitigate noise emissions during construction, as the manager of a wind farm planning department of one utility (E-Org04) recalls:

> *The fact that the limit value alone was anchored in the authorizations naturally meant that the issue of noise protection was very high on our risk map. This was particularly because we were unable to estimate what the authorities would do if we were unable to comply with this value, as there were no suitable noise reduction systems on the market, for example. (...) It didn't take long for the issue to reach the very top of the board's agenda. (E-Org04, Offshore engineering manager)*

At the time, the utilities were searching in vain for new technical solutions. An industry association provided a public forum to discuss the options available, and representatives from all the utilities decided to systematically search for technical solutions together by setting up a joint research project, the offshore manager continues: "*We then sat down with the partners through [a foundation] and thought about what we could do. (...) On a technical and scientific level, we had a special working group, which eventually led to this research project.*"

These quotes indicate that the offshore wind industry initiated a joint R&D project to compare existing technical solutions to meet regulatory requirements, to generate basic knowledge on underwater noise emissions and, most importantly, to initiate innovation projects in the offshore wind industry. A joint R&D project based on both public and industry support has been set up to act as a "catalyst" for the creation of a market for noise abatement systems, as the same expert explains:

> *We earn our money afterwards with the wind farm. This means that although we saw ourselves as a catalyst for initiating developments through this project, it was clear from the outset that we would buy the noise reduction service on the market. (E-Org04, Offshore engineering manager)*

System developers are a third major actor in the field, alongside regulators and large utilities, as a representative of a large utility points out: "*This noise protection is characterized by large companies like [names anonymized] or small companies that operate like start-ups*" (E-Org05, Expert noise mitigation). The main clients of these system developers are construction companies commissioned by the large utilities. The contractors integrate the system developers' technical solutions into their wind farm installation procedures, as specified by the utility manager: "*At the end of the day, noise control is just a purchased part for us, like a hammer. There is also no installer who develops his own noise control systems. That's not our job, but then you go to the market and ideally the internal development is so far advanced that you know what you want*" (E-Org04, offshore engineering manager).

The empirical cases discussed in this chapter tell the story of two system developers offering two different systems for reducing noise emissions. Case E deals with a noise abatement system, while in case F, the developer company wanted to introduce a "quieter" foundation system by adapting a state-of-the-art technology used in the oil and gas industry. In both cases, the system developers were newcomers to the offshore wind energy sector who saw the new environmental regulations as a business opportunity.

The final major actor included in the research was a certified measurement organization. A representative of this body described the organization as officially authorized to measure noise emissions during offshore construction and to assess system suppliers on behalf of the public licensing authority: "*We are independent. We evaluate all noise control manufacturers and are in great demand by the federal authorities in our advisory role*" (E-Org06, Measurement specialist and consultant).

In summary, two development projects were observed in an emerging area of technology development around new environmental regulations in the offshore wind industry. As shown in Figure 7.1, this field emerged from interactions between four key actors: (1) a public authority; (2) utilities and wind farm planning companies; (3) offshore engineering specialists and system developers; and (4) a certified measurement body. In contrast to the examples of incremental and radical innovation discussed in the previous two chapters, neither technical standards nor innovation networks had yet been established in this field. The projects had to create both technical and working standards from scratch.

Figure 5: An emerging field of technology development

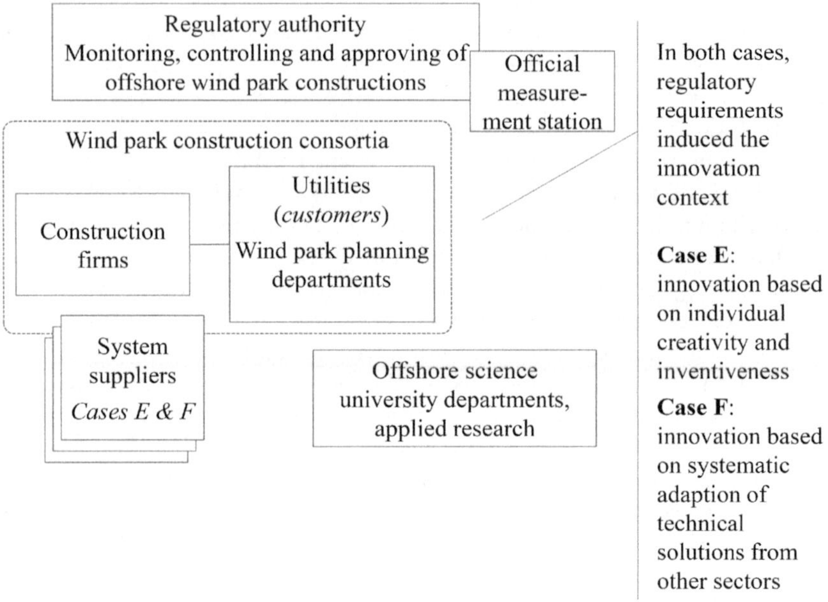

7.1.3 Cases E & F: Two system suppliers, two solutions

Both cases involve an engineering service provider that saw the new environmental regulations in the offshore wind industry as a business opportunity. Both companies were newcomers to the sector, but differed in terms of size, competence and practical experience in implementing projects for the offshore wind energy industry.

Case E deals with noise abatement systems, which are used to reduce noise emissions caused by the construction of offshore wind farms. Typically, offshore engineering services are contracted by large utilities planning the installation of offshore wind farms. One of the system suppliers involved in the investigation was an entrepreneur specializing in steel construction. This company was a newcomer to the offshore wind industry, as he explains:

> *I have to say that I was still pretty green behind the ears in that sector back then. (...) I had to completely rethink things. There wasn't as much literature about it as there is today that you could fall back on. (E-Org02, Managing director)*

In addition to this firm, a second supplier of noise mitigation systems was also interviewed for *case E.* Relying on decades of experience as a solution provider to the offshore industry, this firm turned into the entrepreneur's main competitor. Its managing director stated: "*We mainly specialise in coming to the customer's aid when they are experiencing a problem. Their needs are met by something that is tailored precisely to them.*" (E-Org03-Managing director).

In *case F*, the focal firm was a well-established engineering service provider in the international offshore oil and gas industry. This firm also perceived the offshore wind energy industry as a new market and designed an alternative foundation procedure for offshore wind turbines that is far more silent than the established method of pile ramming, as the firm's senior manager (F-Org01) stresses:

> *It has been proven that a foundation with [this procedure] would represent a quantum leap in noise reduction. (...) If you put it in popular scientific terms, then this is a low-noise foundation in comparison (...) We are now in the process of using this innovative technology for wind turbines, because that is where the ecological added value can be found.*

The next section shows how both companies established collaborative knowledge integration processes despite the lack of technical and working standards in this emerging field.

7.2 Analysed practices of knowledge integration

After introducing the major players in the emerging field of noise mitigation in the offshore wind industry, this section shows how the two engineering firms studied developed technical solutions despite the fact that no technical standards, working standards or innovation networks had been established in the field. In fact, at the time of the research, no technology existed that could meet the new regulatory requirements, as two experts pointed out:

> *Nowadays, there is no system that fulfils all requirements to the same extent. The requirements are good manageability at sea, i.e. small and relatively low weight as well as maximum noise reduction. There is no such system. (E-Org07, R&D noise mitigation system)*

> *There is no serial system that can be said to work in every case. (E-Org05, Expert wind park permission)*

Below, it will be shown that both firms combined their technological know-how gained in other sectors such as steel construction or offshore oil and gas with the technical requirements of the offshore wind energy industry to develop new technical solutions. However, the two companies pursed different strategies. The entrepreneur in *case E* mainly drew on her/his inventiveness to create a solution "*in [her/his] mind*", while the firm in *case F* adapted a technical standard from the offshore oil and gas industry and drew on scientific knowledge gained in an earlier joint R&D project.

7.2.1 Case E: Relying on individual creativity and inventiveness

The solution for a noise reduction system in Case E was developed by an entrepreneur and newcomer to the wind energy industry. During the economic crisis that hit German industry after 2008, the entrepreneur saw the new environmental regulations as an opportunity to expand his business, he recalls: "*That was in 2009. The [alpha ventus wind farm] was in its early stages, people were desperately looking for noise control solutions, and I took part in a symposium and realized that there was a lot of development and production potential here*" (E-Org02, Managing Director and Entrepreneur). For his first invention, the entrepreneur drew mainly on his technical experience in steel construction and combined this knowledge with the technical requirements of installing offshore wind turbines, as the expert continues:

> *In terms of statics alone, I was able to learn a lot from steel construction. I was also able to learn something about construction and sound insulation, although sound insulation under water is different from sound insulation in the air, but once you have understood the basic principle, you can still draw a lot on this knowledge.*

The entrepreneur's innovation strategy relied mainly on his individual creativity and inventiveness, as well as his ability to quickly implement technical ideas based on his own manufacturing facilities, as he explains: "*What was a big advantage in the whole story was that I have my own production company. This means that I can definitely come up with new ideas every day and implement them immediately without having to look for manufacturing companies*" (E-Org02). In this way, the entrepreneur creatively invented a new technical solution in the absence of technical standards.

Thus, in this case, knowledge integration took place very much in the mind of an entrepreneur who was able to draw on his own creativity, ingenuity, and pragmatism to combine steel construction know-how with the technical requirements of installing offshore wind turbines. A strategy of collaborative innovation with other development partners was not pursued, as the entrepreneur openly stated:

> *The ideas for my systems only ever come from me. (E-Org02, Managing director and entrepreneur)*

> *[This entrepreneur] (...) knows down to the last detail how everything works. But he can also realize it because he has a steel construction company, because he welds, because he has a cutting machine. He did everything on the system himself, right down to the procedures. He has everything in his head. (E- Org05, Expert noise mitigation system)*

7.2.2 Case F: Technology transfer from oil and gas

While case E is an example of an entrepreneur who relied mainly on individual know-how and creativity to invent a new prototype, in case F an engineering service provider tried to adapt a technical standard for offshore constructions in the oil and gas industry to the installation of offshore wind turbines.

To accomplish this technology transfer, the company drew on its technological and logistical expertise gained over "*decades*" of construction projects for clients in the oil and gas industry, as the senior manager (F-Org01) explains: "*We have done a lot of work on steel structures for oil and gas. This could then be applied more or less one-to-one when it came to designing the foundation structure.*" Thus, in contrast to the entrepreneur in Case E, who was a newcomer to the offshore industry, this firm was able to draw on professional offshore engineering competencies3 that included a broad bundle of technological knowledge and skills, such as simulation-based engineering routines and experience with offshore logistics, as the manager continues:

> *[We were able to learn what equipment can be used to install something like this quickly and effectively. (...) We also brought in all the experience of how to go from production to loading to transportation and installation at sea. But also the calculations, the proof and the forecasting of the weather window in which something like this can be done are experiences that have been gathered here for decades. We can also take a very critical look at an operation, looking at what works and what doesn't.*

The company's innovation strategy was to adapt an installation procedure and foundation structure used for converter stations to the technical requirements of the offshore wind energy industry, he adds: "*It has been considered to apply this concept to the foundations of wind turbines, but there are some difficulties at the moment. The loads are different and we don't know exactly how the geotechnics and the soil will react.*" To solve such problems, the company's experts usually work completely independently of external specialists. The manager (F-Org01) explains that when designing a new technology, they can rely on internally standardized, software-based engineering procedures:

> *With external partners to the extent that we bring in specialist expertise. If we have very specific soil mechanics problems, the question arises as to who we can work with to solve them. (...) Otherwise, we actually solve everything ourselves. We have software that is also recognized by international classification societies and inspectors. This means that we are in line with the international standard.*

However, during the study, the interviewees emphasized that additional basic scientific knowledge was needed for the implementation of the project. In particular, the experts needed geotechnical knowledge to adapt the new foundation structure to the loads and weights of the wind turbines mounted on the foundation structure, as the manager (F-Org01) points out: "*From the point of view of design, the load on the structure is extremely different from that of fixed platforms, because you have to deal with these oscillation problems, for example, in a constructive way.*" To gain access to the necessary geotechnical expertise, the company participated in a joint R&D project with scientists from an applied research institute and a university department specializing in the calculation and simulation of foundation structures, as the expert explains:

> *First you have to create a model and have an idea of what is important. Then I have to create a mathematical model that can map all the effects. Then I have to carry out element experiments. For example, I can carry out small laboratory tests with the model. (...) Then you hope that the FE model, which simulates the prototype, will have the same behavior as in reality. (...) You don't just press a button and then the things are finished. It's basically manual work. It takes time. (F-Org03, Expert geotechnics)*

The scientific expert describes the engineering skills needed to develop a quieter foundation structure as manual work. The manager of the focal company adds that these skills also include information systems that allow the simulation of new foundation structures, but which are too specialized to be available internally, as the design engineer (F-Org01) specifies: "*There is special R&D software for geotechnical problems, i.e. finite elements. We don't need it often enough. On the other hand, there is still a lot of research going on in this area, and new soil models are being developed all the time.*"

To conclude, in this case the focal company developed a prototype of a new foundation structure and installation procedure, mainly by adapting a technical standard established in the offshore oil and gas industry. This technology transfer was possible because the company had the necessary technological know-how and skills (such as engineering and offshore logistics) gained from decades of construction projects. In addition, the company strategically collaborated with scientific experts to fill its knowledge gaps:

> *This means that the geotechnical design basics are passed on to the relevant institutes. We are then told that they should give us an assessment or evaluation. Of course, this has to end with us being told whether it is possible or not. (F-Org01, Senior manager)*

7.3 Realizing technology development

The previous section presented two examples of offshore engineering firms attempting to introduce a new technology into an emerging technology field. For both companies, the implementation of new environmental regulations for the construction of offshore wind farms opened up new business opportunities.

It could be shown that both firms followed different knowledge integration strategies. In case E, an entrepreneur relied mainly on his personal ability to invent technical solutions by creatively combining know-how gained in steel construction with the technical requirements of wind turbine installation.

In case F, a small engineering firm relied on its professionalized engineering routines and expertise gained from decades of construction projects for the offshore oil and gas industry to transfer an existing technical standard to the offshore wind industry. In contrast to the first case, this company collaborated with scientists to develop fundamental knowledge and gain access to testing facilities. This section analyzes in more detail how each company attempted to establish a position as a systems supplier in this new field.

7.3.1 Case E: Technical invention vs. trial-and-error learning

Below we show how the entrepreneur in Case E tried to establish a position in the offshore wind energy industry. His innovation strategy is elaborated by contrasting it with that of his main competitor. In fact, the reader will learn that the competitor was able to establish a position as a trusted system supplier, while the entrepreneur failed to do so until the time of the interviews.

7.3.1.1 Imagining new solutions "in the mind"

The entrepreneur entered the offshore wind energy sector at a time when utilities were "*desperatel*y" searching for technical solutions to meet new environmental regulations, as the managing director (E-Org02) recalls: "*There was a desperate search for [technical solutions]. I attended a symposium and realized that there was a huge potential for development and production.*" Drawing on his creativity and experience in reducing noise emissions in other industries, the entrepreneur quickly invented a first solution, which he offered to all potential customers in the offshore wind energy sector:

> *I had an idea and thought that could be used. That was [solution A]. I suggested it and from one day to the next, within a week, I was known to the whole group. There was only one provider at the time.*

Since the entrepreneur did not find a buyer for this solution A, he developed solution B by adapting a technical principle already established in the field and offered by his main competitor: "*I stood there and thought about what I would do if there was no need and what I would do then. (...) Then I came up with [solution B]*" (E-Org02, manager and entrepreneur). Within a few weeks, the entrepreneur reports, he/she sold this solution to a customer who was under pressure to incorporate noise abatement into an ongoing offshore construction project: "*Then I went [to the client] and we talked about the system. I also described the process, what the project looked like and how it worked. I didn't have a drawing, nothing. Not even a picture. Nothing at all. Just my stories. This is how we would do it and this is how it works*" (E-Org02, Manager and entrepreneur).

As these findings show, the entrepreneur's first solution, which was basically invented from scratch, did not find customers, but – in line with P3 – the second solution was successful because it was an adaptation of a solution that was already in use. The entrepreneur built this solution and quickly established first customer relationships mainly by relying on personal creativity, ingenuity and pragmatism rather than strategic collaboration with external partners.

The entrepreneur did not take a strategic approach to collaborative innovation, but mainly did technology development "in the head. At the time of market entry, the entrepreneur (E-Org02) admits that she/he had no further insight into related scientific expertise: "*I had no idea about impedance jumps and frequencies and speed of sound* (laughs)." Over the course of two interviews, the CEO came across as a typical entrepreneur, relying on his or her unique individual skills to perform autonomous technology development and come up with quick technical solutions: "*I have it in my head and then I try to communicate it to the people. That way we can be as efficient as possible because we're immediately faced with the product and don't have to spend a lot of time at the drawing board thinking and calculating whether it fits.*" In this particular case, the entrepreneur's cognitive ability to imagine technical solutions "in his head" and a supporting "gut feeling" were the source of technology development:

> *Alone, when you've already reached a certain age – that may sound a bit arrogant – but then you have a certain gut feeling. And that's pretty strong in my case and it hasn't let me down very often. And you can let the context of what's happening run completely through your head. (E- Org02, Managing director and entrepreneur)*

In conclusion, the entrepreneur in this case did not take a strategic approach to collaborative innovation. Technology development took place mainly "in the head" of an entrepreneur who adapted a technical solution from a competitor, but – more interestingly – creatively combined know-how gained in steel construction with the technical requirements of installing wind turbines, thereby imagining new technical solutions and quickly establishing new customer relationships.

7.3.1.2 Personal conviction instead of collaborative innovation

Above it appeared that the entrepreneur did not try to develop a technical solution together with external partners. In fact, the entrepreneur describes her/his position in the field as that of a "lone fighter" with little support from partners, for example in the form of financial risk sharing: "*I would approach the market a bit differently. Maybe I would also look for a partner who would support the whole investment from the beginning and make money out of it, because I am always the lone fighter and I have realized that I am alone in the wilderness and I have no one. Anyone can talk my system to pieces if they want to, even though it's undoubtedly good.*"

Against this background, it was interesting to observe that the entrepreneur's main competitor company was more successful in strengthening its position as a trusted system supplier. According to the entrepreneur, he/she had the "*lobby*" and "*experience*" that the main competitor possessed, which was experience in offshore engineering services for over three decades, as the entrepreneur explains:

> *[My direct competitor], for example, has been on the market for 30 years and has a completely different lobby to [me]. You don't know the [new entrepreneur]. He's never been noticed anywhere, suddenly arrives and offers [his own system]. That's something that really bothers me and that's how the customers outside react. We'd rather go with someone who has the experience.*

The entrepreneur's main competitor has decades of practical experience as an offshore solution provider, as its managing director (E-Org03) explains: "*I've been traveling the world for [the company] since the early 80s. (...) What we do is everything that has to do with oil on the water and air in the water. We don't do oil spill response, we make the equipment for it.*"

The entrepreneur, on the other hand, was a newcomer to the offshore wind industry. With few references and limited engineering capacity, his company struggled to establish a position in the field based on stable customer relationships, as the CEO (E-Org02) suggests:

> *But I don't have a lobby. (...) First of all, I'm not based by the sea. Secondly, I'm fairly new to the market and thirdly, I don't have a manufacturing company with 20 engineers and designers, I do it on my own and nobody has any confidence in that.*

During the investigation, it became clear that the entrepreneur was unable to establish a position as a trusted system supplier. In contrast, the entrepreneur's main competitor succeeded in doing so. This was because, unlike the competitor, the entrepreneur did not take a strategic approach to collaboration and financial risk-sharing, as the following quote from the entrepreneur (E-Org02) illustrates: "*Before we now build [solution A] on a large scale, [which] costs several million, the question remains: is it any good at all? We won't get any research funding for it. Zero! We're doing it all on our own."*

Apart from shouldering the financial risks alone, the entrepreneur also hardly cooperated with scientists to gain access to new knowledge, as the following quote shows: "*At the end of the day, the research institutions are just a confirmation of what I was doing. It confirmed to me that I was on the right track and that I had done my work properly and thought it through technically. That's all it really did for me. It's always good, I'm more of a practical thinker.*

In summary, the entrepreneur managed to quickly invent technical solutions without the support of development partners. His innovation strategy did not include strengthening the FRM's position as a system supplier by sharing financial risks or systematically collaborating with scientific experts to improve the system. Thus, instead of collaborative innovation, personal "conviction" or visionary thinking was the dominant mechanism for introducing a new technology into an emerging technological field, as one of the entrepreneur's employees points out:

> *His conviction was his motivation to drive the system forward in the way he did, so that he could then deliver the performance to satisfy the customer. Nobody does that unless they are so convinced that it won't work the way they have designed it in their head. (E-Org02, Technical assistant)*

7.3.1.3 A collaborative approach to technical invention

In the technology development case described above, one entrepreneur's technical creativity, visionary thinking, and personal conviction emerged as the dominant mechanism for introducing a new technical solution into an emerging field. The entrepreneur's competitor, however, seemed to have adopted an opposite strategy: a strategic approach to collaborative innovation.

The competitor was already an established system supplier when the entrepreneur entered the field. The competitor had adapted a solution that was already in use to mitigate noise from submarine explosions. The competitor incrementally improved this idea in close coordination with scientists, customers, and government regulators.

For example, from the start of its involvement in the offshore wind energy industry, the company has worked with scientists responsible for measuring and reporting noise emissions to regulatory authorities, as the managing director (E-Org03) explains: "*For example, we often work with [a measurement facility]. It is a very fruitful connection. (...) Because they have measured and said what can be done better, you also have opportunities or see ways in which something can be done better.*"

One of the scientists involved (E-Org06) confirms this "*close cooperation*" in which trial-and-error learning and system testing were improvised. As the expert explains, the partners combined practical knowledge with theoretical knowledge of underwater acoustics to improve the technical solution step by step during the construction of offshore wind farms:

> *A relatively close cooperation then developed and we spent a lot of time at sea together with [the competitor]. You then realized that you would like to try out one thing or another and he/she then said whether you can do it or whether it is simply not technically feasible. (...) You then approach it from both the theoretical and the practical side and simply try out a few questions.*

Comparing the entrepreneur with his competitor, a strategic approach to establishing a collaborative innovation praxis was observed only in the latter case. The competitor collaborated with scientists to improve offshore system testing, facilitate trial-and-error learning, and further adapt the company's technical solution to the needs of the wind energy industry, as the following quote illustrates:

> *If you have built a noise protection system, the technical aspects are restricted. During operation, you can't completely rebuild it, but you can vary the set screws within certain limits. That was considered at the time and it really is done bilaterally. (E-Org06, Measurement specialist and consultant)*

For the competitor, these collaborative relations not only provided access to offshore system tests, but also enabled trust-building and the establishment of a shared innovation praxis. For example, as the managing director of the competitor firm (E-Org03) suggests, collaborating with scientists enabled her/him to explain to the functioning of the system to customers, thereby establishing some trust that the solution was working:

> *Of course, it also depends on whether you have the physicist with you when you talk to the customer. He/she will explain that the floor is constructed in such a way that the pile does not penetrate as quickly and vibrates more. He/she can simply explain this better. In return, she/he is the made woman or man.*

In another example, the competitor explains that working with scientists strengthens the company's position vis-à-vis the regulatory authorities, as the manager (E-Org03) adds: "*When the [scientist] explains it to the [authority], everyone understands. We also had a joint presentation once, which was great. I did all the practical work and she/he did the theory.*" In retrospect, this strategy of building trust and strengthening social relations with relevant innovation partners appeared to be particularly successful in an emerging field of technology development where reliable technical standards were lacking, as one expert suggests:

> *No one will give a guarantee for a certain value [of noise reduction] because the technology is still being tested and developed. (E-Org05, Expert wind farm approval)*

These findings illustrate that, in contrast to the entrepreneur who remained socially isolated, the competitor strategically collaborated with scientists to gain access to offshore system tests, to flexibly adapt the firm's solution to specific wind farm construction projects, to explain the functioning of the solution to customers and representatives of public approval authorities, and thus to build trust in the solution. In this way, the competitor was able to establish an innovation praxis and strengthen the company's position in the field. As confirmed by the entrepreneur (E-Org03), customers perceived the competitor as a "*safe*" supplier:

> *The large corporations see the secure suppliers first. You have to see it that way: They also carry out risk assessments. (...) Now the small [entrepreneur] comes along... What if he/she stretches his/her wings in between? (...) So let's take a company that is supposedly efficient and use it. Even if this company then costs three million euros more? It doesn't matter, we'll have peace of mind. That's how the large corporations think. (E-Org02, Managing director and entrepreneur)*

As a result, after almost five years in the offshore wind industry, the entrepreneur has decided to leave the sector, as she explains: "*But regardless, I am in the process of selling my company. Completely gone. This dishonest fight is not my profession. I've been in business too long to play these games and I don't want to*" (E-Org02, manager and entrepreneur). In fact, looking back on his experience, the entrepreneur admits that he did not build enough trust in the eyes of customers and public authorities: "*I would present myself differently. Probably with other partners too, so that I can carry more weight for my company. People always say: 'Oh, is that going to work with [the entrepreneur]? So there are always these doubts in the room.*"

The entrepreneur admits that a strategic approach to establishing a joint innovation praxis with external partners might have been more effective: "*That's why I would maybe look for a cooperation partner. This could be an installer or a large company that would support the whole thing financially and also make a profit from it. That would give me a lot more security and I wouldn't have to take a big risk on my own*" (E-Org02, manager and entrepreneur).

At this point in time, innovation processes in this field were far from being regulated. However, as one expert mentions, personal trust was no longer sufficient to prove the effectiveness of technologies, which is a sign of the professionalization of technology development in the sector. Thus, according to the expert, companies began to demand "experience", technical references and even contractual guarantees for system performance:

> *On the other hand, experience is welcome, the results from previous projects, what can you really count on and what can be guaranteed. I know from the construction*

companies that the contract system has changed completely this year. (E-Org06, Researcher and consultant)

7.3.1.4 Preliminary conclusions

Based on the empirical case of an entrepreneur introducing a noise reduction system in the field of offshore wind energy, some first conclusions can be drawn. In sect. 3.3 assumed that an *innovation project operating in an emerging field of technology development is likely to adapt technical solutions from adjacent fields* (P3). The results of Case E only partially support this assumption.

It could be shown that one entrepreneur adapted the solution of a competitor already established in the new field. Most interestingly, the entrepreneur relied on personal "*conviction*" and technical imagination to invent a new solution independently of external partners. Technology development took place mainly "*in the mind*" of the entrepreneur. Personal determination and visionary thinking thus appeared to be the dominant mechanism for introducing the new technology into the emerging field. However, a strategic approach to establishing an innovation praxis was not found.

It was also interesting to observe that the entrepreneur did not establish a position as a trusted system supplier, while its competitor succeeded in doing so. It could be shown that the competitor firm strategically collaborated with scientists to improvise its offshore system tests and incrementally improve its solution based on trial-and-error learning. In a field characterized by high technological uncertainty, this innovation praxis built trust with customers and government regulators and strengthened the competitor's position as a trusted system provider. The competitor thus relied on personal trust as the dominant mechanism of technology development.

Table 18: Innovation praxis in emerging fields

Technical standards	Working standards
In an emerging field, no technical standards are available	In the example of the entrepreneur, technology development was based on individual creativity, personal conviction and technical imagination (no strategic approach to collaborative innovation was found)
	In the example of the entrepreneur's competitor, collaborating with scientists allowed the firm to improvise offshore system tests and establish trust among customers and authorities

7.3.2 Case F: Creatively combining technical standards

The previous section illustrated the case of an entrepreneur who relied on individual creativity, personal conviction, and technical imagination to introduce technical solutions to an emerging field. In the second case discussed in this chapter, an engineering service provider specializing in technology development for the offshore oil and gas industry pursued a very different strategy. The company worked with scientists to adapt a technical standard from the offshore oil and gas industry to the needs of wind farms, as the senior manager (F-Org01) puts it:

> *The other point is that we have now completed the first research project. We have a positive result. Everybody knows it works. Now it would be nonsense to say we've done a great study and then put it in a drawer and that's it. That can't be the case. Now we have to put it into practice.*

This company tried to realize a technology transfer from the oil and gas industry by relying solely on its professionalized engineering skills.

7.3.2.1 A unique offshore engineering competence

In contrast to the entrepreneur, the engineering firm in Case F had technical problem-solving competencies, especially for offshore environments, that it had acquired over decades. To remind the reader, competence is defined here as a "*generative ability of actors or systems to cope with concrete tasks and solve problems, but to apply general, cross-situational knowledge in the process*" (Sydow, 2014a, p. 311; own translation). Case F zooms in on the competence of adapting a technical standard from an adjacent field to the technical requirements of the offshore wind energy industry.

In offshore engineering projects, as the senior manager of the company (F-Org01) explains, the main development partner is usually the customer-usually a large technology company specializing in energy technologies such as converter stations, oil and gas platforms, or wind turbines: "*The requirement comes from the design of the energy technology manufacturer. On the other hand, you have to operate the interface, which the shipyard can do. (...) These are practically the cooperation interfaces that we need. The composition comes from that. This is a normal project. At least for us.*"

In addition to customers, offshore engineering projects involve shipyards that provide additional technical expertise and build the required technologies. As a result, offshore engineering projects typically rely on a "complex collaboration matrix" to address both technical and logistical issues,[38] as the expert puts it:

> *In practice, this is a relatively complex matrix of requirements that must be examined from both a cost and a speed-of-assembly perspective.*

Offshore engineering projects are interesting to study because offshore technologies must be customized to specific contexts of use by creatively combining the technical expertise and requirements of different project partners, while also addressing non-technical, logistical challenges. However, in order to control the complexity inherent in such projects, customers tend to clearly define the technical interfaces between the collaborating partners. As a result, innovation tends to occur within each component, as in the case of an engineering service provider that adapted a foundation structure from an adjacent field, the offshore oil and gas industry, to the requirements of offshore wind farms. The technical standards provided by other project partners are then simply incorporated into the respective component, as the senior manager (F-Org01) points out:

> *Basically, we are not developing new technology. We build on our experience. We know what the steel grades are. We know how to build [a foundation structure]. We know what the welding technology is. So there is little change. The changes are in the heart of the plant. That is the plant technology. We have absolutely no influence on that. We are pure designers. If you like, we'll build a beautiful*

38 4For example, logistic questions refer to the transportation and lifting of components, which requires specialized ships with enough space and loading capacity. Logistic questions also involve the coordination of construction works within tight weather windows or under conditions of high waves/special soil characteristics, the elaboration of detailed work procedures, health and security precautions, deploying systems during ongoing installations, controlling the costs of offshore working hours (e.g. 250,000 – 500,000 Euro for an installation vessel per day), or maintenance work under water, for instance.

> *table here, but we don't really care what you put on it. (...) We just react to the requirements. (F-Org01, Senior manager)*

In Case F, the engineering service provider needed not only technological and logistical know-how and practical experience, but also creativity to integrate the technical expectations of the project partners into a working wind energy technology. Like "architects," says the senior manager, the company's engineers combined the customer's technical requirements with its in-house technical expertise to develop a foundation structure that could be installed under the customer's offshore wind turbines: "*How do you combine the top [of the system] with the bottom? (...) In principle, it's like an architect planning a house. One prefers the Bauhaus style, the other the Tyrolean style. That's how you have to think about it. (F-Org01, Senior manager)*

These quotes illustrate what enabled the engineering services provider to introduce an innovation to the offshore wind energy sector. Based on technological knowledge, logistical know-how, practical experience and creativity, the technology specialist was able to adapt an existing technical standard from a related field to a new application context. In this way, the company created a customized solution to meet the needs of a specific wind farm. As the senior manager (F-Org01) puts it, the work of combining different technical standards was done "in dialog" with different parties (e.g. technology developers, system manufacturers and certification bodies). Metaphorically speaking, the offshore engineering specialist "*pieced together*" a new technology:

> *That's how you put it together. That's how it comes about afterwards. So that means that you can never say that this thing has only one signature. The basic concept of what it looks like is already there. The details come in the dialog.*

The company's unique innovation capability was thus rooted in a project organization that involved all relevant partners. As the senior manager (F-Org01) explains, the company generally designs new offshore solutions based on close, face-to-face interaction with other partners: "*We basically have a project team here. Then we have a mirror team on the other side. On the one hand, this involves exchanging plans. But at these project meetings it's also important to exchange ideas personally. So you have regular team meetings to check how everything is being implemented and what the requirements are. It's quite an illustrious bunch that sits together.*

The project organization therefore played an important role in bringing together "an illustrious bunch of experts" from different organizations, as the expert put it. Through inter-company "design loops", the manager continues, the partners combined their technical requirements and controlled the development effort: "*The implementation always also means what costs will be incurred, so a product is always created in dialogue or in coordination. The design features are constantly reviewed and updated. Loops are run*“ (F-Org01, Senior manager). In the end, the project resulted in an individualized technical standard for a specific offshore wind farm, as the senior manager (F-Org01) concludes:

> *Standardization certainly stops when you look at the floor. There is no standard floor. The floor is different in every place. But by standardization I also mean coordinating the design and standardizing the installation methods so that you can rely on the existing installation vessels and technologies. and technologies. (F-Org01, Senior Manager)*

In conclusion, this case demonstrated a unique, professionalized offshore engineering competence. Based on a broad bundle of knowledge and skills – technological knowledge, logistical know-how, decades of practical experience, and a cross-company project organization – the offshore engineering company was able to creatively and collaboratively adapt technical standards from an adjacent field and individualize a foundation structure to the specific requirements of offshore wind farms. An “*extreme creativity*", as the senior manager (F-Org01) puts it, is an important component of such innovation competence:

> *If we weren't international, we wouldn't exist. We wouldn't be able to make a living from it. There is a lot of competition in the standard sector. There are a lot of them, and you're just one of many. We can't serve the German market with the creativity we have here. That extreme creativity is not necessary. That's why we're better positioned and that's why there are actually very few offices in Germany that have the continuity that you have in oil and gas. In this respect, the others retreat into standard designs for port or bridge construction. (F-Org01, Senior manager)*

7.3.2.2 A strategic approach to trust-building

It has been shown above that the engineering service provider in Case F has developed a professionalized offshore engineering competence that involves the creative and collaborative adaptation of technical standards from the oil and gas industry as well as the individualization of technical solutions to the context of specific wind farms. In addition, the offshore engineering company has also strategically collaborated with scientific experts to improve its system and build trust in the eyes of customers, as the senior manager (F-Org02) explains: “*The crucial factor with this system is how the foundation behaves in the long term in terms of soil mechanics and geotechnics, but also how to deal with any scour that may occur.*"

The technology specialist joined a joint R&D consortium that included partners from applied research institutes and university departments. The company worked with these scientists to gain access to geotechnical expertise and testing facilities, This allowed the company to simulate offshore system tests, conduct engineering experiments, and prove the functionality of its prototype.

During the course of the project, the applied research institute coordinating the R&D project also attempted to recruit a utility company as a potential partner that would be willing to provide access to system testing under real-world conditions, i.e., in the context of an offshore wind farm construction project. However, the research project manager (F-Org02) reported that at the time of the investigation, German utilities and wind farm operators showed little interest in such collaborative testing of a new foundation structure:

> *Large companies tend to be risk-averse. They only ever assess risk. In other words, they want to shift the risks somewhere else, if possible, or have them eliminated. (...) That's why there are two main lines in the project. One is experimental and the other is prototyping.*

The research project manager (F-Org02) points out that the main objective of the R&D project was to create new science-based knowledge in order to compete in the emerging market for offshore solutions. A major competitor in this endeavor was the Danish utility company Ørsted (formerly Dong Energy), which specializes in offshore energy production technologies:

> *We, in turn, say that we must also examine the fundamentals. They are not clear. Dong Energy is saying the same thing. I have the impression that they are more courageous in this respect. But they also have more confidence because they have been working in this direction for more than ten years, and they are also artists at sea.*

These findings indicate that the engineering firm took a strategic approach to building trust with potential clients by working with scientists and proving the functionality of the new foundation structure. Given the lack of technical standards in the field, the project manager explains that building trust was a key focus, relying on systematic, science-based, collaborative engineering, testing, and certification:

> *[When somebody puts it [at sea], it brings the simple message that it works and that they have the confidence to put it there. It should work, but everybody knows that there are some reserves in terms of load-bearing capacity that are not in a book. that are not in a book, but nobody gives us that. We can't call them up and ask what ratio they're using to get that verification. You have to do it yourself. There is no guideline either. You can't look at some standard and say you should use this and that. So it's research and development until Germanischer Lloyd or BAM [Federal Institute for Materials Testing] or some working group comes up with design rules and makes them binding. It's not there yet. It's not state of the art.*

In summary, the offshore engineering firm, together with scientists, established a collaborative innovation praxis of adapting a technical standard from the oil and gas industry to the technical requirements of offshore wind turbine installation. In contrast to Case E of an entrepreneur who autonomously designed a new noise mitigation system, this firm strategically pursued a trust-building strategy based on collaborative system testing and certification. Collaboration with scientists provided the company with access to basic scientific knowledge and systematic, simulation-based offshore system testing, as the following statement by the senior manager (F-Org02) illustrates:

> *We wanted to work with [a central German university] because they have more geotechnical expertise and they also have a large testing center. (...) They can test steel structures for fatigue strength. (F-Org01, Senior manager)*

Despite these efforts to build trust, the senior manager (F-Org01) points out that at the time of the study, the new foundation structure had not yet been introduced to the offshore wind energy sector. The main challenge was to find a German utility willing to participate in the innovation project by providing access to real-world system testing: "*The [research institute] is on the ball, so the question is, which of the wind farm operators can we motivate to give us a site within a field where we can test this prototype? (...) This would have the advantage that the infrastructure could also be used. So there is a grid that you can feed into" (F- Org01, Senior manager).*

Compared to the entrepreneur who quickly invented and implemented a new solution, the second solution, the second innovation project discussed in this chapter was still in the basic research stage at the time of the interviews. The absence of a wind farm planning company in the R&D consortium left the innovation network incomplete.

7.3.2.3 Preliminary conclusions

Based on these findings, some additional conclusions can be drawn about the social processes underlying technology development. P3 suggested that *if an innovation project is operating in an emerging field of technology development, it is likely to adapt technical solutions from adjacent fields.* In Case F, it was found that an offshore engineering specialist adapted a technical standard from the oil and gas industry to develop a quieter foundation structure for wind turbines. This supports the predictions of P3.

To realize the technology transfer, the engineering firm drew on a unique engineering expertise that it had professionalized over decades of involvement in offshore construction. Based on a broad bundle of knowledge and skills – technological and logistical know-how, practical experience and a cross-company project organization – the offshore specialist creatively and collaboratively combined technical standards to customize its technology to the specific context of offshore wind farms.

In addition to its professionalized offshore engineering expertise, the company used trust building as another innovation strategy. For example, the engineering firm worked with scientists to adapt its technical solution to the geotechnical conditions of offshore wind turbines. This collaboration also gave the company access to testing facilities and simulation-based testing methods, which helped certify the technology and build trust with customers.

But the innovation network remained incomplete. No utility or customer was part of the innovation project. In other words, the innovation praxis was not fully established at the time of the study. As the results indicated, an established innovation praxis would likely become more hierarchical because the customer would (1) grant access to system testing at sea, (2) select system suppliers, and thus (3) define membership rules.

The two examined examples of technology development in an emerging technological field provide additional empirical evidence in support of the author's main argument that a collaborative innovation praxis is key to the introduction of complex technologies. In emerging fields where technical standards and technology markets are lacking, innovation partners such as firms, scientific institutes, and certification or licensing authorities must be integrated into the innovation praxis. In this praxis, technical standards are combined in a creative and collaborative way.

Table 19: Innovation praxis in emerging fields

Technical standards	**Working standards**
A technical standard from the offshore oil and gas industry is adapted to the installation of offshore wind turbines	Creatively and collaboratively combining technical standards (based on technological and logistic know-how, decades of practical experience, and an inter-firm project organization)
	Collaborating with scientists to access basic scientific knowledge, testing facilities and simulation-based system tests as a means towards certifying the technology and building up trust in the eyes of customers

7.4 Institutional barriers and what they caused

At the time of the study, neither technology company had established a stable position as a trusted system supplier in the industry. In fact, while the entrepreneur was about to leave the sector (case E), the offshore engineering specialist (case F) lacked a customer willing to participate in the innovation project. Both firms remained excluded from established system supply networks, an observation that is interpreted as an unintended outcome.

7.4.1 Case E: Lacking trust in system suppliers

In Case E, the entrepreneur did not establish a position as a system supplier, an outcome that is linked here to the entrepreneur's inability to build trust in the eyes of customers and licensing authorities.

At the time of the study, all noise control systems in the field were still at the prototype stage, which meant that there was no technical standard to meet the newly introduced environmental regulations, as one expert pointed out: "*Noise protection is of course a huge problem, because there is no state of the art or proven method for it, and especially in our project we were driven through the village by the approval authorities with ever higher and additional requirements*" (E-Org05, Expert foundation structures).

Respondents from customers and large utilities explained that their choice of noise mitigation system is based on empirical evidence, rather than assessing system performance based on standardized engineering procedures, as the head of an offshore wind farm planning department pointed out (E-Org04): "*Our biggest challenge is that we still work very empirically. (...) That's a risk, because it's like a dance every time.*"

Typically, the same executive continued, the performance of systems is evaluated on the basis of simulation-based engineering routines. In this emerging field of technology development, however, decisions are based on "*gut feeling*" or trial-and-error learning:

> *Ultimately, probability values are needed for a risk assessment. This is normally the result of a numerical simulation. What is the probability that we will exceed 160 dB? At the moment, it's a lot of gut feeling. (...) Ideally, we would design the system so that we simulate it and know relatively precisely that the system will give us a value of plus/minus five decibels for this soil, this pile, this hammer and this thickness. At the moment it's trial and error. (E-Org04, Offshore engineering manager)*

Under such conditions of high technological uncertainty, contractual control over system suppliers was not possible. At the same time, technology development could not be based on trust in the technological competence of system suppliers, as the same expert suggests: "*The system has to be tested a year in advance. If it doesn't work, or if it turns out during the year that it doesn't work, you won't get a construction permit*" (E-Org05, Expert wind farm permit). In a mature technology field, trust could grow based on the proven effectiveness of a noise mitigation system, which is critical for offshore projects that are characterized by high costs, technological risks, and hardly controllable weather conditions. However, in the case studied, neither the customers nor the system suppliers were able to predict the performance of the system as specified by the manager:

> *We know relatively well what a system has to do. (...) But the point is that I can't prove it mathematically. On the other hand, the provider can't prove to me mathematically that he can do it either. Of course, the moment we ask a provider whether he is contractually liable if I want him to pay me a million euros in damages, he will immediately fall to his knees. (E- Org04, Offshore engineering manager)*

As these quotes show, contractual control of noise abatement system suppliers was not a viable option. Large utilities have little confidence in system suppliers who are unable to develop solutions based on standardized engineering procedures.

When it comes to more established offshore technologies, trust usually comes from standardized engineering procedures and methods such as Computational Fluid Dynamics (CFD). Using numerical simulations, utility engineers then estimate system performance, define the technical requirements for a specific wind farm project and select a suitable system supplier, the same manager adds: "*If you are not clear about the simulation, it is not so easy to define the system parameters.*"

In the case of the noise abatement system, not only was there a lack of standardized, simulation-based engineering methods, but also a lack of basic scientific knowledge to improve the system's effectiveness. As a result, technology development has had to rely on trial-and-error learning in parallel with ongoing offshore construction, as the representative of a utility company points out:

> *What I have always valued, especially in relation to [the noise mitigation system], is that the theoretical foundations have actually not been explored. Research is being conducted, things are being done, and the same questions keep coming up, but no one takes the trouble to answer them. It's more of a trial-and-error approach. (E-Org05, Expert noise mitigation)*

These results show that in the absence of standardized, simulation-based engineering praxis and basic scientific knowledge, customers have little confidence in the effectiveness of a new technology such as a noise control system. At the same time, purchasing off-the-shelf solutions and contractually controlling system suppliers is not a viable option in the absence of technical standards. Therefore, it would be necessary to establish personal trust between the system supplier and the customer.

As a result, without trust in system suppliers, customers themselves have engaged in trial-and-error learning to improve the effectiveness of noise mitigation. That is, utilities improvised system tests during ongoing construction, "*playing*" with different system parameters and using the resulting empirical evidence to improve the systems they were using, according to representatives of two different utilities:

> *During each ramming operation, measurements were actually taken. An attempt was made to establish correlations between the introduced air, the compressor pressure, and the noise emissions. (...) We then started experimenting with this in collaboration with the researchers. For example, we made the holes narrower or wider and observed how that affected the results. (E-Org05, Expert foundation structures)*

> *The biggest challenge is that you get very variable values out there. That means it's not the case that when you make a change, it consistently results in the same noise reduction gain. (...) You really have to conduct a lot of measurements at many different locations so that, over time, it becomes clear what is actually the true effect. (E-Org05, Expert wind park permission)*

> *At the moment, I have to design my system for the worst location and then use it in the same way at all other locations. (E-Org04, Offshore engineering manager)*

It was interesting to observe that the knowledge created in the field of offshore noise mitigation was largely socially constructed, rather than the result of systematic technology development. For example, one expert points out that some licensing decisions seemed to be based on "beliefs", which in turn were based on individual recommendations: "*There were also reports from various BMUV-funded projects that contained recommendations. However, these were neither scientifically substantiated nor questioned. In [the regulatory authority], they became beliefs.*" (*E-Org-05, Expert on noise abatement*).

Similarly, the entrepreneur interviewed expressed the impression that individuals have a strong influence on approval decisions when system performance can hardly be assessed on the basis of objective technical criteria:

> *There are few decision-makers here, because there are no committees responsible for making soundproofing decisions. It could be just one person who, for example, is convinced that a particular supplier is excellent.*

In conclusion, in this case the entrepreneur did not succeed in establishing a position as a trusted system supplier in the field. This was related to the entrepreneur's inability to build trust with customers and public regulators. In more mature fields, trust generally comes from standardized, simulation-based engineering that allows customers to buy off-the-shelf technologies in markets and to contractually control their system suppliers. When technical standards are lacking, building trust based on an established engineering praxis is not a viable option. Under such conditions of high technological uncertainty, a more successful innovation strategy is to build trust based on collaborative, pragmatic trial-and-error learning. This strategy was used successfully by the competitor, but not by the entrepreneur, who worked largely autonomously. At the time of the study, however, this situation was about to change, as one expert pointed out:

> *As recently as last year, installation companies were not required to guarantee noise levels to wind farm operators. In the meantime, some have started demanding guarantees, as otherwise, financial discussions arise. Increasingly, these contractual provisions are also being passed on to noise protection manufacturers, for example, requiring a certain state of the art or a specific noise protection value to be guaranteed. (E-Org06, Scientist and consultant)*

7.4.2 Case F: Lacking customer cooperation

While in case E the entrepreneur eventually left the field, in case F the offshore engineering graduate was still looking for a customer willing to grant access to system tests under real conditions at the time of the interviews. Despite these efforts, the company had not yet managed to establish a stable position as a trusted system supplier:

> *We are looking for a wind farm operator who is capable of installing a wind turbine. (F-Org01, Senior manager)*

Normally, the senior manager (F-Org01) continues, it is common praxis in offshore engineering that the customer is also an important cooperation partner: "*The customer is actually always also a cooperation partner. They have an idea of what kind of equipment they want, and we have an idea of how to implement it*" (F-Org01, Senior Manager). Furthermore, since the technical interfaces between the various components of an offshore structure (e.g. a converter station) are clearly defined, different system suppliers merely exchange technical requirements with each other.

In this case, however, no German utility supported the innovation project. As the interviewees explained, large utilities generally prefer to externalize the technical risks associated with the engineering, procurement, commissioning and installation (EPCI) of offshore wind farms. In an ideal world, utilities therefore contractually control an entire offshore project on the basis of a single large contract – a so-called EPCI contract, as explained by the senior manager (F-Org01):

> *If you want to put it very simply, this is turnkey construction. Essentially, it's the worry-free package for a wind farm operator. Their involvement is then limited to a supervisory role. They don't have to get involved in engineering or push through any permits. They can delegate that and might pay a bit more for it, but their team is relieved of the burden.*

In contrast to German utilities, foreign wind farm planning companies such as Ørsted (formerly Dong Energy) take a different approach. According to the senior manager (F-Org01), foreign companies with a long tradition in the offshore oil and gas industry have an international customer network and rely on sophisticated technical departments. These companies are largely able to internalize the technical risks of offshore wind farm construction and develop offshore solutions in close coordination with trusted partners from industry and academia:

> *That is exactly the difference between a company like Dong Energy, which has a large team of engineers and brings its own designs to the market. They come from the oil and gas sector and are used to this approach. They are also well connected with laboratories, test facilities in Denmark, and universities. The corporate philosophy there is different. (F-Org01, Senior manager)*

In fact, the corporate communications officer of one of these foreign wind farm developers confirms that its offshore engineering expertise is deeply rooted in technical standards that are well established in the oil and gas industry: "*Offshore wind technology is so specific and specialized that you can't just copy and paste things. But when it comes to project planning, you can. (...) Certain standards have been adopted from the oil and gas industry. If you just look at the substations, they are built in a similar way.*"

These findings provide empirical evidence that the development of offshore wind technologies is moving towards the creation of technical standards controlled by a few large utilities and their exclusive innovation networks. However, at the time of the research, the offshore engineering specialist included in this study had not become part of such a network.

7.5 Interim conclusions

The findings of this chapter reinforce the author's main argument that a common innovation praxis is key to the development of innovative complex technologies. In the absence of technical standards and technology markets, as in an emerging field, the forced imposition of standards is not a viable innovation strategy. Instead, an innovating firm needs to establish a stable position as a trusted, accepted and reputable development partner.

The observed engineering firms were active in the emerging fields of offshore noise abatement and offshore wind turbine foundations. In case E, an entrepreneur invented a new noise mitigation system. In case F, an offshore engineering specialist attempted to adapt a technical standard already established in the offshore oil and gas industry to the installation of offshore wind farms. However, both companies did not establish a position as a trusted system supplier.

This chapter first described the field of offshore wind energy technologies and its main players. Second, the practices of knowledge integration observed in the two cases were analysed. Thirdly, it showed how the collaboration was organized in each case, and fourthly, it discussed the project's unintended outcomes. This section summarizes the main findings of the chapter.

Table 20: Emerging technology fields

	Case E: Noise mitigation system	**Case F: Alternative foundation procedure**
Knowledge Integration	Relying on individual creativity, inventiveness and pragmatism to combine technical knowledge from steel construction with the requirements of wind parks	Drawing on professionalized competences such as creatively and collaboratively combining technical standards, or individualizing solutions to a specific context of use
Realizing technology development	Relying on the individual ability to quickly invent a new technology (entrepreneur) vs. trust-building based on pragmatically improving offshore system tests (competitor)	Creatively combining technical standards from different industries based on a unique, professionalized offshore engineering competence
Institutional barriers	Attempt of trust-building (would require simulation-based engineering or improvised offshore system tests)	Remaining excluded from existing innovation networks as well as from the creation of technical standards (a process controlled by large utilities)

The two companies followed two different knowledge integration strategies. In Case E, the entrepreneur and newcomer to the offshore wind industry relied mainly on his individual creativity to quickly realize a new technical solution. In this case, knowledge integration took place mainly "in the mind" of the entrepreneur, who combined his technical experience gained in other industries with the technical requirements of installing offshore wind turbines, including technical principles used by a competitor.

In Case F, an offshore engineering specialist adapted a technical standard from the offshore oil and gas industry, relying on an acquired, professionalized competence to creatively combine technical standards and customize solutions to specific application contexts. In contrast to the entrepreneur, this company engaged in collaborative research to gain access to scientifically based testing procedures and facilities.

Overall, the results of this chapter only partially support the assumption that an innovation praxis operating in an emerging field of technology development is likely to adapt technical solutions from adjacent fields (P3). Such a strategy was only observed in the second case analyzed above. While the entrepreneur remained a "lone fighter", the offshore engineering specialist tried to establish an innovation praxis together with a large utility company in order to build trust in the eyes of the customer and public approval authorities. However, the company remained excluded from existing industry networks that create new technical standards for the offshore wind industry. Thus, there was a lack of innovation praxis that included large utilities.

The results showed that even in emerging fields of offshore wind energy technologies, new technologies are developed by hierarchically organized innovation networks, with utilities at the top controlling technical standards, selecting system suppliers, granting access to offshore wind farms, and thus defining membership rules. In both cases, the engineering firms studied did not become part of such an innovation network.

8. Conclusions

The author of this book used a sociological perspective to analyze the management of collaborative innovation that draw on different sources of knowledge within and outside the development firm (cf. Chesbrough, 2003, 2006a; Tell, 2017). Based on six empirical cases of technology development in the wind energy industry, the author discussed the extent to which the innovation partners were able to establish a collaborative innovation praxis based on shared working standards. It was expected that such an innovation praxis would normatively bind representatives of different organizations despite their different interests and cognitions.

The author's overall aim was to identify the regulative and normative elements that explain why innovation projects do not achieve their intended outcomes (cf. Scott, 2008). In particular, the author has analysed how the social process of establishing a collaborative innovation praxis differs across innovation contexts. It was found that innovation can take place in three different context. Incremental innovation (within a technology life cycle) rather happen in organized and stable but changing fields; radical innovation (beyond the present technology cycle) is most likely to occur in organized and unstable fields that are open to transformation; while unorganized or emerging fields provide opportunities for new actor constellations and technologies (cf. Fligstein & McAdam, 2011, p. 11; Foucart & Li, 2021). The associated innovation praxis is described below.

The findings of the author of this book advance our understanding of the management of collaborative innovation, a topic of intense debate among innovation scholars and practitioners alike. The study provides empirical evidence that the management of collaborative innovation must be understood as a social process of establishing shared standards that normatively integrate professionals from all relevant organizations. It will be argued that such a collaborative innovation praxis is particularly important for those innovation projects that aim to create new knowledge beyond established technological architectures.

This chapter provides a brief overview of this argument. It also summarizes the empirical findings and draws conclusions about the institutional barriers to collaborative innovation.

8.1 The author's main argument

The introductory chapter argued that complex innovation projects can be called collaborative when professionals from formally independent organizations work together to develop a new technology in a particular sector. An innovation project is realized when a new technology is commercialized in markets or applied in a firm's production processes. Complex technologies such as wind turbines are particularly suitable for analyzing collaborative forms of firm innovation processes. Wind turbines are technological architectures composed of different subsystems and components (Huenteler et al., 2016a, b). Due to the associated technological interdependencies between the components, which touch on different bodies of science-based technical knowledge, such as information technology, sensor technology or new materials, but also due to extensive regulatory requirements as well as customer demands, the introduction of complex wind energy technologies usually relies on the collaboration of experts from different organizations, such as system developers, supplier companies, research institutes, certification bodies, public authorities or technology users.

The author of this book assumes that because the member organizations specialize in different areas of expertise, collaborative innovation is necessarily confronted with different cognitive frames, but also potentially conflicting interests of the professionals involved as representatives of different organizations in the field. Therefore, the author of this book argues that professionals involved in collaborative innovation need to define common meanings, interpretations, and norms. The resulting system of inter-organizational shared working standards normatively integrates the different professionals, thereby facilitating technical problem solving and compromise in spite of potentially conflicting self-interests.

It has been proposed that each innovation project engages in social processes of establishing working standards, such as a shared concept of time (e.g., milestones), exclusive communication channels between project managers (e.g., single points of contact), or shared simulation-based engineering routines between relevant development partners such as customers, system developers, component suppliers, or certifiers. Such shared working standards, created in the process of technology development, normatively bind the innovation partners together and 'bridge' knowledge boundaries between them. In fact, the praxis of reflexively defining shared working standards is argued to be crucial for the management of collaborative innovation.

From this perspective, the management of collaborative innovation is not only about efficiency and new technologies, but also about a largely social process of establishing shared working standards (cf. Jackwerth, 2017;

Lawrence, 2010; Lawrence & Suddaby, 2006). This collective effort to norm the distributed work creates the collective agility needed to rapidly combine technical knowledge distributed across organizations (cf. Zheng et al., 2010). Shared working standards provide a common cognitive framework that informs stakeholders about the 'rules of the game' in an innovation project (North, 1990) as well as the consequences of deviating from the jointly established 'ways of doing things' (Elster, 2007). The social process of collaboratively norming distributed technology development thus plays a key role in understanding the outcome of innovation projects.

8.2 Advancing innovation management research

This book contributes to the debate on the management of collaborative (or open) innovation. As shown in chapter 2, there is an intense debate in the management literature on the management of innovation projects. In particular, the open innovation approach postulates that inter-firm collaboration is positively associated with better products, services and processes (Chesbrough, 2003, 2006b). A literature review of empirical studies on open innovation in Chapter 2 identified three factors that influence the outcome of open innovation projects: the type of collaboration (horizontal/vertical), the specificity of knowledge (broad/specific), and appropriability regimes (formal/informal knowledge protection rules) or the rationality of management decisions such as 'strategic openness'. However, the open innovation approach has also been criticized for relying only on success stories of technology development to show how openness leads to innovation.

The lack of a theory of open innovation is the reason why management scholars cannot explain the outcomes of collaborative innovation. In fact, tracing the social process of innovation is not the primary research interest of open innovation scholars, as (Bogers & West, 2012, p. 65) point out: "*The core research questions in open innovation research are how and when firms can commercialize the innovations of others and commercialize their valuable innovations through others.*" Because of this theoretical blind spot of open innovation, which is fixated on the business goal of commercialization of technical knowledge, the author of this book has taken a sociological perspective to uncover the institutional conditions that hinder the potential of collaborative innovation.

As discussed in Chapter 2, a relatively new strand in the management literature, the knowledge integration approach, takes a more theory-oriented view of the challenges of managing collaborative forms of learning and innovation. Founded by Robert M. Grant, recent contributions and empirical studies from a knowledge integration perspective illustrate that in technology-based industries organized around complex technologies, such as energy production, automotive manufacturing, heavy electrical equipment, telecommunications, or tooling, it is typical for innovation projects to integrate specialized knowledge from different professions, organizations, and sectors (Berggren et al., 2011a). However, the literature on knowledge integration also shows that in such industries, technologies are typically introduced through hierarchical, pyramidal networks dominated by large incumbents at the top. These empirical findings show that managing collaboration requires understanding how powerful actors define the 'rules of the game' or 'how things are done' in a given industry (cf. Edquist, 2005; Elster, 2007; North, 1990, p. 427).

The author of this book adopted the insight from the knowledge integration literature that network structures influence the outcome of innovation projects. Empirical studies have shown that within the boundaries of established technology-based industries, technologies are typically introduced through hierarchical innovation networks. Therefore, social interactions in innovation projects within a single industry, as well as power asymmetries between incumbents and challengers in the field, are important to study from a knowledge integration perspective (cf. Fligstein & McAdam, 2011, 2012). By rejecting the economists' assumption that sectors are homogeneous social systems whose boundaries are defined abstractly by "*broad and related product groups, (...) similar existing or emerging demands, needs and uses, (...) common knowledge bases*" (Malerba & Adams, 2014, p. 188), the knowledge integration approach thus looks specifically at different forms of collaborative combination of knowledge that may could come from very different sectors.

In addition to looking at practices of knowledge integration across organizations, management scholars also argue that cognitive structures can hinder collaborative innovations. In particular, knowledge boundaries are understood as institutionalized barriers to collaborative innovation (Berggren et al., 2017; Orlikowski & Gash, 1994; Tell, 2017). This literature assumes that as long as innovation partners share similar epistemic backgrounds (e.g., professional education, individual training, tacit knowledge, personal experiences, theories, language, identities, or value systems), they form what sociologists call epistemic communities (Håkanson, 2010). Because of their fairly homogeneous cognitive frameworks, members of an epistemic community can easily exchange information even over large geographic distances. Management scholars assume that at least a minimal overlap of knowledge between innovation partners is necessary to be able to collaborate, but also to maintain efficient work processes.

However, as this book has shown, collaborative innovations typically rely on collaboration between organizations with different specializations. As a result, cognitive frameworks are likely to be highly heterogeneous, and knowledge overlap is difficult to achieve. Innovation projects run the risk of suffering too much from unintended outcomes if cognitive differences or knowledge boundaries between all relevant innovation partners are not 'bridged' by routines, rules or standards of knowledge integration that normatively integrate the professionals involved. However, the social praxis that 'bridges' such knowledge boundaries have remained an open question.

To fill this research gap, the author of this book approaches the management of collaborative innovation as a social praxis. Its social 'production' can be analyzed by looking at the practices of collaboratively combining expertise across professional, organizational and sectoral boundaries (*practices of knowledge integration*), which are influenced by more or less institutionalized rules, norms or standards (*such as examples, models, levels, norms of technology development*) concerning the design, construction and testing of a new technology (cf. Elster, 2011). This – in theory – creates a praxis of collaborative innovation.

Supported by the empirical analysis, the author of this book considers the praxis of establishing shared rules and norms as the key for the management of collaborative innovation (cf. Lawrence, 2010; Lawrence & Suddaby, 2006). Innovation projects aimed at the development of new technologies are rarely a harmonious endeavor, but usually involve different cognitive frameworks and self-interests that compete with each other. The praxis of collaborative innovation thus refers to the constant (re)creation of shared rules and norms that provide professionals with a common cognitive frame that informs them about the 'rules of the game' (e.g., design rules) that apply in a particular innovation project, as well as the consequences of deviating from the established standards of technology development (e.g., warranty claims). Thus, the praxis of establishing shared working standards exerts the normative power necessary to bind innovation partners together despite their different cognitions and interests.

All in all, from a sociological perspective, the management of collaborative innovation is based on a praxis of establishing a shared standards of collaboratively combining knowledge and solving technical problems. Working standards then contain typified ways of solving problems that, because they are routinized, make collaboration predictable, relieve collaboration partners of the need to calculate each step, and provide recipes (recipe knowledge) for dealing with technical problems (cf. Berger & Luckmann, 2009, p. 58).

The author's main research objective was to empirically evaluate this key argument. For this purpose, it was theorized that collaborative innovation can be realized on the basis of three strategies: 1) An innovation project may incrementally improve an existing technology architecture, 2) it may aim to introduce a radically new technology by reconfiguring an architecture or creating a new one, or 3) it may operate in emerging technology fields where neither technical standards nor innovation networks are yet established and thus new collaborations need to be created. Therefore, the following three propositions guided the empirical evaluation:

> *Proposition 1 (P1): The praxis of innovation is mainly shaped by the monitoring of technical standards and the sanctioning of nonconformity when innovation projects are initiated in organized and stable fields.*

> *Proposition 2 (P2): When a radically new technology is being developed, the praxis of innovation is likely to be shaped by newly created procedures and methods for solving collaborative problems.*

> *Proposition 3 (P3): When an innovation praxis has to establish itself in an emerging sector, it is likely to adapt technical standards from adjacent fields.*

In P1, the innovation praxis of coordinating the ongoing (re)creation of shared rules and norms is largely limited to monitoring established technical standards and sanctioning nonconformity. In P2, the innovation praxis refers to the creation of new shared work standards, while in P3 the innovation praxis is directed towards finding and adapting technical solutions from other fields. These strategies were evaluated in chapters 5 to 7 on the basis of empirical findings from six innovation projects in the wind energy industry. These results are summarized below.

8.3 Summarizing the empirical findings

Based on the empirical evaluation of six innovation projects, this section discusses the extent to which shared rules and norms influence the outcome of firms' innovation processes. To present the results, the findings are first summarized separately for each type of innovation, namely incremental innovation, radical innovation, and emerging technologies. In particular, for each type of innovation, the findings are presented with respect to the underlying practices of knowledge integration, a key challenge in managing collaborative innovation.

Table 20 provides an overview of the empirical results. The author of this book found three innovation praxis. One referred to the coercive imposition of technical standards found in the incremental innovation examples. However, enforced imposition also runs the risk of reducing innovative projects to mere contract development rather than innovation. The second praxis is the reliance on personal trust in the cases of radical innovation. A third innovation praxis, found in the examples of emerging technologies, is individual technical imagination or collaborative trial-and-error learning. The latter two mechanisms are less effective in realizing collaborative innovations, which provides empirical support for the proposition that the creation of new technologies – especially those, which deviate from established technology architectures – depend on an inter-organizationally shared innovation praxis, as will be discussed below.

Table 21: Summary of the findings

Innovation type	**Integrating knowledge**	**Realizing technology development**	**The innovation praxis**	**Institutional barriers**
Incremental innovation	Based on centrally controlled enginee-ring and manufacturing procedures	Using various contracts to predefine innovation projects	Coercive power (based on contracts, technical standards, homogeneous knowledge)	Coercive rules reduce innovation projects to mere order development
Radical innovation	Based on a newly established network in case C, and a boundary spanner in case D	Establishing a praxis of material testing (case C) or using a technical specification sheet to gain some control (case D)	Relying on personal trust (to gain some control over the innovation process)	Relevant development partners were not sufficiently integrated
Emerging technologies	Based on individual abilities (case E) or unique offshore engineering competences (case F)	Relying on technical inventions (case E) or creatively combining technical knowledge (case F)	Technical imagination vs. trial-and-error learning (case E), collaborative engineering with scientists (case F)	No stable position as a trusted system supplier establis-hed in the field

8.3.1 Using coercive power to impose technical standards

The first two cases compared two component suppliers working with a large European wind turbine manufacturer (WTM) to design and build a new component for wind turbines. In Case A, a medium-sized component supplier, an established specialist and market leader in large components, worked with a WTM. In case B, another medium-sized component supplier, formerly specialized in the rail vehicle industry, collaborated with another large WTM. In both cases, the collaboration took the form of a hierarchical innovation network, with the WTM at the top controlling technology development. Horizontal collaboration, which is typical for the development of new technologies, was hardly observed.

The knowledge integration process took different directions in the two cases. In case A, the WTM imposed its technical expectations and largely predefined the entire innovation project based on detailed technical specifications. The component supplier relied on highly standardized engineering and manufacturing processes, mainly to combine different types of technical standards (such as industry standards, customer expectations, or internal guidelines) to develop a prototype. In this case, the practices of knowledge integration were already well established among the innovation partners.

In Case B, the component supplier was a newcomer to the wind energy industry and therefore an outsider to established supply networks. The supplier initiated an innovation project and, together with a WTM, developed a new component for stopping rotors that was radically new compared to established component technologies in the field. In this case, knowledge integration and collaborative innovation were observed only at the beginning of the innovation process, when the supplier company collaborated with an applied research institute to develop a first prototype. Later, after the product was introduced to the wind energy industry, knowledge integration took place mainly within the organizational boundaries of the supplier firm, which created additional product versions to attract new customers. Interestingly, the innovation partnership between the supplier and its main customer, WTM, quickly turned into a mere contract development. Thus, the partnership became a hierarchical market relationship that was strictly controlled by the WTM and left little room for collaborative innovation.

In addition to the knowledge integration processes, this study also analyzed how the two innovation projects were organized. In Chapter 3, it was suggested that incremental innovation projects are organized through practices of monitoring technical standards and sanctioning nonconformity (P1). The innovation project in Case A was organized in three ways: First, the customer largely imposed its technical expectations based on various contractual agreements (e.g., framework contracts, development contracts, and non-disclosure agreements). Second, it could also be shown that the customer centrally controlled the external technology development. Both partner organizations were structurally coupled based on a common understanding of time (e.g., milestones), direct communication channels between project managers (single points of contact; SPOCs), and a homogeneous knowledge base. Interestingly, centralized control, based on well-defined process standards, quality standards, and transparency standards, also included personal inspections. These findings hardly support P1, which assumes that in incremental innovation projects collaboration tends to be horizontal and even the most powerful actor cannot rely on coercive power to realize a project due to functional interdependencies and knowledge complementarities. In this case of an incremental innovation project, however, coercion based on contracts and the imposition of technical standards emerged as the dominant mechanism of collaborative innovation. Rather than establishing a shared praxis of collaborative innovation, coercive rules reduced the project work to mere contract development.

Similarly, Case B also showed few signs and efforts of collaborative innovation. On the contrary, although the component supplier collaborated with a large WTM to introduce a radically new product, this collaborative innovation partnership quickly turned into a simple market transaction. The customer, i.e. the WTM, centrally controlled the supply relationship by imposing product prices and interface data on the component supplier. Thus, in contrast to P1, centralized power-based control emerged as the dominant mechanism of technology development. Mutual dependencies and knowledge complementarities typical of collaborative innovation were not found. In this case, technical standards (e.g., technical interfaces) were used instrumentally to minimize knowledge integration and to control the entire component supply network. Similar to the first case of incremental innovation, coercive rules reduced the innovation project to a mere order development.

Overall, in both projects, coercive power was the dominant strategy. In case A, however, this praxis could be linked to a loss of innovation capability of the organizations. The established rules can be interpreted as an institutional barrier to collaborative innovation. The results showed that the imposition of technical standards limited the creativity of component suppliers. In addition, it was shown that technological interdependencies between the major components of a wind turbine (such as the rotor, gearbox and generator) can be optimized based on closer collaboration with all relevant component suppliers. However, in this empirical case, WTM actively prohibited such horizontal information sharing. Therefore, the author of this book concludes that when coercive rules of technology development prevent wind turbine component suppliers from collaborating with others to optimize the technological architecture of the wind turbine, it leads to rigidity and reduces the innovative capacity of an entire innovation network.

Case B showed a similar picture. Because WTM, the supplier's main customer, explicitly prohibited further major technical improvements, the component supplier could not expand its product range and engage in additional innovation projects with other large customers. The lack of such collaborative innovation partnerships was the reason why the supplier remained trapped in a market niche.

The strategy of coercive power that systematically inhibits collaborative innovations and socially reduces the innovation projects into a pure order development relationship is illustrated in Table 21 below.

Table 22: The praxis of innovation

Cases	Strategies	Innovation praxis
A & B	Coercive imposition of technical standards	Reduced innovation capability of the collective of organizations
C & D	Relying on personal trust	The social closure of the innovation process is constantly being undermined
E & F	Individual imagination of technical solutions (case E) Trial-and-error learning (competitor firm in case E) Collaborative engineering with scientists (case F)	The innovator lacks legitimacy in the eyes of the partners who are crucial for the development and the deployment.

8.3.2 Relying on personal trust to gain some control

The third and fourth cases presented two radical innovation projects. In Case C, a German rotor blade factory and subsidiary of a large European WTM introduced a robotic rotor blade coating line. Coating rotor blades in an assembly line-like fashion was radically new to the wind energy industry. In Case D, a small German start-up company pursued its radical idea of a new support structure for wind turbines using wood as a construction material instead of steel or concrete.

The practices of knowledge integration were organized differently than in cases A and B. Both companies – the rotor blade factory and the start-up – initiated the innovation process, set up a project organization, and collaborated with partners specialized in previously unknown areas of expertise. For example, the factory collaborated with process automation experts specializing in automotive manufacturing, while the start-up collaborated with various experts specializing in wood engineering. However, these collaborations were less horizontal than expected in a context of radical innovation.

In Case C, a general contractor located several hundred kilometers from the factory designed, built, and tested the new technology. Other key project partners had little influence on the innovation process. For example, the factory and its main customer could only rely on a local, trusted technology specialist and boundary spanner to specify the project idea, using the technical specification sheet as a boundary object to control at least part of the external technology development process. However, a coherent collaborative innovation praxis between the three main actors – the client, the general contractor and the technology specialist – was hardly observed.

In Case D, a start-up company successfully coordinated an innovation network and collaborated with specialists from different fields of expertise to design the first prototype of a 'wooden wind turbine'. In this case, it was interesting to observe that once the prototype was developed, the public authorities responsible for approving the new design took control of the innovation process. In order to prove that the new design met public safety expectations, the approval authority imposed additional technical experiments on the project. As a result, the start-up company expanded its innovation network to include more wood engineering experts from university departments and material testing institutes. In fact, the start-up company established a praxis of collaborative testing of the 'wooden wind turbine' and developed new technical solutions with scientists to improve the prototype. By formulating additional technical requirements, the approval authority also became a relevant development partner, but was integrated too late in the entrepreneurial innovation process of the start-up company.

In the two cases of a robot-based rotor blade coating system and the 'wooden wind turbine', technology development was less horizontal than expected on the basis of proposition 2 outlined in chapter 3. A praxis of collaborative innovation was observed only for specific tasks or stages of the innovation process, such as material testing and science-based experimentation in case D, or the specification of customers' technical requirements in case C. Furthermore, in both cases not all relevant development partners were sufficiently integrated into the innovation processes, which might have significantly caused the unintended outcomes (project delays, quality defects). Based on these findings, the original assumption that radical innovation projects are organized on the basis of newly created procedures and methods of collaborative problem solving (P2) can only be partially supported.

In case C, P2 must be partially refuted, because a collaborative innovation praxis was found only in the stage of technical conception, when the rotor blade factory worked together with various external specialists to negotiate technical solutions and elaborate a technical specification sheet. At this stage, an external technology specialist and trusted partner of the factory management played the role of facilitator and boundary spanner. However, the later stages of technology development remained under the control of the general contractor and system supplier: a common interest in collaborative innovation and "*knowledge transfer*", as one interviewee put it, was not observed. Instead, the project work was characterized by large geographical distances, mistrust, and tactics of keeping proprietary knowledge secret.

In this sense, Case C suggests that a shared praxis of collaborative innovation is necessary for the success of radical innovation. In the case of the development of a robotics-based rotor blade coating system, the lack of a shared innovation praxis led to 'blind spots' in technology development that caused significant quality defects that could only be resolved several months behind the project schedule. Relying on personal trust, on the other hand, proved to be an inferior strategy for managing radical innovation projects. Relying on personal trust implies that a project team relies on individual expertise instead of defining common 'rules' or 'ways' of developing a new technology. Only such an established innovation praxis would be able to socially integrate all relevant development partners.

Case D shows a similar picture. A collaborative innovation praxis was found during the approval process. In order to get the prototype of a 'wooden wind turbine' approved for construction, the start-up company collaborated with experts from material testing and scientific institutes to prove the safety of its design. However, it was too late to involve the regulatory authorities in the innovation process. Due to the radical nature of using wood as a construction material for wind turbines, the constant interpretation of standards kept the innovation process open and delayed the approval decision. Thus, in contrast to P2, the approval authority centrally dominated this later stage of the innovation process. In the end, the start-up relied on the personal trust that the public approval authority placed in a renowned wood engineering expert to socially close the innovation process.

In conclusion, the example of the 'wooden wind turbine' supports the conclusion that in radical innovation projects, the process of establishing a collaborative innovation praxis and the social integration of all relevant development partners – here: approval and material testing authorities – can create the normative power to socially close an innovation process and to bridge incongruent technological frames by defining common working standards. However, the example of Case D also shows that if the approval authorities are not integrated into the innovation process at an early stage, time-consuming experiments and norm interpretations are likely to delay the realization of the project. In our case, the project was completed ten months behind schedule. Another finding of Case D is that because radical innovation projects are uncertain, long-term, and expensive, simply relying on reputable experts, individual assessments, tacit knowledge, or idiosyncratic decisions to develop a new technology is a risky strategy, especially for small firms that need to commercialize new technologies quickly and lack the resources to develop further technologies if a previous initiative has failed.

8.3.3 Individual imagination vs. trial-and-error learning

The fifth and sixth cases illustrate how two engineering service providers attempted to introduce a new technology into an emerging field of technology development in the offshore wind energy sector. The empirical findings showed how a new technology field emerged in the German offshore wind energy industry as a result of new environmental regulations imposed by a public licensing authority to protect marine fauna from noise emissions caused by installation work at sea. The findings support the proposition that "*in the wake of a significant new piece of legislation, we are likely to see organizations or groups move in to take advantage of the new opportunities for strategic action it creates*", thereby creating a new field, as Fligstein & McAdam (2011, p. 13) assert.

For new fields, it was assumed in Chapter 3 that neither technical standards nor innovation networks are established, so that innovation projects have to adapt technical solutions from adjacent fields (P3). This is reflected in the two cases studied, where technology firms that previously served customers in other industries perceived the new field as a business opportunity to gain new customers. Thus, both firms were newcomers to the offshore wind industry. However, each company had a different strategy for developing a technical solution to meet regulatory requirements. At the time, all the major utilities in the industry were desperately searching for such a solution in order to get approval for the construction of their planned offshore wind farms.

In Case E, the focal firm was dominated by a single entrepreneur. Before entering the wind energy industry, this individual had worked for foundries and aircraft manufacturers. After hearing about new technical requirements in the offshore wind energy industry, the entrepreneur invented a solution by creatively combining his technical knowledge gained in steel construction with the unique technical requirements of installing offshore wind turbines. The entrepreneur was not immediately successful, but he quickly found another solution. He adapted a technological principle that, at the time of the research, was well established in the field and used by the company's main competitor.

In this case, technology development took place largely in the mind of the entrepreneur, who essentially imagined technical solutions independently of established scientific knowledge, standardized engineering routines, or external partners. As predicted by P3, the entrepreneur relied on experience gained in other industries and adapted technical ideas from adjacent fields. The entrepreneur's main competitor followed a different strategy. This firm improvised collaborative trial-and-error learning and system testing during ongoing construction projects. The studied entrepreneur's firm did not pursue such a collaborative innovation approach, but instead relied on the individual creativity, determination, and technical imagination of its CEO. This creativity and determination emerged as the dominant mechanism shaping the technology development in case E.

In Case F, a more collaborative approach to the introduction of a technical solution in a new field was observed. The focal company was an engineering service provider specializing in the design and installation of foundation structures for drilling platforms used in the offshore oil and gas industry. The company was attempting to transfer an oil and gas technology to the wind energy industry by developing a quieter foundation process for the installation of offshore wind turbines. In contrast to Case E, this company developed a prototype by relying on professional offshore engineering skills. Based on a broad bundle of technological know-how as well as simulation-based engineering routines and logistical skills gained from "*decades*" of offshore construction projects, the company was highly experienced in combining the technical requirements of different project partners to develop creative solutions, as described in P3. This competence was key to the technology transfer from the offshore oil and gas industry to the wind energy industry.

In contrast to the individual entrepreneur in Case E, the focal firm in Case F strategically collaborated with external partners. In particular, it worked with scientists to gain access to science-based engineering routines and testing facilities to adapt its new foundation structure to the technical requirements of the offshore wind energy industry. In this way, the company was able to establish a collaborative innovation praxis that resulted in a technology suited to the unique requirements of offshore wind turbine installation. Thus, in this case, trust building based on collaborative engineering and science-based system testing appeared to be an effective mechanism of technology development. However, as in Case E, the engineering firm were unable to establish a stable position in the field because it barely partnered with a large utility willing to use the new technology in an offshore wind farm.

Thus, at the time of the investigation, neither company had established stable customer relationships with large utilities, which prevented these companies from establishing a strong position in the new field. It can be concluded that neither the reliance on individual skills (such as creativity, determination or imagination), as observed in case E, nor the reliance on professional offshore engineering skills, as in case F, is sufficient to successfully introduce a new technology and establish a firm as a trusted system supplier based on certified, proven technologies. Both companies did not establish a power position and their technologies remained prototypes. As a result, one firm was unable to prevail against its competitor (Case E), while the other firm remained excluded from offshore innovation networks (Case F). In both cases, the observed outcome was rooted in a lack of collaborative innovation praxis with a large utility willing to provide access to real-world system testing at sea.

Based on these findings, it could be argued that even in emerging technology fields, such as noise mitigation or quiet foundations in the offshore wind industry, new technologies tend to be introduced through hierarchical innovation strategies because utilities and wind farm operators select system suppliers, define membership rules, and provide access to collaborative offshore system testing, which is a prerequisite for adapting technical solutions to new environments. Only the ability to establish a stable position as a trusted, accepted and reputable system supplier ensures the survival of a development company in an emerging field.

8.4 Synthesis: The institutional barriers to collaborative innovation

The previous section summarized the empirical findings of this study. Based on these findings, this section analyses the institutional barriers to collaborative innovation.

The author argues that the key to managing collaborative innovation is the praxis of establishing shared standards for designing, building, and testing new technologies. In the case of new technologies, characterized by intricate technological interdependencies between components, this process is necessarily collaborative in nature and requires knowledge input into the firm's innovation processes from various fields of expertise outside the innovating firm. It has been expected that the praxis of establishing shared standards can normatively bind together different innovation partners despite the different self-interests associated with the respective actors' positions in the field (cf. Lawrence, 2010; Lawrence & Suddaby, 2006). Particularly in the case of radical innovations, the establishment of a common innovation praxis was seen as crucial for ensuring collaboration between previously unfamiliar innovation partners.

In short, the establishment of a collaborative innovation praxis was expected to play a key role in the management collaborative innovation. Shared working standards provide 'rules of the game' (e.g., design rules) and inform actors about the consequences of violating commonly accepted 'ways of doing things' (e.g., warranty claims). Working standards were defined in Chapter 3 as voluntarily decided rules or impositions of normatively connotated procedures and methods of technology development (Ortmann, 2014; Ahrne & Brunsson, 2010). In the context of this study on the wind energy industry, working standards refer to examples, models, levels, or norms for the design, construction, and testing of a new technology that is part of wind turbines, integrated into production processes, or used for the installation of offshore wind turbines. If this innovation praxis is not established, innovation projects are likely to produce a series of unintended outcomes, incurring costs as well as delaying and degrading quality. In the following, this argument is specified with regard to three different technology fields.

8.4.1 Incremental innovation: Incumbents are bound to existing technical standards

In the two examples of incremental innovation among the empirical cases studied in this book, a largely established praxis of collaborative innovation seemed to be visible. However, as both innovation projects were hierarchically controlled by a WTM, a collaborative innovation praxis characterized by openness to new solutions and equal cooperation based on knowledge complementarities and technical interdependence was hardly observed. Thus, coercive power appeared as the dominant strategy, which reduced the innovation project to a mere order development and also reduced the innovative potential of the two project networks as a whole.

These findings suggest that for incumbent firms such as large WTM, establishing an innovation praxis would mean integrating new and previously unknown technical standards and technology specialists into their corporate innovation processes. If they don't, the incumbents' own rules will limit their capability to change the technical standards that have served them well in the past, as Fligstein & McAdam (2011, p. 14) also note: "*[I]ncumbents are both products and architects of the worldview and set of rules they helped to create. They are now dependent on it, and this dependence limits their ability to imagine alternative courses of action.*" As a result, when incumbents are not open to the contributions of other partners, they are not open to change and innovation.

8.4.2 Radical innovation: The inability to build coalitions with powerful actors

In the two cases of radical innovation, a coherent approach to establishing a collaborative innovation praxis was found only in single stages of the innovation process, such as the definition of technical requirements for a new rotor blade coating facility, or the material testing and science-based experimentation in the case of a 'wooden wind turbine'. In these examples, the project partners gained some control over the outcome of each stage by relying on personal trust between individuals. However, when it came to implementing the new technology, the peer-to-peer collaboration quickly gave way to more hierarchical, centrally controlled network relationships. This led to unintended outcomes such as time delays and serious quality defects.

To avoid such outcomes in the creation of radically new technologies, it would be crucial to establish a shared innovation praxis even in the later stages of the innovation process. For this, innovative component suppliers in established technology fields would depend on coalitions with powerful field actors who control technical standards and the 'rules of the game' (cf. Fligstein & McAdam, 2011, p. 7). In the two empirical cases of radical innovation studied, the rotor blade factory had to convince a specialist in automation systems to transfer his established expertise to the context of rotor blade manufacturing, while in the case of the 'wooden wind turbine' the start-up firm had to convince a licensing authority to certify its new design. In both cases, however, the focal firms were unable to build a stable coalition with these powerful actors, which might explain the observed outcomes.

8.4.3 Emerging fields of technology development: The lacking legitimacy of system suppliers

Similar to the cases of radical innovation, no coherent strategy of collaborative innovation was found in the last case pair of emerging technology development in the German offshore wind industry. In one case (noise reduction), an entrepreneur relied on individual technical imagination instead of (re)creating common working standards, while in the other case (a more quiet founding process), a professional offshore engineering firm could not establish a stable position in the field.

To introduce a new technology in an emerging field and to establish a shared innovation praxis, firms may need what Fligstein & McAdam (2011, p. 7) refer to as cognitive, empathetic, and communicative skills to secure the willing cooperation of others and to build the legitimacy needed to establish entirely new technical standards. In the words of Fligstein and McAdam (ibid.), socially skilled actors have the ability to transcend their own individual and group self-interest and consider the interests of multiple groups in order to mobilize support from those groups for a particular shared worldview. In the empirical case of a new field emerging around public regulations for minimizing noise emissions during the construction of wind farms, social skill would have enabled the two developers of a noise mitigation system and a quieter foundation process to build trust in the eyes of large utilities and regulatory agencies involved in the planning and permitting of offshore wind farms at the time. However, neither innovator was able to establish a stable position as a trusted, accepted and reputable system supplier.

Based on these findings, it can be concluded that the praxis of establishing the regulatory, normative, and cultural-cognitive foundations of firm openness is key to the development and adoption of complex new technologies. In the words of Scott (2008, p. 48), an interorganizational shared innovation praxis together with its associated activities and resources, provides stability and meaning to social life. In this context, to the collaborative development of new technologies. If the establishment of such a praxis across organizations is hindered, collaborative innovation are likely to miss their objectives.

This brings us to an answer to the research question formulated in Chapter 1 of this book. The author seeks to contribute to sociological theory-building around the management issues of 'knowledge integration'. Indeed, theory building should be a primary goal of all qualitative research based on a multiple case study design, meaning that the analyst should derive valid, relevant, and testable hypotheses from the empirical material (Eisenhardt & Graebner, 2007; Eisenhardt, 1989). This study examines the relationship between innovation project outcomes and institutional barriers. In empirical cases, such results took the form of untapped innovation potential, serious quality defects, or excessive delays. The author identifies three institutional barriers to collaborative innovation:

1. Powerful firms that have control over incumbent technologies whose architecture could be changed by innovation do not grant legitimacy to innovative firms that might be able to introduce new technical standards. This would result in loss of power over industry technical standards. Innovative companies should therefore engage in industry-specific discourse in order to mobilize support for their innovative position.
2. Incumbents do not integrate innovative solutions from unfamiliar fields of expertise into their innovation practices. This institutional barrier is evident when incumbents use coercive rules to control technology development. In this way, the incumbent firms are able to retain full power over the praxis of innovation. On the other hand, established players could bridge the gap to innovators with the help of boundary spanners with professional experience in several specialist disciplines (Carlile, 2004).
3. Innovative firms seeking to introduce radical innovations may not be able to secure the support of powerful actors such as incumbents or regulatory bodies (e.g., certification/licensing agencies) that control existing standards for developing technology in an established field. The ability to gain support from incumbents would in turn be a factor in the overcoming of this institutional barrier. This could happen when innovative firms use intermediary institutions to partner with established firms or to

reduce regulatory uncertainty and integrate normative expectations into their solutions (Borrás & Edler, 2014).

In summary, strategies for overcoming institutional barriers in the context of collaborative innovation are not purely technical in nature. Rather, they require social-strategic skills in the sense of Fligstein & McAdam's (2011) Social Skill Theory: the ability to understand the power positions of influential actors, the ability to form coalitions, to balance interests and to establish common interpretations of innovation. Companies that are aware of this social dimension significantly increase their chances of success in collaborative innovation processes. Ideally, future research should test these findings with more empirical cases.

8.5 Theoretical relevance

The study shows that the management of collaborative innovation is not purely technical in nature, but must be understood as a social praxis. It is essentially about establishing common working standards that hold the innovation team together despite differing interests and cognitive frames. This is an important development of the open innovation approach (Chesbrough, 2003, 2006), which has so far neglected the institutional and social context of innovation projects. While open innovation focuses on the benefits of external knowledge sources, this study shows that collaborative innovation often fails to realize its potential due to institutional barriers shaped by societal expectations of technology development and power dynamics between the actors involved.

The study also makes an important contribution to the theory of knowledge integration by showing that not only do knowledge boundaries need to be bridged, but that the key to knowledge integration lies in a praxis that overcomes barriers of cognition and power, which must be consciously constructed (Grant, 1996; Berggren et al., 2011). By examining three collaborative innovation praxis (imposing technical standards, relying on personal relationships, and individual imagination), we show how knowledge integration can succeed or fail in different innovation contexts. In particular, relying on personal trust seems to be an inferior innovation strategy.

With regard to knowledge integration, the book also extends our understanding of the concept of "epistemic communities" (Håkanson, 2010). It is shown that collaborative innovation practice is not only the result of knowledge sharing, but is also the result of shared norms and standards of technology development.

The author of the book has used field theory to understand collaborative innovation as an institutionally embedded social practice (Fligstein & McAdam, 2011). The three innovation contexts (incremental, radical, emergent) reflect different institutional conditions under which organizations have pursued specific innovation strategies for knowledge integration.

This book builds on the work of North (1990) and Elster (2007). It argues that working standards as informal institutions that constrain and structure agency, and that the distinction between formalized norms (e.g. through certification) and implicit rules (e.g. social norms in the innovation process) is particularly relevant for innovation management in regulated industries such as wind energy.

Finally, the study shows how powerful actors (e.g. large companies or regulatory authorities) can enable or hinder innovation efforts by outsiders in fields by setting standards or controlling access to knowledge and networks. This book, therefore, also expands our understanding of the concept of social closure by showing that organizations are closed not only by hierarchies or market mechanisms, but also by technical standards, regulatory requirements, and professional norms. This can be well observed in the contexts of collaborative innovation.

Overall, this book makes an important contribution to innovation and organizational theory by showing that implementing collaborative innovation requires a social practice that is characterized by shared norms, social closure, and interorganizational power dynamics. This opens new perspectives on open innovation, institutional barriers, and interorganizational collaboration for the study of innovation management.

8.6 Practical relevance

The findings in this book are also relevant to practitioners. The applied sociological perspective provides a deeper understanding of how to manage collaborative innovation. Specifically, the book's author shows that companies must develop not only technological but also social strategies to overcome power asymmetries and effectively implement innovation projects. Encouraging and moderating the power dynamics and the social process of involving all relevant innovation partners would then be a core capability of innovation management.

The findings of this book also sensitize practitioners to the institutional work involved in collaborative innovation. Particularly in the case of radically new technologies, technology development requires not only the negotiation of shared working standard, but also the establishment of social norms such as a sense of duty, trustworthiness, secrecy, solidarity, etc. The existence of such social norms could provide informal rules of collective behavior of organizations. The existence of such social norms can compensate for the social conflicts between innovation partners that are likely to arise when diverse actors come together to develop radically new, complex technologies.

It has also become clear that regulatory authorities have a crucial role to play in radical innovation, as they can either facilitate or impede the innovation process by means of standards and certification procedures. It has also become clear that innovation networks, which are composed of several organizations, have to be shaped not only by the knowledge, but also by the social and political skills of the actors involved. This is a crucial innovation capability.

The empirical results also show that digital solutions can have an important role in the facilitation of knowledge integration in collaborative innovation projects. In particular, it is emphasized that the digitization of technical information using standardized simulation methods (e.g., Finite Element Methods (FEM), Failure Mode and Effects Analysis (FMEA)) supports combining and developing knowledge. Future research should deepen this aspect.

8.7 Limitations and implications for future research

While this study has valuable insights into the social processes of collaborative innovation, it has several limitations that should be taken into account in future research.

First, the study focuses on companies outside of large research and development (R&D) departments and is based on six empirical case studies from the wind energy industry. Only the case of a robotics-based rotor blade coating facility was located within a large WTM, albeit with little support from the central R&D department. Apart from this case, all three types of innovation contexts included mostly newcomers to the wind energy industry. This means that key players such as established wind turbine manufacturers – such as Enercon, Vestas, Siemens or General Electric – are largely ignored. Here, studies can be conducted to examine whether incumbent firms, with their innovation networks and existing power structures, manage collaborative innovations differently from newcomers.

Second, the qualitative case study method allows for in-depth insights into social dynamics of innovation, but is prone to selective perception and retrospective bias. Furthermore, a simple classification of innovation types (incremental, radical, emergent) has been used so far. Other relevant categories have not been systematically considered. For example, innovation classification could better distinguish between technical components, technological architectures, and service innovations, as the latter require more collaboration. Also, quantitative or mixed-methods approaches may be appropriate to investigate causal relationships between innovation practices and project outcomes.

Third, the study emphasizes the importance of social processes. However, the role of power and strategic behavior of incumbent actors remains unclear. The rules of the game are often in the hands of powerful companies or regulatory authorities. They can either be the promoters of innovation or the controllers of innovation networks through institutional barriers. For example, the case studies show that dominant wind turbine manufacturers force their suppliers into a purely contractual relationship through strict technical standards. This limits the potential for collaborative innovation. Studies that show how incumbents deliberately set innovation standards in order to secure competitive advantage could be informative here.

In summary, several avenues of research can be derived from the limitations of the study: 1) Cross-industry analyses can verify the generalizability of the results. 2) Quantitative studies could reveal the causal relationships between innovation efforts and project outcomes. 3) Power and political perspectives should be included to analyze strategic interests in innovation networks.

9. Appendix

9.1 Interview guide

1) Innovating company's knowledge and networks relevant for the innovation
   - Could you generally describe how the company has grown in the sector over time?
   - What rendered the entry into or involvement in the sector difficult? What made it easier?
   - What is the importance of collaborations with external parties for the company?
2) Main barriers to introducing the innovation into the sector
   - Why was the project initiated?
   - What were the greatest barriers to introducing the innovation into the sector?
   - To what extent did you try to protect the innovation against competitors?
3) General overview of the project work
   - Of which tasks were you in charge during the project work?
   - What were the objectives of the project?
   - Could you describe the progress of the project work? (Duration, phases)
   - What were the biggest challenges?
4) Daily collaboration with colleagues or other internal departments
   - What knowledge was particularly important for the project? What knowledge were you able to draw on internally?
   - Who are your most important contacts internally (for example colleagues, other departments)?
   - What knowledge did those colleagues or internal departments provide to the project?
   - What were the greatest challenges in cooperating with those internal contacts?
   - Can you give examples of how you collaborated with those internals contacts?
5) Daily collaboration with external partners / organizations
   - For which tasks are you working particularly closely together with external partners?
   - What knowledge do bring these external partners to the project?
   - Where do you see the biggest challenges in using their knowledge?

- What factors encourage or make it difficult to use their knowledge?
- How was the collaboration regulated (by contract)?
- What, in your view, were the greatest challenges in collaborating with those external partners?
- Could you give examples of how collaboration with external partners proceeds?
- To what extent did the collaboration initiate technological innovations or lead to internal knowledge generation?
- To what extent could the externals partners access your internal knowledge?
- To what extent did you protect your internal knowledge from unwanted intrusion by externals?

6) Retrospective assessments and outlook
   - To what extent did the project touch national or international industry standards?
   - To what extent did the project work differ from other customers, projects or industries you were previously involved in?
   - To what extent would you reconsider the why in which the collaboration with external partners is organized in the future?
   - Key performance indicators (employees, sales)

Bibliography

Ahrne, G., & Brunsson, N. (2010). Organization outside organizations: The significance of partial organization. *Organization, 18*(1), 83–104. https://doi.org/10.1177/1350508410376256

Alexy, O., & Dahlander, L. (2014). Managing open innovation. In M. Dodgson, D. M. Gann, & N. Phillips (Eds.), *The Oxford handbook of innovation management* (pp. 442–461). Oxford University Press.

Alexy, O., & Reitzig, M. (2013). Private–collective innovation, competition, and firms' counterintuitive appropriation strategies. *Research Policy, 42*(4), 895–913. https://doi.org/10.1016/j.respol.2012.12.003

Alexy, O., West, J., Klapper, H., & Reitzig, M. (2017). Surrendering control to gain advantage: Reconciling openness and the resource-based view of the firm. *Strategic Management Journal, 39*(6), 1704–1727. https://doi.org/10.1002/smj.2736

Allen, R. H., & Sriram, R. D. (2000). The role of standards in innovation. *Technological Forecasting and Social Change, 64*(2–3), 171–181. https://doi.org/10.1016/S0040-1625(99)00105-7

Arora, A., Athreye, S., & Huang, C. (2016). The paradox of openness revisited: Collaborative innovation and patenting by UK innovators. *Research Policy, 45*(7), 1352–1361. https://doi.org/10.1016/j.respol.2016.03.019

Arthur, W. B. (2007). The structure of invention. *Research Policy, 36*(2), 274–287. https://doi.org/10.1016/j.respol.2006.11.005

Ates, A. (2022). Impeding factors for the generation of collaborative innovation performance in ecosystem-based manufacturing. *International Journal of Productivity and Performance Management, 72*(8), 2225–2246. https://doi.org/10.1108/IJPPM-06-2021-0320

Bachmann, R., Gillespie, N., & Priem, R. (2015). Repairing trust in organizations and institutions: Toward a conceptual framework. *Organization Studies, 36*(9), 1123–1142. https://doi.org/10.1177/0170840615599334

Bachmann, R., & Inkpen, A. C. (2011). Understanding institutional-based trust building processes in inter-organizational relationships. *Organization Studies, 32*(2), 281–301. https://doi.org/10.1177/0170840610397477

Bachmann, R., & Zaheer, A. (2014). Trust in inter-organizational relations. In S. Cropper (Ed.), *The Oxford handbook of inter-organizational relations* (pp. 533–554). Oxford University Press.

Baldwin, C., & von Hippel, E. (2011). Modeling a paradigm shift: From producer innovation to user and open collaborative innovation. *Organization Science, 22*(6), 1399–1417. https://doi.org/10.1287/orsc.1100.0618

Baldwin, C. Y., & Clark, K. B. (2000). *Design rules: The power of modularity* (Vol. 1). MIT Press.

Barley, S. R. (1986). Technology as an occasion for structuring: Evidence from observations of CT scanners and the social order of radiology departments. *Administrative Science Quarterly, 31*(1), 78–108. https://doi.org/10.2307/2392767

Baumstark, B. A. (2020). Barriers in profiting from external knowledge: The role of organizational design. *Industrial and Corporate Change, 29*(4), 979–995. https://doi.org/10.1093/icc/dtaa018

Beck, N., & Walgenbach, P. (2005). Technical efficiency or adaptation to institutionalized expectations? The adoption of ISO 9000 standards in the German mechanical engineering industry. *Organization Studies, 26*(6), 841–866. https://doi.org/10.1177/0170840605054593

Bengtsson, L., Lakemond, N., Laursen, K., & Tell, F. (2017). Managing knowledge integration across multiple boundaries. In F. Tell, C. Berggren, S. Brusoni, & A. van de Ven (Eds.), *Managing knowledge integration across boundaries* (pp. 87–105). Oxford University Press.

Berger, P., & Luckmann, T. (2009). *Die gesellschaftliche Konstruktion der Wirklichkeit: Eine Theorie der Wissenssoziologie* (22. Aufl.). Frankfurt am Main: Fischer Taschenbuch Verlag.

Berggren, C., Bergek, A., Bengtsson, L., Hobday, M., & Söderlund, J. (2011a). *Knowledge integration and innovation: Critical challenges facing international technology-based firms.* Oxford University Press.

Berggren, C., Bergek, A., Bengtsson, L., & Söderlund, J. (2011b). Exploring knowledge integration and innovation. In C. Berggren, A. Bergek, L. Bengtsson, M. Hobday, & J. Söderlund (Eds.), *Knowledge integration and innovation: Critical challenges facing international technology-based firms* (pp. 3–19). Oxford University Press.

Berggren, C., Sydow, J., & Tell, F. (2017). Knowledge boundaries and reflective agency in path-dependent processes. In F. Tell, C. Berggren, S. Brusoni, & A. van de Ven (Eds.), *Managing knowledge integration across boundaries* (pp. 57–71). Oxford University Press.

Bijker, W. E. (1995). *Of bicycles, bakelites, and bulbs: Toward a theory of sociotechnical change.* MIT Press.

Bijker, W. E. (2010). How is technology made? – That is the question! *Cambridge Journal of Economics, 34*(1), 63–76. https://doi.org/10.1093/cje/bep042

Bijker, W. E., Hughes, T. P., & Pinch, T. J. (Eds.). (1987). *The social construction of technological systems: New directions in the sociology and history of technology.* MIT Press.

Bitektine, A. (2007). Prospective case study design. *Organizational Research Methods, 11*(1), 160–180. https://doi.org/10.1177/1094428106292900

Bjornali, E. S., Giones, F., & Billstrom, A. (2017). Reveal or conceal? Signaling strategies for building legitimacy in cleantech firms. *Sustainability, 9*(10), 1815. https://doi.org/10.3390/su9101815

Blättel-Mink, B. (2015). Das persönliche Element im Wirtschaftsleben – Joseph A. Schumpeter. In B. Blättel-Mink & R. Menez (Eds.), *Kompendium der Innovationsforschung* (pp. 67–81). Springer Fachmedien.

Blättel-Mink, B., & Menez, R. (2015). *Kompendium der Innovationsforschung* (2. Aufl.). Springer Fachmedien.

Blind, K. (2012). The influence of regulations on innovation: A quantitative assessment for OECD countries. *Research Policy, 41*(2), 391–400. https://doi.org/10.1016/j.respol.2011.08.008

Blind, K., Petersen, S. S., & Riillo, C. A. (2017). The impact of standards and regulation on innovation in uncertain markets. *Research Policy, 46*(1), 249–264. https://doi.org/10.1016/j.respol.2016.11.003

Blumer, H. (1954). What is wrong with social theory? *American Sociological Review, 19*(1), 3–10. https://doi.org/10.2307/2088165

Bø Lyng, H., & Brun, E. C. (2020). Innovating with strangers: Managing knowledge barriers across distances in cross-industry innovation. *International Journal of Innovation and Technology Management, 17*(1), 2050008. https://doi.org/10.1142/S0219877020500083

Bogers, M., Bekkers, R., & Granstrand, O. (2012). Intellectual property and licensing strategies in open collaborative innovation. In C. de Pablos Heredero & D. López (Eds.), *Open innovation in firms and public administrations* (pp. 37–58). IGI Global.

Bogers, M., & West, J. (2012). Managing distributed innovation: Strategic utilization of open and user innovation. *Creativity and Innovation Management, 21*(1), 61–75. https://doi.org/10.1111/j.1467-8691.2011.00622.x

Borrás, S., & Edler, J. (2014). *The governance of socio-technical systems: Explaining change.* Edward Elgar Publishing.

Boxenbaum, E., & Jonsson, S. (2008). Isomorphism, diffusion and decoupling. In R. Greenwood, C. Oliver, R. Suddaby, & K. Sahlin-Andersson (Eds.), *The SAGE handbook of organizational institutionalism* (pp. 78–98). SAGE.

Brown, J. S., & Duguid, P. (2001). Knowledge and organization: A social-practice perspective. *Organization Science, 12*(2), 198–213. https://doi.org/10.1287/orsc.12.2.198.10116

Brunsson, N., Rasche, A., & Seidl, D. (2012). The dynamics of standardization: Three perspectives on standards in organization studies. *Organization Studies, 33*(5–6), 613–632. https://doi.org/10.1177/0170840612450120

Brubaker, E.R., Sheppard, S.D., Hinds, P.J., & Yang, M.C. (2023). Objects of Collaboration: Roles and Sequences of Objects in Spanning Knowledge Group Boundaries in Design. *Journal of Mechanical Design*. https://doi.org/10.1115/1.4056798

Caccamo, M., Pittino, D., & Tell, F. (2023). Boundary objects, knowledge integration, and innovation management: A systematic review of the literature. *Technovation, 122*, 102645. https://doi.org/10.1016/j.technovation.2023.102645

Carlile, P. R. (2002). A pragmatic view of knowledge and boundaries: Boundary objects in new product development. *Organization Science, 13*(4), 442–455. https://doi.org/10.1287/orsc.13.4.442.2953

Carlile, P. R. (2004). Transferring, translating, and transforming: An integrative framework for managing knowledge across boundaries. *Organization Science, 15*(5), 555–568. https://doi.org/10.1287/orsc.1040.0094

Carlile, P. R., & Rebentisch, E. S. (2003). Into the black box: The knowledge transformation cycle. *Management Science, 49*(9), 1180–1195. https://doi.org/10.1287/mnsc.49.9.1180.16564

Cassiman, B., & Valentini, G. (2015). Open innovation: Are inbound and outbound knowledge flows really complementary? *Strategic Management Journal, 37*(6), 1034–1046. https://doi.org/10.1002/smj.2375

Cheng, C. C., & Huizingh, E. K. (2014). When is open innovation beneficial? The role of strategic orientation. *Journal of Product Innovation Management, 31*(6), 1235–1253. https://doi.org/10.1111/jpim.12148

Chesbrough, H. (2003). *Open innovation: The new imperative for creating and profiting from technology.* Harvard Business School Press.

Chesbrough, H. (2006a). Open innovation: A new paradigm for understanding. In H. Chesbrough, W. Vanhaverbeke, & J. West (Eds.), *Open innovation* (pp. 1–12). Oxford University Press.

Chesbrough, H. W. (2006b). *Open innovation: The new imperative for creating and profiting from technology.* Harvard Business Press.

Chesbrough, H. W., & Bogers, M. (2014). Explicating open innovation: Clarifying an emerging paradigm for understanding innovation. In H. W. Chesbrough, W. Vanhaverbeke, & J. West (Eds.), *New frontiers in open innovation* (pp. 3–28). Oxford University Press.

Cohen, W. M., & Levinthal, D. A. (1990). Absorptive capacity: A new perspective on learning and innovation. *Administrative Science Quarterly, 35*(1), 128–152. https://doi.org/10.2307/2393553

Cook, K. S., & Gerbasi, A. (2011). Trust. In P. Hedström & P. S. Bearman (Eds.), *The Oxford handbook of analytical sociology* (pp. 218–241). Oxford University Press.

Cropper, S., & Palmer, I. (2009). Change, dynamics, and temporality in inter-organizational relationships. In S. Cropper, C. Huxham, M. Ebers, & P. S. Ring (Eds.), *The Oxford handbook of inter-organizational relations* (pp. 635–663). Oxford University Press.

Crozier, M., & Friedberg, E. (1979). *Macht und Organisation: Die Zwänge kollektiven Handelns* (3. Aufl.). Athenäum-Verlag.

Czarnitzki, D., & Spielkamp, A. (2000). Business services in Germany: Bridges for innovation. *Discussion Paper / ZEW, Zentrum für Europäische Wirtschaftsforschung GmbH Industrial Economics and International Management, 2000*(52), Mannheim: ZEW.

Dahlander, L., & Gann, D. M. (2010). How open is innovation? *Research Policy, 39*(6), 699–709. https://doi.org/10.1016/j.respol.2010.01.013

Dannenberg, L. (2013). Technische Rahmenbedingungen. In J. Böttcher (Ed.), *Handbuch Offshore-Windenergie, BWL 10–2012* (pp. 289–352). Oldenbourg.

Davidson, E., & Pai, D. (2004). Making sense of technological frames: Promise, progress, and potential. In T. Kaplan, D. P. Truex III, D. Wastell, A. T. Wood-Harper, & J. I. DeGross (Eds.), *Information systems research* (pp. 473–491). Springer US.

Davis, J. P., & Eisenhardt, K. M. (2011). Rotating leadership and collaborative innovation: Recombination processes in symbiotic relationships. *Administrative Science Quarterly, 56*(2), 159–201. https://doi.org/10.1177/0001839211428131

Dekkers, M. (2014). Die Stärkung der Innovationskraft als gemeinsame Aufgabe von Wirtschaft, Politik und Gesellschaft. In M. Mai (Ed.), *Handbuch Innovationen* (pp. 55–72). Springer Fachmedien.

DiMaggio, P. (1988). Interest and agency in institutional theory. In L. G. Zucker (Ed.), *Research on institutional patterns: Environment and culture* (pp. 3–21). Ballinger Publishing Co.

DiMaggio, P., & Powell, W. W. (1983). The iron cage revisited: Institutional isomorphism and collective rationality in organizational fields. *American Sociological Review, 48*(2), 147–160. https://doi.org/10.2307/2095101

Dodgson, M., & Gann, D. M. (2014). Technology and innovation. In M. Dodgson, D. M. Gann, & N. Phillips (Eds.), *The Oxford handbook of innovation management* (pp. 375–393). Oxford University Press.

Dodgson, M., Gann, D. M., & Phillips, N. (2014). Perspectives on innovation management. In M. Dodgson, D. M. Gann, & N. Phillips (Eds.), *The Oxford handbook of innovation management* (pp. 3–25). Oxford University Press.

Dokko, G., Nigam, A., & Rosenkopf, L. (2012). Keeping steady as she goes: A negotiated order perspective on technological evolution. *Organization Studies, 33*(5–6), 681–703. https://doi.org/10.1177/0170840612443627

Dörrenbächer, C., & Gammelgaard, J. (2011). Subsidiary power in multinational corporations: The subtle role of micro-political bargaining power. *Critical Perspectives on International Business, 7*(1), 30–47.

Dosi, G., & Nelson, R. R. (2010). Technical change and industrial dynamics as evolutionary processes. In *Handbook of the economics of innovation* (pp. 51–127). North-Holland.

Dougherty, D. (2001). Reimagining the differentiation and integration of work for sustained product innovation. *Organization Science, 12*(5), 612–631. https://doi.org/10.1287/orsc.12.5.612.10096

Dougherty, D., & Dunne, D. D. (2011). Organizing ecologies of complex innovation. *Organization Science, 22*(5), 1214–1223. https://doi.org/10.1287/orsc.1100.0615

Easterby-Smith, M., Golden-Biddle, K., & Locke, K. (2007). Working with pluralism: Determining quality in qualitative research. *Organizational Research Methods, 11*(3), 419–429. https://doi.org/10.1177/1094428107308072

Ebers, M., & Maurer, I. (2014). Connections count: How relational embeddedness and relational empowerment foster absorptive capacity. *Research Policy, 43*(2), 318–332. https://doi.org/10.1016/j.respol.2013.10.017

Edgerton, D. (2008). *The shock of the old: Technology and global history since 1900.* Profile Books.

Edquist, C. (2002). Innovation policy—a systemic approach. In *The globalizing learning economy* (pp. 219–238). Oxford University Press.

Edquist, C. (2005). Systems of innovation: Perspectives and challenges. In J. Fagerberg, D. C. Mowery, & R. Nelson (Eds.), *The Oxford handbook of innovation* (pp. 181–208). Oxford University Press.

Egbekokun, A., & Svin, I. (2015). Absorptive capacity and innovation: When is it better to cooperate? In A. Pyka (Ed.), *The evolution of economic and innovation systems* (pp. 373–399). Springer.

Engstrand, Å.-K., & Enberg, C. (2020). The power in positionings: A Foucauldian approach to knowledge integration processes. *Management Learning, 51*(3), 336–352. https://doi.org/10.1177/1350507619889028

Eisenhardt, K. M. (1989). Building theories from case study research. *The Academy of Management Review, 14*(4), 532–550. https://doi.org/10.5465/amr.1989.4308385

Eisenhardt, K. M., & Graebner, M. E. (2007). Theory building from cases: Opportunities and challenges. *The Academy of Management Journal, 50*(1), 25–32. https://doi.org/10.5465/amj.2007.24160888

Elster, J. (2007). *Explaining social behavior: More nuts and bolts for the social sciences.* Cambridge University Press.

Elster, J. (2011). Norms. In P. Hedström & P. S. Bearman (Eds.), *The Oxford handbook of analytical sociology* (pp. 195–217). Oxford University Press.

Emirbayer, M. (1997). Manifesto for a relational sociology. *American Journal of Sociology, 103*(2), 281–317. https://doi.org/10.1086/231209

Esser, H. (2000). *Soziologie. Spezielle Grundlagen: Institutionen* (Vol. 5). Campus Verlag.

Faems, D., Looy, B. V., & Debackere, K. (2005). Interorganizational collaboration and innovation: Toward a portfolio approach. *Journal of Product Innovation Management, 22*(3), 238–250. https://doi.org/10.1111/j.0737-6782.2005.00120.x

Fagerberg, J. (2005). Innovation: A guide to the literature. In J. Fagerberg, D. C. Mowery, & R. R. Nelson (Eds.), *The Oxford handbook of innovation.* Oxford University Press.

Feldman, M. S. (2016). Routines as process: Past, present, and future. In J. Howard-Grenville, C. Rerup, A. Langley, & H. Tsoukas (Eds.), *Organizational routines: How they are created, maintained, and changed* (pp. 23–46). Oxford University Press.

Feldman, M. S., & Pentland, B. T. (2003). Reconceptualizing organizational routines as a source of flexibility and change. *Administrative Science Quarterly, 48*(1), 94–118. https://doi.org/10.2307/3556620

Fiss, P. C. (2009). Case studies and the configurational analysis of organizational phenomena. In D. Byrne & C. C. Ragin (Eds.), *The SAGE handbook of case-based methods* (pp. 424–440). SAGE Publications.

Flick, U. (2002). *Qualitative Sozialforschung: Eine Einführung.* Rowohlt Taschenbuch Verlag.

Fligstein, N., & McAdam, D. (2011). Toward a general theory of strategic action fields. *Sociological Theory, 29*(1), 1–26. https://doi.org/10.1111/j.1467-9558.2010.01385.x

Fligstein, N., & McAdam, D. (2012). *A theory of fields.* Oxford University Press.

Fornahl, D., Hassink, R., Klaerding, C., Mossig, I., & Schröder, H. (2012). From the old path of shipbuilding onto the new path of offshore wind energy? The case of Northern Germany. *European Planning Studies, 20*(5), 832–855. https://doi.org/10.1080/09654313.2012.667908

Foss, N. J., Laursen, K., & Pedersen, T. (2011). Linking customer interaction and innovation: The mediating role of new organizational practices. *Organization Science, 22*(4), 980–999. https://doi.org/10.1287/orsc.1100.0584

Foucart, R., & Li, Q. C. (2021). The role of technology standards in product innovation: Theory and evidence from UK manufacturing firms. *Research Policy, 50*(2), 104157. https://doi.org/10.1016/j.respol.2020.104157

Freeman, C., & Soete, L. (1999). *The economics of industrial innovation* (3rd ed.). Pinter.

Gallini, N. (2014). Cooperating with competitors: Patent pooling and choice of a new standard. *International Journal of Industrial Organization, 36*, 4–21. https://doi.org/10.1016/j.ijindorg.2014.03.006

Gambardella, A., & Panico, C. (2014). On the management of open innovation. *Research Policy, 43*(5), 903–913. https://doi.org/10.1016/j.respol.2013.12.002

Garriga, H., von Krogh, G., & Spaeth, S. (2013). How constraints and knowledge impact open innovation. *Strategic Management Journal, 34*(9), 1134–1144. https://doi.org/10.1002/smj.2049

Garud, R., Jain, S., & Kumaraswamy, A. (2002). Institutional entrepreneurship in the sponsorship of common technological standard: The case of Sun Microsystems and Java. *Academy of Management Journal, 45*(1), 196–214. https://doi.org/10.5465/3069292

Gerring, J., & Cojocaru, L. (2016). Selecting cases for intensive analysis: A diversity of goals and methods. *Sociological Methods & Research, 45*(3), 392–423. https://doi.org/10.1177/0049124116631692

Gibbert, M., & Ruigrok, W. (2010). The "what" and "how" of case study rigor: Three strategies based on published work. *Organizational Research Methods, 13*(4), 710–737. https://doi.org/10.1177/1094428109351319

Gibbert, M., Ruigrok, W., & Wicki, B. (2008). What passes as a rigorous case study? *Strategic Management Journal, 29*(13), 1465–1474. https://doi.org/10.1002/smj.722

Giddens, A. (1984). *The constitution of society: Outline of the theory of structuration.* Polity Press.

Grigoriou, K., & Rothaermel, F. T. (2016). Organizing for knowledge generation: Internal knowledge networks and the contingent effect of external knowledge sourcing. Strategic Management Journal, 37(3), 431–454. https://doi.org/10.1002/smj.2489

Granstrand, O., & Holgersson, M. (2014). The challenge of closing open innovation: The intellectual property disassembly problem. *Research-Technology Management, 57*(5), 19–25. https://doi.org/10.5437/08956308X5705257

Grant, R. M. (1996a). Prospering in dynamically-competitive environments: Organizational capability as knowledge integration. *Organization Science, 7*(4), 375–387. https://doi.org/10.1287/orsc.7.4.375

Grant, R. M. (1996b). Toward a knowledge-based theory of the firm. *Strategic Management Journal, 17*(S2), 109–122. https://doi.org/10.1002/smj.4250171110

Gurca, A., Bagherzadeh, M., Markovic, S., & Koporcic, N. (2020). Managing the challenges of business-to-business open innovation in complex projects: A multi-stage process model. *Industrial Marketing Management, 89*, 191–207. https://doi.org/10.1016/j.indmarman.2020.03.016

Habersang, S., Küberling-Jost, J., Reihlen, M., & Seckler, C. (2018). A process perspective on organizational failure: A qualitative meta-analysis. *Journal of Management Studies, 56*(1), 19–56. https://doi.org/10.1111/joms.12341

Hage, J., & Hollingsworth, J. R. (2000). A strategy for the analysis of idea innovation networks and institutions. *Organization Studies, 21*(5), 971–1004. https://doi.org/10.1177/0170840600215003

Håkanson, L. (2010). The firm as an epistemic community: The knowledge-based view revisited. *Industrial and Corporate Change, 19*(6), 1801–1828. https://doi.org/10.1093/icc/dtq052

Heidenreich, M. (1997). Zwischen Innovation und Institutionalisierung. In B. Blättel-Mink & O. Renn (Eds.), *Zwischen Akteur und System: Die Organisierung von Innovation* (pp. 177–206). VS Verlag für Sozialwissenschaften.

Heidenreich, M., Kädtler, J., & Mattes, J. (Eds.). (2017). *Kollaborative Innovationen: Die innerbetriebliche Nutzung externer Wissensbestände in vernetzten Entwicklungsprozessen*. Universitätsverlag Göttingen.

Hendry, C., & Harborne, P. (2011). Changing the view of wind power development: More than "bricolage." *Research Policy, 40*(5), 778–789. https://doi.org/10.1016/j.respol.2011.03.004

Henkel, J., Schöberl, S., & Alexy, O. (2014). The emergence of openness: How and why firms adopt selective revealing in open innovation. *Research Policy, 43*(5), 879–890. https://doi.org/10.1016/j.respol.2013.12.006

Henttonen, K., Hurmelinna-Laukkanen, P., & Ritala, P. (2016). Managing the appropriability of R&D collaboration. *R&D Management, 46*(S1), 145–158. https://doi.org/10.1111/radm.12172

Heras-Saizarbitoria, I., & Boiral, O. (2012). ISO 9001 and ISO 14001: Towards a research agenda on management system standards. *International Journal of Management Reviews, 15*(1), 47–65. https://doi.org/10.1111/j.1468-2370.2012.00328.x

Herstad, S. J., Sandven, T., & Ebersberger, B. (2015). Recruitment, knowledge integration and modes of innovation. *Research Policy, 44*(1), 138–153. https://doi.org/10.1016/j.respol.2014.07.015

Hoffman, A. J. (1999). Institutional evolution and change: Environmentalism and the U.S. chemical industry. *Academy of Management Journal, 42*(4), 351–371. https://doi.org/10.5465/257008

Hofman, E., Halman, J. I. M., & van Looy, B. (2016). Do design rules facilitate or complicate architectural innovation in innovation alliance networks? *Research Policy, 45*(7), 1436–1448. https://doi.org/10.1016/j.respol.2016.05.008

Hollingsworth, J. R., & Boyer, R. (1997). Coordination of economic actors and social systems of production. In J. R. Hollingsworth & R. Boyer (Eds.), *Contemporary capitalism: The embeddedness of institutions* (pp. 1–47). Cambridge University Press.

Hollingsworth, R. J. (2000). Doing institutional analysis: Implications for the study of innovations. *Review of International Political Economy, 7*(4), 595–644. https://doi.org/10.1080/096922900750034575

Holzner, B. (1972). *Reality construction in society*. Schenkman Publishing.

Horn, A., Urias, E., Klein, J. T., Hess, A., & Zweekhorst, M. B. M. (2023). Expert and non-expert at the same time: Knowledge integration processes and dynamics in interdisciplinary teamwork. *Sustainability Science, 18*(5), 2357–2371. https://doi.org/10.1007/s11625-023-01305-3

Huenteler, J., Ossenbrink, J., Schmidt, T. S., & Hoffmann, V. H. (2016). How a product's design hierarchy shapes the evolution of technological knowledge—Evidence from patent-citation networks in wind power. *Research Policy, 45*(6), 1195–1217. https://doi.org/10.1016/j.respol.2016.03.014

Huenteler, J., Schmidt, T. S., Ossenbrink, J., & Hoffmann, V. H. (2016). Technology life-cycles in the energy sector—Technological characteristics and the role of deployment for innovation. *Technological Forecasting and Social Change, 104*, 102–121. https://doi.org/10.1016/j.techfore.2015.09.022

Hughes, T. P. (1987). The evolution of large technological systems. In W. E. Bijker, T. P. Hughes, & T. J. Pinch (Eds.), *The social construction of technological systems: New directions in the sociology and history of technology* (pp. 51–82). MIT Press.

Huxham, C., & Beech, N. (2010). Inter-organizational power. In S. Cropper, M. Ebers, C. Huxham, & P. S. Ring (Eds.), *The Oxford handbook of inter-organizational relations* (pp. 555–579). Oxford University Press.

Idelchik, M., & Kogan, S. (2012). GE's open collaboration model. *Research-Technology Management, 55*(4), 28–31. https://doi.org/10.5437/08956308X5504085

Jackwerth, T. (2009). *Die Einführung von Informationssystemen und ihre Auswirkungen auf die Arbeit und Kommunikation im Unternehmen: Eine empirische Untersuchung dreier SAP-Einführungsprojekte bei einem Unternehmen aus der Transport- und Logistikbranche*. Kovač.

Jackwerth, T. (2014). Studie zum Windenergiesektor. Eine empirische Analyse der betrieblichen Nutzung verteilten Wissens. *Oldenburger Studien zur Europäisierung und zur transnationalen Regulierung*, (23), 1–24.

Jackwerth, T. (2017). Formen der Wissensintegration in Innovationsnetzwerken: Das Beispiel der Windenergie. In M. Heidenreich, J. Kädtler, & J. Mattes (Eds.), *Kollaborative Innovationen* (pp. 163–192). Universitätsverlag Göttingen.

Jacobsson, S., & Karltorp, K. (2013). Mechanisms blocking the dynamics of the European offshore wind energy innovation system—Challenges for policy intervention. *Energy Policy, 63*, 1182–1195. https://doi.org/10.1016/j.enpol.2013.08.077

Johnsen, T. E., Lamming, R. C., & Harland, C. M. (2009). Inter-organizational relationships, chains, and networks. In S. Cropper, M. Ebers, C. Huxham, & P. S. Ring (Eds.), *The Oxford handbook of inter-organizational relations* (pp. 61–89). Oxford University Press.

Kaldellis, J. K., & Zafirakis, D. (2011). The wind energy (r)evolution: A short review of a long history. *Renewable Energy, 36*(7), 1887–1901. https://doi.org/10.1016/j.renene.2011.01.002

Kamp, L. M., Smits, R. E., & Andriesse, C. D. (2004). Notions on learning applied to wind turbine development in the Netherlands and Denmark. *Energy Policy, 32*(14), 1625–1637. https://doi.org/10.1016/S0301-4215(03)00134-4

Kappelhoff, P. (2014). Kompetenzentwicklung in Netzwerken: Die Sicht der Komplexitäts- und allgemeinen Evolutionstheorie. In A. Windeler & J. Sydow (Eds.), *Kompetenz, Organisation und Gesellschaft* (pp. 109–223). VS Verlag für Sozialwissenschaften.

Karnøe, P., & Garud, R. (2012). Path creation: Co-creation of heterogeneous resources in the emergence of the Danish wind turbine cluster. *European Planning Studies, 20*(5), 733–752. https://doi.org/10.1080/09654313.2012.667923

Kash, D. E., & Rycroft, R. (2002). Emerging patterns of complex technological innovation. *Technological Forecasting and Social Change, 69*(6), 581–606. https://doi.org/10.1016/S0040-1625(01)00168-8

Katzy, B., Turgut, E., Holzmann, T., & Sailer, K. (2013). Innovation intermediaries: A process view on open innovation coordination. *Technology Analysis & Strategic Management, 25*(3), 295–309. https://doi.org/10.1080/09537325.2013.764982

Knights, D. (2009). Power at work in organizations. In M. Alvesson, T. Bridgman, & H. Willmott (Eds.), *The Oxford handbook of critical management studies* (pp. 144–165). Oxford University Press.

Kogut, B., & Zander, U. (1992). Knowledge of the firm, combinative capabilities, and the replication of technology. *Organization Science, 3*(3), 383–397. https://doi.org/10.1287/orsc.3.3.383

Kriegesmann, B., & Kerka, F. (2014). Unternehmerisches Innovationsmanagement. In M. Mai (Ed.), *Handbuch Innovationen* (pp. 73–87). Springer Fachmedien.

Krücken, G. (2016). Paul J. DiMaggio und Walter W. Powell: The iron cage revisited—Institutional isomorphism and collective rationality in organizational fields. In *Schlüsselwerke der Wirtschaftssoziologie* (pp. 195–200). Springer Fachmedien.

Kumar, Y., Ringenberg, J., Depuru, S. S. S. R., Devabhaktuni, V. K., Lee, J. W., Nikolaidis, E., Andersen, B., & Afjeh, A. (2016). Wind energy: Trends and enabling technologies. *Renewable and Sustainable Energy Reviews, 53*, 209–224. https://doi.org/10.1016/j.rser.2015.07.129

Langhof, A., Hahn, L., Bergmann, J., & Wagner, G. (2014). Einführende Überlegungen zum Scheitern aus organisations- und wirtschaftssoziologischer Perspektive. In J. Bergmann, M. Hahn, A. Langhof, & G. Wagner (Eds.), *Scheitern – Organisations- und wirtschaftssoziologische Analysen* (pp. 9–28). Springer Fachmedien.

Laursen, K., & Salter, A. (2006). Open for innovation: The role of openness in explaining innovation performance among U.K. manufacturing firms. *Strategic Management Journal, 27*(2), 131–150. https://doi.org/10.1002/smj.507

Laursen, K., & Salter, A. J. (2014). The paradox of openness: Appropriability, external search and collaboration. *Research Policy, 43*(5), 867–878. https://doi.org/10.1016/j.respol.2013.10.004

Lawrence, T. B. (2008). Institutions and organizations. In R. Greenwood, C. Oliver, R. Suddaby, & K. Sahlin-Andersson (Eds.), *The SAGE handbook of organizational institutionalism* (pp. 170–197). SAGE.

Lawrence, T. B. (Ed.). (2010). *Institutional work: Actors and agency in institutional studies of organizations* (1st paperback ed.). Cambridge University Press.

Lawrence, T. B., & Suddaby, R. (2006). Institutions and institutional work. In S. R. Clegg, C. Hardy, T. B. Lawrence, & W. R. Nord (Eds.), *The Sage handbook of organization studies* (pp. 215–254). SAGE.

Lawrence, T. B., Suddaby, R., & Leca, B. (2010). Introduction: Theorizing and studying institutional work. In T. B. Lawrence, R. Suddaby, & B. Leca (Eds.), *Institutional work: Actors and agency in institutional studies of organizations* (pp. 1–27). Cambridge University Press.

Lee, S., Park, G., Yoon, B., & Park, J. (2010). Open innovation in SMEs—An intermediated network model. *Research Policy, 39*(2), 290–300. https://doi.org/10.1016/j.respol.2009.12.009

Lema, R., Nordensvärd, J., Urban, F., & Lütkenhorst, W. (2014). Innovation paths in wind power: Insights from Denmark and Germany. *German Development Institute / Deutsches Institut für Entwicklungspolitik (DIE).*

Lewin, A. Y., Massini, S., & Peeters, C. (2011). Microfoundations of internal and external absorptive capacity routines. *Organization Science, 22*(1), 81–98. https://doi.org/10.1287/orsc.1100.0525

Lijphart, A. (1971). Comparative politics and the comparative method. *American Political Science Review, 65*(3), 682–693. https://doi.org/10.2307/1955513

Love, J. H., Roper, S., & Vahter, P. (2013). Learning from openness: The dynamics of breadth in external innovation linkages. *Strategic Management Journal, 35*(11), 1703–1716. https://doi.org/10.1002/smj.2170

Luhmann, N. (2006). *Organisation und Entscheidung* (2. Aufl.). VS Verlag für Sozialwissenschaften.

Lyng, H. B., & Brun, E. C. (2020). Innovating with strangers: Managing knowledge barriers across distances in cross-industry innovation. *International Journal of Innovation and Technology Management, 17*(1), 2050008. https://doi.org/10.1142/S0219877020500083

Maitlis, S., & Christianson, M. (2014). Sensemaking in organizations: Taking stock and moving forward. *The Academy of Management Annals, 8*(1), 57–125. https://doi.org/10.1080/19416520.2014.873177

Mäkitie, T. (2019). Corporate entrepreneurship and sustainability transitions: Resource redeployment of oil and gas industry firms in floating wind power. *Technology Analysis & Strategic Management*. Advance online publication. https://doi.org/10.1080/09537325.2019.1668553

Malerba, F., & Adams, P. (2014). Sectoral systems of innovation. In M. Dodgson, D. M. Gann, & N. Phillips (Eds.), *The Oxford handbook of innovation management* (pp. 183–203). Oxford University Press.

March, J. G. (1991). Exploration and exploitation in organizational learning. *Organization Science, 2*(1), 71–87. https://doi.org/10.1287/orsc.2.1.71

Mariotti, F., & Delbridge, R. (2012). Overcoming network overload and redundancy in interorganizational networks: The roles of potential and latent ties. *Organization Science, 23*(2), 511–528. https://doi.org/10.1287/orsc.1100.0568

Markard, J. (2011). Transformation of infrastructures: Sector characteristics and implications for fundamental change. *Journal of Infrastructure Systems, 17*(3), 107–117. https://doi.org/10.1061/(ASCE)IS.1943-555X.0000056

Mattes, J. (2014). Formalisation and flexibilisation in organisations – Dynamic and selective approaches in corporate innovation processes. *European Management Journal, 32*(3), 475–486. https://doi.org/10.1016/j.emj.2013.10.003

Mautz, R. (2012). Sozioökonomische Dynamik der Energiewende. In P. Bartelheimer, S. Fromm, & J. Kädtler (Eds.), *Berichterstattung zur sozioökonomischen Entwicklung in Deutschland* (pp. 223–241). VS Verlag für Sozialwissenschaften.

McEvily, B., Perrone, V., & Zaheer, A. (2003). Trust as an organizing principle. *Organization Science, 14*(1), 91–103. https://doi.org/10.1287/orsc.14.1.91.12814

McKenna, R., van der Leye, P. O., & Fichtner, W. (2014). Key challenges and prospects for large wind turbines. *Renewable and Sustainable Energy Reviews, 53*, 1212–1221. https://doi.org/10.1016/j.rser.2014.02.015

Meyer, J. W., & Rowan, B. (1977). Institutionalized organizations: Formal structure as myth and ceremony. *American Journal of Sociology, 83*(2), 340–363. https://doi.org/10.1086/226550

Meyer, J. W., & Rowan, B. (1991). Institutional organizations: Formal structure as myth and ceremony. In W. W. Powell & P. J. DiMaggio (Eds.), *The new institutionalism in organizational analysis* (pp. 41–62). University of Chicago Press.

Meyer, U. (2016). *Innovationspfade: Evolution und Institutionalisierung komplexer Technologie.* VS Verlag für Sozialwissenschaften.

Nakagaki, P., Aber, J., & Fetterhoff, T. (2012). The challenges in implementing open innovation in a global innovation-driven corporation. *Research-Technology Management, 55*(4), 32–38. https://doi.org/10.5437/08956308X5504086

Narayanan, V., & Chen, T. (2012). Research on technology standards: Accomplishment and challenges. *Research Policy, 41*(8), 1375–1406. https://doi.org/10.1016/j.respol.2012.02.003

Nieto, M. J., & Santamaría, L. (2007). The importance of diverse collaborative networks for the novelty of product innovation. *Technovation, 27*(6–7), 367–377. https://doi.org/10.1016/j.technovation.2006.10.001

Nightingale, P. (2000). The product-process-organisation relationship in complex development projects. *Research Policy, 29*(7–8), 913–934. https://doi.org/10.1016/S0048-7333(00)00130-2

Nightingale, P. (2014). What is technology? Six definitions and two pathologies. *SPRU Working Paper Series, SWPS 2014–19*, 1–29.

Nooteboom, B. (2014). Learning and innovation in inter-organizational relationships. In S. Cropper, C. Huxham, M. Ebers, & P. S. Ring (Eds.), *The Oxford handbook of inter-organizational relations* (pp. 606–634). Oxford University Press.

North, D. C. (1990). *Institutions, institutional change and economic performance.* Cambridge University Press.

North, D. C., & Thomas, R. P. (1976). *The rise of the Western world: A new economic history.* Cambridge University Press.

Ohlhorst, D. (2009). *Windenergie in Deutschland.* VS Verlag für Sozialwissenschaften.

Orlikowski, W. J. (2001). Due duality of technology: Rethinking the concept of technology in organizations. In C. G. A. Bryant (Ed.), *The contemporary Giddens* (pp. 62–96). Palgrave.

Orlikowski, W. J. (2002). Knowing in practice: Enacting a collective capability in distributed organizing. *Organization Science, 13*(3), 249–273. https://doi.org/10.1287/orsc.13.3.249.2776

Orlikowski, W. J. (2007). Sociomaterial practices: Exploring technology at work. *Organization Studies, 28*(9), 1435–1448. https://doi.org/10.1177/0170840607081138

Orlikowski, W. J. (2010). The sociomateriality of organisational life: Considering technology in management research. *Cambridge Journal of Economics, 34*(1), 125–141. https://doi.org/10.1093/cje/bep058

Orlikowski, W. J., & Gash, D. C. (1994). Technological frames: Making sense of information technology in organizations. *ACM Transactions on Information Systems, 12*(2), 174–207. https://doi.org/10.1145/196734.196745

Ortmann, G. (1999). Innovation als Paradoxieentfaltung. In D. Sauer & C. Lang (Eds.), *Paradoxien der Innovation* (pp. 249–263). Campus Verlag.

Ortmann, G. (2014). Das Driften von Regeln, Standards und Routinen. In J. Bergmann, M. Hahn, A. Langhof, & G. Wagner (Eds.), *Scheitern – Organisations- und wirtschaftssoziologische Analysen* (pp. 31–59). Springer Fachmedien.

Ortmann, G., Sydow, J., & Windeler, A. (2000). Organisation als reflexive Strukturation. In G. Ortmann, J. Sydow, & K. Türk (Eds.), *Theorien der Organisation* (pp. 315–354). VS Verlag für Sozialwissenschaften.

Owen-Smith, J., & Powell, W. W. (2008). Networks and institutions. In R. Greenwood, C. Oliver, R. Suddaby, & K. Sahlin-Andersson (Eds.), *The SAGE handbook of organizational institutionalism* (pp. 596–623). SAGE Publications.

Pisano, G. P., & Teece, D. J. (2007). How to capture value from innovation: Shaping intellectual property and industry architecture. *California Management Review, 50*(1), 278–296. https://doi.org/10.2307/41166428

Powell, W. W. (1990). Neither market nor hierarchy: Network forms of organization. *Research in Organizational Behavior, 12*, 295–336.

Powell, W. W. (1996). Weder Markt noch Hierarchie: Netzwerkartige Organisationsformen. In P. Kenis & V. Schneider (Eds.), *Organisation und Netzwerk* (pp. 213–271). Campus-Verlag.

Powell, W. W., & Giannella, E. (2010). Collective invention and inventor networks. In B. H. Hall & N. Rosenberg (Eds.), *Handbook of the economics of innovation* (Vol. 2, pp. 575–605). Elsevier North-Holland.

Powell, W. W., Koput, K. W., & Smith-Doerr, L. (1996). Interorganizational collaboration and the locus of innovation: Networks of learning in biotechnology. *Administrative Science Quarterly, 41*(1), 116–145. https://doi.org/10.2307/2393988

Rammert, W. (2007). *Technik – Handeln – Wissen*. VS Verlag für Sozialwissenschaften.

Rau, C., Möslein, K. M., & Neyer, A.-K. (2015). Playing possum, hide-and-seek, and other behavioral patterns: Knowledge boundaries at newly emerging interfaces. *R&D Management, 46*(S2), 341–353. https://doi.org/10.1111/radm.12164

Reckwitz, A. (2002). Toward a theory of social practices: A development in culturalist theorizing. *European Journal of Social Theory, 5*(2), 243–263. https://doi.org/10.1177/13684310222225432

Rodrigues, S., Restrepo, C., Kontos, E., Pinto, R. T., & Bauer, P. (2015). Trends of offshore wind projects. *Renewable and Sustainable Energy Reviews, 49*, 1114–1135. https://doi.org/10.1016/j.rser.2015.04.092

Rossoni, A. L., Vasconcellos, E. P. G. de, & Rossoni, R. L. de C. (2024). Barriers and facilitators of university-industry collaboration for research, development and innovation: A systematic review. *Management Review Quarterly, 74*(4), 1841–1877. https://doi.org/10.1007/s11301-023-00349-1

Salter, A., & Alexy, O. (2014). The nature of innovation. In M. Dodgson, D. M. Gann, & N. Phillips (Eds.), *The Oxford handbook of innovation management* (pp. 26–49). Oxford University Press.

Sandholtz, K. W. (2012). Making standards stick: A theory of coupled vs. decoupled compliance. *Organization Studies, 33*(5–6), 655–679. https://doi.org/10.1177/0170840612443621

Sankowska, A., & Söderlund, J. (2015). Trust, reflexivity and knowledge integration: Toward a conceptual framework concerning mobile engineers. *Human Relations, 68*(6), 973–1000. https://doi.org/10.1177/0018726714542732

Schaffarczyk, A. (2013). Technische Rahmenbedingungen. In J. Böttcher (Ed.), *Handbuch Windenergie* (pp. 163–263). Oldenbourg Verlag.

Schmidt, C. (2004, Mai). Analyse von Leitfadeninterviews. In U. Flick, E. v. Kardorff, & I. Steinke (Eds.), *Qualitative Forschung* (pp. 447–456). Rowohlt Taschenbuch Verlag.

Schroll, A., & Mild, A. (2012). A critical review of empirical research on open innovation adoption. *Journal für Betriebswirtschaft, 62*(2), 85–118. https://doi.org/10.1007/s11301-012-0080-4

Schubert, C., Sydow, J., & Windeler, A. (2013). The means of managing momentum: Bridging technological paths and organisational fields. *Research Policy, 42*(8), 1389–1405. https://doi.org/10.1016/j.respol.2013.04.010

Schumpeter, J. A. (1934). *The theory of economic development: An inquiry into profits, capital, credit, interest, and the business cycle.* Harvard University Press.

Schumpeter, J. (2006). *Theorie der wirtschaftlichen Entwicklung.* Duncker & Humblot GmbH.

Scott, W. R. (2008). *Institutions and organizations: Ideas and interests* (3rd ed.). SAGE.

Silva, P. C., & Klagge, B. (2013). The evolution of the wind industry and the rise of Chinese firms: From industrial policies to global innovation networks. *European Planning Studies, 21*(9), 1341–1356. https://doi.org/10.1080/09654313.2012.755842

Simmie, J. (2012). Path dependence and new technological path creation in the Danish wind power industry. *European Planning Studies, 20*(5), 753–772. https://doi.org/10.1080/09654313.2012.667924

Star, S. L., & Griesemer, J. R. (1989). Institutional ecology, translations and boundary objects: Amateurs and professionals in Berkeley's Museum of Vertebrate Zoology, 1907–39. *Social Studies of Science, 19*(3), 387–420. https://doi.org/10.1177/030631289019003001

Stones, R. (2009). Power and structuration theory. In S. Clegg & M. Haugaard (Eds.), *The SAGE handbook of power* (pp. 89–107). SAGE Publications.

Swärd, A. (2016). Trust, reciprocity, and actions: The development of trust in temporary inter-organizational relations. *Organization Studies, 37*(12), 1841–1860. https://doi.org/10.1177/0170840616655481

Swedberg, R., & Granovetter, M. (2018). Introduction to the third edition. In M. Granovetter & R. Swedberg (Eds.), *The sociology of economic life* (pp. xiii–xli). Routledge.

Sydow, J. (2010). Management von Netzwerkorganisationen: Zum Stand der Forschung. In J. Sydow (Ed.), *Management von Netzwerkorganisationen* (pp. 373–470). Gabler Verlag.

Sydow, J. (2014). Organisation als reflexive Strukturation: Grundlage. In J. Sydow & C. Wirth (Eds.), *Organisation und Strukturation* (pp. 17–55). Springer Fachmedien.

Sydow, J., Schüßler, E., & Müller-Seitz, G. (2016). *Managing inter-organizational relations: Debate and case.* Palgrave Macmillan.

Takeichi, A. (2002). Knowledge partitioning in the interfirm division of labor: The case of automotive product development. *Organization Science, 13*(3), 321–338. https://doi.org/10.1287/orsc.13.3.321.2772

Tassey, G. (2000). Standardization in technology-based markets. *Research Policy, 29*(4–5), 587–602. https://doi.org/10.1016/S0048-7333(99)00091-6

Teece, D. J. (2018). Profiting from innovation in the digital economy: Enabling technologies, standards, and licensing models in the wireless world. *Research Policy, 47*(8), 1367–1387. https://doi.org/10.1016/j.respol.2018.05.011

Tell, F. (2011). Knowledge integration and innovation: A survey of the field. In C. Berggren, A. Bergek, L. Bengtsson, M. Hobday, & J. Söderlund (Eds.), *Knowledge integration and innovation: Critical challenges facing international technology-based firms* (pp. 20–58). Oxford University Press.

Tell, F. (2017). Managing across knowledge boundaries. In F. Tell, C. Berggren, S. Brusoni, & A. van de Ven (Eds.), *Managing knowledge integration across boundaries* (pp. 19–38). Oxford University Press.

Timilsina, G. R., van Kooten, G. C., & Narbel, P. A. (2013). Global wind power development: Economics and policies. *Energy Policy, 61*, 642–652. https://doi.org/10.1016/j.enpol.2013.06.091

Tucci, C. L., Chesbrough, H., Piller, F., & West, J. (2016). When do firms undertake open, collaborative activities? Introduction to the special section on open innovation and open business models. *Industrial and Corporate Change, 25*(2), 283–288. https://doi.org/10.1093/icc/dtw002

Tushman, M. L. (1977). Special boundary roles in the innovation process. *Administrative Science Quarterly, 22*(4), 587–605. https://doi.org/10.2307/2392402

Un, C. A., Cuervo-Cazurra, A., & Asakawa, K. (2010). R&D collaborations and product innovation. *Journal of Product Innovation Management, 27*(5), 673–689. https://doi.org/10.1111/j.1540-5885.2010.00744.x

Vanhaverbeke, W., & Cloodt, M. (2014). Theories of the firm and open innovation. In H. Chesbrough, W. Vanhaverbeke, & J. West (Eds.), *New frontiers in open innovation* (pp. 256–278). Oxford University Press.

Veer, T., Lorenz, A., & Blind, K. (2016). How open is too open? The mitigating role of appropriation mechanisms in R&D cooperation settings. *R&D Management, 46*(S3), 1113–1128. https://doi.org/10.1111/radm.12206

Vuillemot, R., Rivière, P., Beignon, A., & Tabard, A. (2021). Boundary objects in design studies: Reflections on the collaborative creation of isochrone maps. *Computer Graphics Forum, 40*(3), 355–360. https://doi.org/10.1111/cgf.14312

Volberda, H. W., Foss, N. J., & Lyles, M. A. (2010). Absorbing the concept of absorptive capacity: How to realize its potential in the organization field. *Organization Science, 21*(4), 931–951. https://doi.org/10.1287/orsc.1090.0503

von Estorff, O., Heitmann, K., Lippert, S., Lippert, T., Reimann, K., Ruhnau, M., & Schwarz, M. (2013). Unterwasser-Rammschall: Eine Herausforderung bei der Errichtung von Offshore-Windparks und für die numerische Simulation. *Lärmbekämpfung, 8*(2), 61–71. https://doi.org/10.1007/s11822-013-0184-1

von Hippel, E. (1994). "Sticky information" and the locus of problem solving: Implications for innovation. *Management Science, 40*(4), 429–439. https://doi.org/10.1287/mnsc.40.4.429

Walsh, J. P., Lee, Y.-N., & Nagaoka, S. (2016). Openness and innovation in the US: Collaboration form, idea generation and implementation. *Research Policy, 45*(8), 1660–1671. https://doi.org/10.1016/j.respol.2016.05.012

Weick, K. E., Sutcliffe, K. M., & Obstfeld, D. (2005). Organizing and the process of sensemaking. *Organization Science, 16*(4), 409–421. https://doi.org/10.1287/orsc.1050.0133

West, J., & Bogers, M. (2014). Leveraging external sources of innovation: A review of research on open innovation. *Journal of Product Innovation Management, 31*(4), 814–831. https://doi.org/10.1111/jpim.12125